THE DYNAMICS OF
ARCHITECTURAL FORM

THE DYNAMICS OF
ARCHITECTURAL FORM

RUDOLF ARNHEIM

BASED ON THE 1975

MARY DUKE BIDDLE LECTURES

AT THE COOPER UNION

UNIVERSITY OF CALIFORNIA PRESS

BERKELEY · LOS ANGELES · LONDON

University of California Press
Berkeley and Los Angeles, California
University of California Press, Ltd.
London, England
Copyright © 1977 by
The Regents of the University of California
ISBN 0-520-03305-1
Library of Congress Catalog Card Number: 76-19955
Printed in the United States of America

1 2 3 4 5 6 7 8 9

CONTENTS

INTRODUCTION

A B O O K on the visual form of architecture requires justification. Are there reasons enough to focus so much attention on the appearance of buildings? And if there are, can such an analysis afford to leave aside most of the social, economical, and historical connotations and all the technology so inseparably involved in the art of building?

Most of us, when walking through the streets, are affected in one way or another by the look of the buildings we pass and their arrangement in space. Moreover, it is hard to escape the impression that visually successful buildings are rarer today than they were in almost any other period or civilization. On what sort of observation are such judgments based? We ask: Does a building display the visual unity that makes it understandable to the human eye? Does its appearance reflect the various functions, physical as well as psychological, for which it was designed? Does it display something of the spirit that animates, or ought to animate, the community? Does it transmit some of the best in human intelligence and imagination? It takes the occasional confrontation with a work of architecture that lives up to these requests to remind us that they are relevant and reasonable; and the elation offered us by such a sight is dampened only by the realization that too often the pleasure is due not to a builder of our own time but to someone long ago.

The persistent discomfort caused by most of the public settings provided today by man for man urged me to explore the visual conditions that influence the psychological effect of architecture. A more positive impulse came from seeing with my own eyes the remains of the Poseidon temple on Cape Sunion, high about the Aegean Sea, or Jörn Utzon's opera house on the promontory in Sydney harbor. I felt inspired by the awesome cube of the Palazzo Farnese in Rome and by the new city hall in Boston; by the cupola of

1

the Pantheon and the poetry in cement by Pier Luigi Nervi; but also by the crystalline mountains of New York's office buildings lit up at night, the generous expanse of Paris streets, and the labyrinths of Venice. Decisive perhaps was the opportunity during my years at Harvard to work in Le Corbusier's Carpenter Center for the Visual Arts. Not simply to visit but to serve and be served by a building of such generous spaces, to be greeted in the morning by the outreach of the curved studios, to walk between the tall columns or up the sweep of the ramp to the third floor, to be impelled to move within the controlled measures of those halls and to try to keep up with them—this added a dimension of practical interaction to the relations between man and man-made form that I had studied in painting and sculpture. It also occurred to me that the perceptual forces which organize visual shapes and endow them with expression were embodied in the geometry of architecture with a purity found elsewhere only in music.

Given the exhilaration of those shapes—*cantique des colonnes*, as Paul Valéry calls it so melodiously—I was puzzled to notice in the practitioners of architecture, professionals, teachers, and students, a kind of malaise, a disillusionment that made them neglect the active study of design or even denounce it as a frivolous diversion from the serious social obligations of the architect. I noticed architects writing books in which they concentrated on reporting about their readings in linguistics, information theory, structuralism, experimental psychology, and Marxism. At times, these excursions seemed to evade the discussion of architecture itself. No doubt, any one of those theoretical approaches can throw light on certain aspects of our subject, but unless that light visibly illuminates the actual products of architecture, that is, the appearance, effect, and use of buildings, the academic talk obscures more than it reveals.

Design, of course, is nothing more or less than the creation of a building's tangible and visible shapes. How then could design come to be considered something that may be done without? Is this merely a reaction to a historical period that tried to revive the temples, churches, and castles of the past in the post offices, banks, and lecture halls of the present? Or is this aversion a protest against a more recent stripping crusade that hid the variety of human impulses in a neat but often empty geometry? Whatever the cause, any attempt to avoid the architect's final responsibility must be futile. One can neglect the shape of an object, but one cannot do without it.

Resistance to the study of form certainly derived in part from the accusation that architects and theorists had taken to treating buildings as pure

2

shapes, without regard to their practical and social functions. Anybody with a live sense of the interplay between buildings and the human community must rebel against such formalism, if only because it must lead to a misinterpretation of the very shapes it wishes to deal with. One cannot understand the shape of a door or a bridge without relating it to its function. And beyond that, it is surely true that only a perverted mind can consider a building anything but a means to an end. What requires scrutiny is the nature of that end and the ways of attaining it.

Material needs would seem to come first. Without well-protected, well-equipped shelter, human life cannot function properly. But it is one thing to be responsibly aware of practical necessity and quite another to try for an easy victory in discussion by denouncing the "formalists." To insist on the importance of material needs and to minimize or even ridicule all others puts the speaker in a strong position. It makes him appear to be someone with his feet on the ground, inspired by a sense of social responsibility, untouched by a frivolous concern with the trifles of taste. He articulates the reality of the cold-water flats, the broken windowpanes, the garbage and the rats. But when it comes to gauging human needs objectively, the easy rhetoric may not suffice.

Later in the this book I shall have occasion to remind the reader that all human needs are matters of the mind. Hunger pangs, the chills of winter, the fear of violence, and the disturbance from noise are all facts of human consciousness. It makes little sense to distinguish between them by attributing some to the body and others to the mind. The hunger, the chill, and the fear are on equal footing with the need for peace, privacy, space, harmony, order, or color. To the best of a psychologist's knowledge, the priorities are by no means self-evident. Dignity, a sense of pride, congeniality, a feeling of ease—these are primary needs, which must be seriously considered when the welfare of human beings is under discussion. And since they are requirements of the mind, they are satisfied not only by good plumbing, heating, and insulation, but equally by light, congenial colors, visual order, well-proportioned space, and so forth.

Here again it is easy to dismiss the problem by maintaining that the average man in the street and in the house does not care about the psychological needs that architects and other creatures of *luxe, calme et volupté* attribute to him. Ask the average person, and he will talk about radiators and drafts, staircases and the laundry, not about color schemes and modules. But he may not talk about light and air, either, and yet be profoundly influenced by their quality. Explicit responses to questionnaires and interviews do not exhaust the factors that determine a person's state of mind. Of many of them, he is not consciously aware.

A building, then, in all its aspects is a fact of the human mind. It is an experience of the senses of sight and sound, of touch and heat and cold and muscular behavior, as well as of the resultant thoughts and strivings. However, I have to do more than make a case for the importance of the aspects of visual form on which this book will dwell. I also have to justify my attempt to discuss visual aspects of architecture without putting them in the historical, social, indeed personal, contexts on which sensory experiences depend.

Would not complete isolation of visual appearance explicitly contradict what I stated a moment ago, namely that the visual form of a building cannot be understood unless one considers its function? It would indeed, as I try to show, for example, in a section comparing architecture and sculpture, where I demonstrate that an object looks different depending on whether one views it as inhabitable or not. Furthermore, my final chapter is devoted entirely to the interrelation between function and the visual expression derived from it.

Even so, some readers might maintain that my descriptions are adrift in space because they do not specify who is doing the looking under what historical, social, and individual conditions. In fact, they will say, I am talking about things existing only in my own mind, since they are bound to be viewed differently by the next person. I reply that my appraoch seems to me indispensable because one must establish what people are looking at before one can hope to understand why, under the conditions peculiar to them, they see what they see. A simple example will make the point. Suppose somebody wishes to investigate the character of the color red. He goes about it by examining individual instances of burning buildings, flags of revolution, slaughterhouses, traffic lights, bullfights, cardinals' robes, sunsets, and the use of red in paintings of the fourteenth, seventeenth, and twentieth centuries. He then tries to extricate from all these reports what the experiences of red have in common. To proceed in this way is not impossible, but it means getting at the facts the hard way. A more promising way of starting the investigation would be to "bracket out" the experience created by a red surface or red light from the context of particular circumstances and examine it under neutral conditions. Strictly speaking, of course, such detachment from particular circumstances is never complete, but it is effective enough to permit all experimental psychology to rely on this procedure. And the closer the facts under observation come to the basic elements of human experience, the more reliable the procedure is. The perceptual phenomena of color contrast or of certain perceptual illusions, for example, are mechanisms of such self-sufficient completeness that individual differences can be ignored. The same is true for the distinction between the experiences of rising and falling and openness and closedness, or the dynamic expression of circular versus parabolic curves.

The results obtained from such inspection are by no means the mere private experiences of individual viewers. They reveal the universal foundation of human perception, the ground floor of mental structure. Once these elementary experiences are ascertained, one can begin to understand what becomes of them under particular circumstances. These perceptual elements are so strong that they are seldom totally overlaid by specific conditions. The overlays merely modulate them. The perceptual elements persist whatever the circumstances, and only when their fundamental aspects are known can we begin to understand an individual instance. How can one hope to realize what distinguishes the experience of the Parthenon in the Athens of the fifth century B.C. from that of a Gothic cathedral in the Bourges of A.D. 1300 if one has no clear notion of the dynamic relations between vertical and horizontal? Not knowing what the Greeks or the French reacted to, how can one speculate on what they saw?

In trying to clarify these relationships for myself, I have been greatly helped by a simple diagram (Fig. 1), in which T indicates the target viewed while A, B, C, D are different observers. If we restrict our analysis to the cultural and individual conditions prevailing in the observers, we proceed without any knowledge of the perceptual object they are receiving; and we are left with the absurd and distressing conclusion that since they all see different things, there can be no shared experience and no communication. If, on the other hand, we restrict our analysis to the target T, we ignore the substantial modifications introduced by the point of view of any individual or collective observer. In this equally one-sided way we can get at the common core, but we cannot tell what happens to it in a particular instance. We can hope, however, to isolate—*in vitro*, as it were—some of the object's qualities most likely to survive the changing tastes of the ages, the timeless values of an Egyptian temple, a Chinese pagoda, or a Rococo hunting lodge, long after the particular connotations of its style cease to be an integral part of the experience. We perceive a unique configuration of readable qualities, which serve to enrich our notion of the many ways in which man can translate his view of life and world into stone or wood.

5

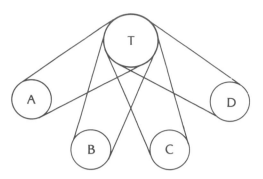

Figure 1

It is a contribution of this kind that the present book hopes to offer. Its approach is partial, but the perceptual core at which it aims can be singled out without producing much distortion by omission. It is as though we were looking at a rose window, whose roundness, tracery, and stained glass design we can appreciate and legitimately analyze, even though its complete meaning derives only from the context of the building. A more thorough understanding would necessarily require inclusion of the historical, social, and individual factors, which in the diagram of Figure 1 I have indicated as A, B, C, and D.

In selecting my examples I constantly had to distinguish between successful and unsuccessful buildings because only the best specimens illustrate visual qualities uncluttered by accidentals. Here again a point of method needs to be made. We are told that the analyst or historian must proceed without making value judgments; he must simply describe what is there. In practice, of course, no such abstinence prevails. But it is demanded in principle because of the same prejudice against which Figure 1 is meant to stand as a warning. The value of an object, it is said, depends entirely on the needs to be satisfied by it. This is surely correct. But the relativist's argument proceeds to assert that since those needs differ from person to person and in accord with the client's social and historical circumstances, it is absurd to interpose one's own judgment and to call, say, the Palazzo Venezia in Rome better architecture than the adjacent monument to Victor Emanuel II. The connoisseur may turn up his nose at the marble wedding cake, but the average patriot or tourist opts differently.

Studies of popular taste are of interest to the social scientist and useful to the businessman. But to be meaningful, they must identify the particular properties inherent in the object on which preference or rejection is based. As a rule, most of an object's qualities exert some sort of effect and are evaluated in some way. The responses range from the most superficial attractions to the deepest human significance. It is to the visual expression of the latter that the present book is devoted.

The qualities that carry values can be described with considerable precision. But many of these descriptions cannot be quantitatively confirmed by the measuring or counting of data. They share this trait with many other facts of mind and nature, and it does not prevent them from existing or being important. Nor does such a lack of numerical proof exclude them from objective discussion. The "ostensive" method of arguing with the index finger by pointing to perceivable facts, making comparisons, and drawing attention to relevant relations is a legitimate way of furthering understanding by common effort.

I have made much use of this method in an earlier book, *Art and Visual Perception*. When I decided to write about architecture, I thought at first of simply applying to this new subject the principles I had developed and illustrated in the earlier book primarily with examples from painting and sculpture. This was, in fact, what students and teachers of architecture had urged me to do; and to some extent I have complied. Yet the present book is less technical, less systematic. Be it because I was reluctant to recapitulate earlier explanations, or because the broader experiential range of architecture invited a different treatment, the present book is more an explorer's report on high spots of the man-made environment than the outcome of a professional analysis.

It is also true that the particular nature of architecture called for additional principles, less relevant or altogether inapplicable to painting or sculpture. The large size of buildings, their agglomeration in settlements, their intimate participation in the inhabitant's practical activities, their having both inside and outside—all these required other concepts. For example, the traditional approach to figure-ground perception, derived from flat figures on paper, had to be overhauled. Most generally, I have come increasingly to believe that the dynamics of shape, color, and movement is the decisive, although the least explored, factor of sensory perception, and for this reason the word "dynamics" figures in the title of this book. It thereby develops its argument from sketchy beginnings presented in 1966 under the title *The Dynamics of Shape* as an issue of *Design Quarterly*.

At the same time I hope devotees of architecture will not begrudge the

7

space I have given to comparisons with other visual arts and also music. One cannot truly understand one's own field without looking at what is going on in the neighbors' gardens, just as one cannot truly know the particular nature of one's own language without learning some others.

Perhaps I should also explain why this book is not as richly illustrated as books on architecture often are these days. The practice of offering a full-fledged photograph with every cursory reference to a work of architecture in the text supplies the reader with a treasure of substitutes for the real experience, enabling him to check on the author's contentions and to extend his own explorations beyond them. But there are also diminishing returns from the pervasive and automatic display of these riches, and I suspect that such abundance can interfere with the training of the visual imagination, for which there is so much need. The drawings that I owe to the collaboration of Robert Rossero, a student at the Cooper Union's School of Architecture, seem to me to maintain just the right level of abstraction between the conceptual principles they are intended to illustrate and the full individuality of the buildings from which they are taken.

Thanks are due also to the School of Art and Architecture of the Cooper Union in New York City for inviting me to give the Mary Duke Biddle Lectures for 1975. The samples from my first four chapters which were read at that occasion led ineluctably to the writing of the rest. I am grateful also to John Gay of London for letting me use a few of his fine photographs, and to Valerie Meyer and Linda Owen of the Department of Art History at the University of Michigan for helping me with the literary sources and the photographic illustrations. My wife, Mary, typed the manuscript, and Mrs. Muriel Bell, my editor, helped make my sentences shiny, lean, and precise. As an architectural historian, Professor Paul Turner of the Art Department at Stanford University contributed a number of valuable corrections and suggestions, and Arvid E. Osterberg looked at my ruminations with the critical eyes of the architect.

R. A.

Ann Arbor, Michigan

I. ELEMENTS OF SPACE

WHAT IS space? There are two ready answers to this question. One of them is spontaneously plausible. It conceives of space as a self-contained entity, infinite or finite, an empty vehicle, ready and having the capacity to be filled with things. Consciously or not, people derive this notion of space from the world as they see it, and unless they are psychologists, artists, or architects, they are unlikely ever to be confronted with the challenge of questioning it. Plato spoke in the *Timaeus* of space as "the mother and receptacle of all created and visible and in any way sensible things." He thought of it as "the universal nature which receives all bodies —that must be always called the same; for while receiving all things she never departs at all from her own nature and never in any way or at any time assumes a form like that of any of the things which enter into her; she is the natural recipient of all impressions, and is stirred and informed by them, and appears different from time to time by reason of them." Space was for Plato a nothingness existing as an entity in the outer world, like the objects it could hold. In the absence of such objects, space would still exist, as an empty, boundless container.

SPACE CREATED BY THINGS

Spontaneously, then, space is experienced as the given that precedes the objects in it, as the setting in which every thing takes its place. Without paying our respects to this spontaneous and universal manner of looking at the world, we could not hope to understand the nature of architecture as an arrangement of buildings placed within a given, continuous space. Nevertheless, this conception neither reflects the knowledge of modern physics nor describes the way the perception of space comes about psychologically.

9

Physically, space is defined by the extension of material bodies or fields bordering on each other, e.g., a landscape of earth and stones adjoining bodies of water and air. The measurable distances within such a rag rug of different materials are aspects of physical space. Beyond that it is the mutual influences of material things that determine the space between them: distance can be described by the amount of light energy that reaches an object from a light source, or by the strength of the gravitational attraction exerted by one body upon another, or by the time it takes for one thing to travel to the next. Apart from the energy that pervades it, however, space cannot be said to exist physically.

The same is true psychologically for the origin of space perception. Although space, once it is established, is experienced as an always present and self-sufficient given, the experience is generated only through the interrelation of objects. This is the second answer to the question: What is space? Space perception occurs only in the presence of perceivable things.

The difference between the two conceptions of space has fundamental consequences. The notion of space as a container that would exist even if it were completely empty is reflected in the Newtonian assumption of an absolute base of reference, against which all distances, velocities, or sizes have equally absolute measurements. Geometrically this corresponds to a system of Cartesian coordinates, to which all locations, sizes, or movements in a three-dimensional space can be related. If, for example, nothing but a single ball-shaped object is given, its spatial position with regard to the framework can be determined by three coordinates indicating the distances from the frame of reference.

This sort of construct makes no sense when we deny the existence of absolute space and instead consider space the creation of existing objects. In this view, no three-dimensional framework exists for the solitary ball suspended in emptiness. There is no up or down, no left or right, neither size nor velocity, and no determinable distance of any kind. Instead there is a single center surrounded quite symmetrically by emptiness in that no direction is distinguishable in any way from any other, and consequently the notion of direction does not come up at all. Space is, in this case, a centrically symmetrical sphere of infinite expanse. It should be noted that the situation I am describing here is not simply physical but experiential, presupposing a consciousness of space that somehow inheres in that single, ball-shaped object.

We can go a step further and separate that consciousness from the target of

10

its attention by assuming the existence of two objects in empty space, an observer and something he observes. Let us assume that astronauts are approaching the earth and, for the time being, have wiped the memory of all other heavenly bodies from their minds. A linear connection forms itself spontaneously between observer and earth, and this connection constitutes the axis of a one-dimensional world. Along this axis there are distances, directions, and velocities, and the empty environment arranges itself symmetrically around the axis in the form of a cylinder of infinite size.

A roughly comparable experience can occur in our terrestrial environment. For example, as one approaches a building towering over a fairly empty plain, the perceptual relation is essentially between the viewer and the target, espccially when the building is the person's destination. The horizontal surface of the plain, although perceived, does not modify the relation between viewer and tower and therefore does not actively enter his spatial conception of the situation. Nor does this happen only when the environment is unoccupied. A stranger trying to reach the one tall building that rises above the city may walk in the direction of his visual target, selecting street after street as it seems to lead him in the right direction, without any more conscious apprehension of the pattern of streets he is traversing than if he were hacking a path through a jungle. Even though a complex physical structure is physically present, the experience is dominated by the primary goal and the single-minded effort to reach it.

Note that the connection established by the observer between himself and his target is experienced as a straight line. In principle, that connection could take any shape among an infinite number of curves, twists, and loops of the most irrational kind. The economical choice of the shortest connection is an elementary application of gestalt psychology's principle of simplicity: any pattern created, adopted, or selected by the nervous system will be as simple as the given conditions permit.

The effects of this principle are better appreciated when we now take a further step and consider a configuration of three, rather than two, points in space (Fig. 2). Suppose a spaceship is navigating in relation to a planet and the sun. According to the principle of simplicity this situation will create a triangular structure in the minds of the astronauts. A flat triangle is the simplest structure compatible with three points. As the astronauts concentrate their attention on their relations to the planet and the sun, their world is no longer one-dimensional but two-dimensional. Functionally, no third dimension exists. For example, the question of how the triangular plane is

11

Figure 2

Figure 3

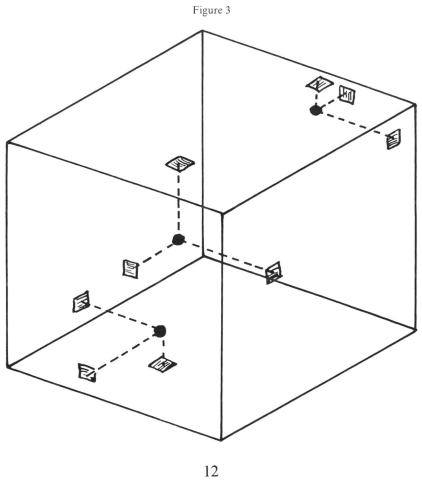

12

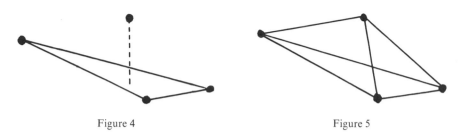

Figure 4   Figure 5

located in space, whether it is oriented horizontally or vertically, or tilted obliquely, has no meaning. Notice here that if space were not created by the three objects involved, but in relation to an external framework of Cartesian coordinates, a different set of spatial relations would result, which could totally exclude the triangular connection between the objects (Fig. 3).

Since we are dealing with the psychological experience of space, much depends on how an observer conceives of and therefore structures the situation. If, for example, further objects venture into the range of the three, the role and function accorded them will influence the resulting constellation. The relative strength of the contending parties will matter. A small asteroid would probably not upset the flatness of the triangular situation, but would be seen as located at some angle to that base (Fig. 4). If, however, the new fourth object is strong, it may create a fuller realization of the now three-dimensional setup: the triangular plane may be replaced by a four-cornered polyhedron (Fig. 5).

ARCHITECTURAL IMPLICATIONS

By way of lofty abstraction we have come across a fundamental principle of practical importance to the architect. In spite of what spontaneous perception indicates, space is in no way given by itself. It is created by a particular constellation of natural and man-made objects, to which the architect contributes. In the mind of the creator, user, or beholder, every architectural constellation establishes its own spatial framework. This framework derives from the simplest structural skeleton compatible with the physical and psychological situation. Under elementary conditions the structure established by the architectural layout as a whole may rule uncontested. For example, in a linear village surrounded by cultivated fields, the main street may serve as a one-dimensional spine to which all particular locations and spatial orientations conform. Usually the situation is more complex. Some components of the whole establish their own spatial framework. A church oriented along an

13

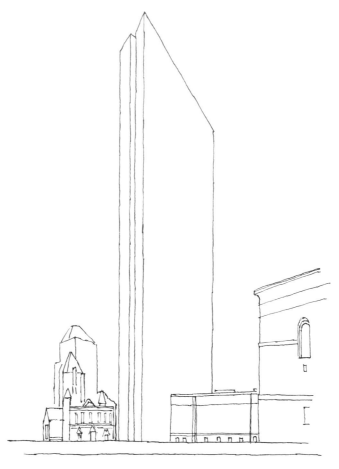

Figure 6

east-west axis may oppose the overall orientation of its environment, and the relation between the two may be complex or even unmanageable, in which case the spatial order comes apart. Take the following recent and particularly dramatic example. The quadrilateral symmetry of Boston's Copley Square, on which H. H. Richardson's Trinity Church and the public library of McKim, Mead, and White face each other, has been pierced visually by a diagonal wedge nearby, the huge rhomboid skyscraper of the John Hancock Tower (Figs. 6 and 7). In such cases the addition may be simply absorbed and subordinated by the existing setting—an unlikely possibility in this case because of the mass and height of the intruder. Or the new structure and the

14

old may reorganize themselves into a new configuration of unified shape. Most probably the clash of two incompatible patterns will result in mutual denial—a disorder that spells visual destruction.

Almost any architectural setting is a highly complex constellation of such spatial systems, some subordinated, some coordinated, some bordering upon each other, some crossing or surrounding others. At its most comprehensive level the setting may be the shape of an entire city, composed of distinguishable boroughs, each of which is made up of isolable parts, with these in turn being subdivided into single streets, squares, buildings. Each building is a constellation of its own, and the subdivision leads all the way down to the furnishings of a single room, in which tables, shelves, or beds each propose a particular spatial framework.

Kevin Lynch's classical description of urban settings makes it clear that at their various levels these spatial systems may be either highly ordered or chaotic. It stands to reason that environments planned as a whole are likely to display a more consistent order than the piecemeal accretions by which most communities grow, although the latter do not necessarily produce disorder. Lynch's analyses show that the more orderly the objectively given spatial structure, the more agreement there is in the images people form of the setting. The more ambiguous the structure, the more the resulting image depends on where an observer happens to anchor his attention, how well acquainted he is with various sections, and so forth.

Figure 7

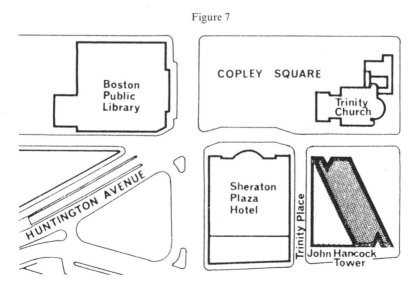

More will be said on this subject in a discussion of order and disorder in Chapter VI. Let me add here that the complexity of the space created by architecture is in part what psychologists call a developmental matter. Three-dimensional space is directly given to the mind only in its crudest extent; the finer interplay of dimensions must be gradually conceived by it. Early spatial conceptions are therefore simple. This is not always evident in the actual constructions since in practice the developmental factor can be overlaid by technical, historical, or personal influences. But it is useful to realize that one of the components at work is a tendency of the mind to proceed from the simplest spatial constructs to increasingly complex ones. In a relatively pure state we may find this tendency manifest in children's block play, in the early experiments of architectural students, or in primitive huts. Psychologically, a first phase may consist in the placement of a single object in neutral space. At a somewhat more developed stage, the relations between objects as well as those between the components of a single object may be essentially two-dimensional, conceived in terms of a flat plane, whether horizontal or vertical. Within such a plane, relations may be limited at first to right-angular ones, proceeding to more intricate obliqueness only later. Similarly, true three-dimensionality limits itself at an early level to right-angular relations, for example in the shape of a cube or an arrangement of cubes.

In this way one can try to establish a scale of increasing complexity, by which spatial imagination proceeds from the simplest structures to the most complex. Of course, in a purely physical sense even the simplest architectural act involves three-dimensionality, since a single brick is a three-dimensional object. But it is essential for the understanding of architectural form to realize that the mere handling of objects in the physical world does not by itself provide an active conception of the dimensions and inherent possibilities of space. This holds true for every human occupation dealing with space, be it engineering, mathematics, physics, medicine, games, or the arts. Spatial imagination must be acquired step by step. In some persons or cultural periods it never reaches beyond fairly elementary relations, either because development stops at an early level or because greater complexity would serve no good purpose. In a few instances, spatial imagination attains the dizzy intricacy displayed by a Borromini or Le Corbusier.

THE FIELDS IN BETWEEN

Let me return to the two conceptions of space from which we started. Spontaneous perception, we said, presents space as a container existing prior

16

to, and independently of, the physical bodies that find their place within it. In such a view, the spaces between things are empty. Everyday experience distinguishes between impenetrable matter, such as mountains or tree trunks or the walls of buildings, and openings that we can pass through. This distinction is fundamental for the architect, since he constantly seeks the proper ratio between the two.

At the same time, however, the architect must be aware of the second conception, suggested to him by the physicist and the psychologist, that space is created as a relation between objects. These relations persist in perceptual experience, even though the man in the street may not spontaneously acknowledge them. There are many aspects of experience of which we are not explicitly conscious that nonetheless tinge our awareness in important ways. The visual relations between objects are of this kind. Space between things turns out not to look simply empty.

Take the example of two buildings, one big and one small, standing at a moderate distance from each other. It is possible to deal with them independently by making statements about one of them without considering the other—for example, by discussing the height of only one of them. That is the sort of disconnected treatment to which we owe the visual, functional, and social chaos of modern life. It derives from the tunnel vision employed for immediate practical ends, especially under social conditions that atomize the human community into a mere aggregate of individuals or small groups, each minding its own business. Perceptually this attitude corresponds to seeing items of the continuous environment in isolation from their context: We readily recognize such dismemberment as a pathological deformation of the natural way of seeing the visual field as a whole. At the less elementary level of viewing social relations, the pathological character of this attitude should be equally evident. Socially as well as perceptually, one cannot understand the nature of either the small house or the large house as long as one considers each only by itself.

Unimpaired vision perceives the two buildings as elements of one image, in which a decrescendo effect leads from the tall house down to the low one, or conversely a crescendo makes our eyes rise from low to high. Also the big mass of the one building is seen as contrasting with the small mass of the other, and vice versa, as the viewer's glance moves back and forth between them. Looking at the two is an eminently dynamic experience, in which the space between the buildings is an inseparable part of the image. Far from being empty, that interstitial space is pervaded by gradients. If the width of the interval were to change, i.e., if the buildings were to be closer together or farther apart, the slope of the gradients would change concomitantly. So would the contrast between the buildings.

It may seem paradoxical that space has a perceptual presence of its own, even though it is not explicitly constructed by the builder and does not appear among the objects constituting the inventory of the visual image. But it is quite common for visual percepts to contain more than what is given in the physical stimulus pattern. A configuration of four dots on a paper may be seen as a square, even though no connections between the dots are drawn in. Perhaps the following example will persuade the reader that what is made does not necessarily correspond to what is seen. For the decoration of an early type of Greek vases, black figures were painted on the red ceramic ground. The inverse procedure was used in later times: the background was covered with black paint, and the figures remained red. If we simplify the technical process somewhat, we may say that on the red-figured vases the artist painted only the background but obtained the figure. Inversely, the architect does not build space but creates it just the same.

A good way to demonstrate that interspaces are not empty is referring to what may be called their density. If one makes small models of our two buildings and moves them back and forth, closer together and farther apart, one observes that the interspace looks looser and thinner as the distance between the buildings increases. Conversely, the interspace becomes denser as the distance diminishes. The observer experiences perceptual compression or decompression in the interval. To my knowledge, this phenomenon has never been systematically investigated, and its conditions are likely to be complex. Although the observed density may be a simple function of the distance between the objects, its absolute level of intensity may depend on other perceptual factors, such as the size of the buildings. Furthermore, if there are additional buildings in the neighborhood, the spaces between them will influence the space we are considering (Fig. 8). Interspace n will look smaller and denser when compared with o; it will look larger and looser when compared with m.

The distance between the buildings also influences the degree of their mutual dependence or independence. If the interspace were entirely eliminated, the two buildings would tend to coalesce into one, with the small one looking like a mere appendage of the large one. At the other extreme, a great distance would extinguish most relations between the buildings. The interspace, then, establishes a particular ratio of remoteness and connectedness, which affects the architectural complex as a whole. When we consider

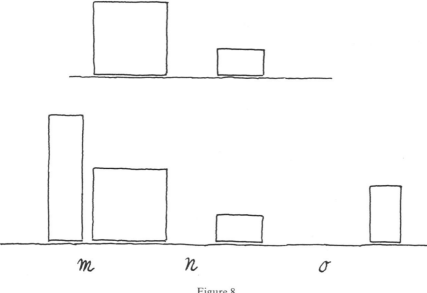

Figure 8

remoteness and connectedness not simply as metric distances but dynamically, we find that they depend on forces of attraction and repulsion. Objects that look "too close" to each other display mutual repulsion: they want to be moved apart. At a somewhat greater distance the interval may look just right or the objects may seem to attract each other.

These forces are at work whenever things are related across space; they determine the spacing of pictures on a wall, the placement of furniture in a room, the proper distances between buildings. We feel impelled to ask whether the distances between the baptistery, the cathedral, and the campanile in Pisa's Piazza del Duomo are just right, and if so, why? What would happen if the distances were altered? The perceptual aspects of the judgments that determine the answers are arrived at intuitively by our sense of sight. They are likely to depend on the strains and stresses activated in the brain field by the particular constellation of stimuli projected upon it by the retinal image. Optimal distances can be measured, but here again the rules governing the phenomenon are not likely to be simple.

In recent years, especially through the work of Edward T. Hall, attention has been drawn to the psychological and social connotations of spatial distances between people in daily intercourse. How close together or far apart people are expected to be when they meet depends on their personal relationship and more generally on the social conventions of the particular cultural setting. These "proxemic" norms influence also the choice of preferred distances between objects, e.g., the placement of furniture, and they are likely to affect the way people determine and evaluate the distances between buildings. What looks oppressively close to one kind of observer may be welcomed as cozily protective by another. These personal and social attitudes overlay and modify the specifically perceptual factors I am discussing here.

Visual distances are judged by the behavior of the perceptual forces generated by them. We feel impelled to juggle the distances between objects until they look just right because we experience these distances as influencing forces of attraction and repulsion. Balancing applies always to forces. If the intervals were experienced as nothing but dead, empty spaces, there would be no criterion, other than practical considerations, for preferring one distance to another. I shall have occasion to make a similar point on the control of proportions in architecture.

EMPTY AND FORLORN

When the distance between buildings increases, the density of the interval lessens and eventually disappears entirely. No longer do we experience any relation between the buildings. It is under such conditions one can say that the space between them is empty. The conditions for perceptual emptiness can be made clear by an analogy to music. Physically, any moment of time during which no music is sounded can be said to be empty. Perceptually, however, the character of such intervals varies greatly. A run of pizzicato notes hangs together like a string of pearls because the small pauses between the tones are entirely absorbed by the continuing sequence. Longer pauses are perceived as silences but nevertheless also as integral parts of the music. During such an interval the tone preceding it acquires its rhythmic weight and meaning by lingering on for the time prescribed by the structure of the composition. These time intervals may be entirely devoid of sound, but they are not empty. They are pervaded by tension. Emptiness, however, is experienced when a movement of a composition comes to an end, its structure is completed, and the performers take a moment's rest and check their instruments before starting again.

This comparison with music shows that the degree to which an interval is filled does not depend simply on its objective length. Visually also, when the two objects bordering on the interval require each other for mutual comple-

20

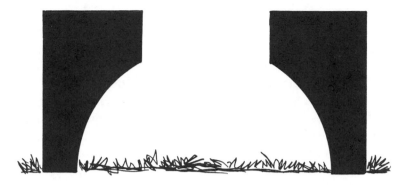

Figure 9a

tion, the interval is more actively and densely filled (Fig. 9a) than if the two shapes are strongly self-contained and independent (Fig. 9b). It follows that perceptual emptiness can be described as a quality of an area whose spatial characteristics are not controlled by the surrounding objects. Extreme emptiness is experienced where there are no objects at all. In darkness, on the ocean, or in outer space, the absence of all points of reference and orientation, the lack of attraction and repulsion, the undefined distances, can cause ultimate terror. Its social equivalent is the experience of a person who feels totally abandoned: the environment is complete without him, nothing refers to him, needs him, calls him, or responds to him. This lack of external definition destroys the internal sense of identity, because a person defines the nature of his own being largely by his place in a network of personal relations.

Figure 9b

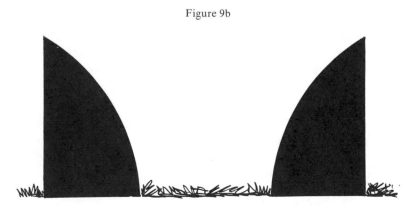

To be sure, a strong personality may cope with aloneness by establishing himself or herself as the center and irradiating the surroundings from that center with a sunburst of forces that animate emptiness. Under such conditions the absence of counteracting obstacles may even create an exhilarating sense of freedom. It is the experience of "covering" the world from a mountain top. Similarly, a monument erected in an empty plain may evoke in the surrounding space a field of perceptual forces whose strength diminishes with increasing distance from the center.

Evidently, emptiness is not simply related to the absence of matter. A space on which nothing is built can be pervaded nevertheless by perceptual forces and filled with density, which we might call a visual substance. Conversely, the fenestrated wall of a high-rise building or a large, homogeneous area in a painting may be experienced as empty even though the architect or painter has put something there for us to look at. The effect of emptiness comes about when the surrounding shapes, e.g., the contours, do not impose a structural organization upon the surface in question. The observer's glance finds itself in the same place wherever it tries to anchor, one place being like the next; it feels the lack of spatial coordinates, of a framework for determining distances. In consequence, the viewer experiences a sense of forlornness.

In the examples I just gave, the viewer feels forlorn because he projects himself onto the place that he scans with his glance; he drifts rudderless within the anonymous expanse. This kind of experience can be more intense when the person finds himself bodily at a place that does not define him spatially, for example, on a shapeless city square or in the vast hall of a museum. He can also diagnose an object as looking forlorn in its setting. This may occur when the placement of the object has no recognizable relation to its surroundings. A piece of sculpture placed injudiciously in a living room, a museum, or a landscape may seem lost. It may drift aimlessly, or it may display a tendency to move to a different place, where it can be anticipated to find spatial definition and therefore rest. The central, symmetrical location of the equestrian statue of Marcus Aurelius on Michelangelo's Capitol Square in Rome is the most obvious instance of a sculpture fully anchored in a highly defined space (Fig. 10). A modern example that has assumed almost mythical qualities among students of architecture—especially since the building has been demolished—is the statue by Georg Kolbe placed by Mies van der Rohe in his German Pavilion for the International Exposition in Barcelona, 1929. The life-sized nude, conspicuous as the only organic shape in a building

Figure 10

formed of rectangular slabs, stood in a corner that otherwise would have escaped the visitors' attention (Fig. 11*a*). It stood on a terrace in a small pool, which was visible through the glass partition of the large internal space, and it was backed by low walls (Fig. 11*b*). The sculpture pool was accessible through a narrow corridor (Fig. 11*c*) that would have led pointlessly to an empty corner without the statue as its visual focus. By giving a special accent to the far corner of the building, the architect stressed the strongly confined rectangularity of the whole design and underscored the diagonal correspondence between the large pool paralleling the longer side of the building near the open entrance and the small, hidden pool marking the building's shortest side at the remote end.

As this example shows, not only does the setting determine the place of the object, but inversely the object also modifies the structure of the setting. Placed in the corner of a terrace, Kolbe's statue gives the rectangular shape of its more immediate environment an eccentric focus, which contrasts with the

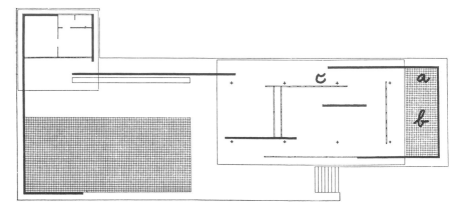

Figure 11

symmetry of the rectangular terrace. The resulting asymmetry creates a tension that must be justified and counterbalanced by the configuration of forces in the building as a whole.

I will report here an experience I had at the time an authentic Japanese house was built in the garden of New York's Museum of Modern Art. The house enclosed a pond of free-form contour, which I admired because, in a way indefinable by measurement and reason, it seemed to establish unalterably a complex spatial relation between the expanse of the water and the landscaping of rocks and shrubs surrounding it. Doubting my judgment, I asked myself whether some arbitrarily different outline might not work equally well. On one visit to the house, however, I noted that somebody had thrown a crumpled-up piece of wrapping paper into the pond. The paper floated on the dark surface of the water as a white patch; and I had to concede that by creating a visually weighty new accent, the intruder had restructured the dynamics of the entire image and disturbed an equilibrium I no longer questioned.

Emptiness and the ensuing sense of forlornness do not come about only when the visual objects needed to determine the field of forces in an open expanse are missing. A similar effect results when such determinants are present but do not add up to an organized structure and thereby cancel one another out. Paul Zucker gives two examples:

New York's Washington Square is laid out as a regular rectangle, framed by houses on all sides—and yet it is not a "closed" square. For its dimensions are so large, the proportions of many of its surrounding structures are so heterogeneous, so irregular, even contradictory, and the location and size of the small triumphal arch are so dissimilar to all the other given factors, that a unified impression cannot result. Disproportion in scale destroys all aesthetic possibilities.

Another factor spoils any aesthetic effect of Trafalgar Square in London: it could have developed into a "nuclear" square had not the tremendous façade of the National Gallery in contrast to the small adjacent blocks of houses and the irregular directions of the streets leading to the "Square" counteracted the effect of the Nelson Column as a space-creating element. But as it is, the column does not become a center of spatial relationships, a kernel of tension.

One could try to describe the disconcerting effect of such a constellation with some precision. One could chart the forces each object generates around itself by its size, mass, location, and direction, and one could show how its particular local field is not supported by those of its neighbors. The object thus does not fit with its neighbors into a superordinate structure, created by them all and containing them as organic parts. The disorientation resulting from a chaos of forces impinging on one another in a disorderly fashion makes it impossible to determine the place and spatial function of any object within the perceptual field. If the observer himself is that object he himself will feel forlorn. A prime source for such perceptual disorientation is the recent fad of reflecting glass walls, which create a surrealistic contradiction between incompatible images. The wall is destroyed, and the reflection shows a space that is not there.

THE DYNAMICS OF SURROUNDING SPACE

Another observation by Zucker suggests that the visual field expands not only in the horizontal dimension but also vertically. He says that an architectural setting induces a definite ceiling to the sky above it:

The subjective impression of a definite height of the sky is caused by the interplay of the height of the surrounding buildings and of the expansion (width and length) of the floor. It is strongly influenced by the contours of eaves and gables, chimneys and towers. Generally the height above a closed square is imagined as three to four times the height of the tallest building on the square. It seems to be higher above squares which are dominated by one prominent building, whereas over wide-open squares, such as the Place de la Concorde in Paris, the visual distance of the sky is only vaguely perceived.

What Zucker calls the "ceiling" of the sky is what I would describe in dynamic terms as the visual field of forces generated by the heights and masses and probably also by the overall relief of the architectural setting, such as that of a city square. A dynamic interpretation of the phenomenon

25

lets us understand the "height of the sky" as the limit of the field of forces that issues from the architecture on the ground but cannot reach beyond a certain distance. With increasing distance the field peters out into the empty sky. This phenomenon is reflected visually in the shape of skylines. A sharply horizontal boundary tends to produce an abrupt break between architecture and sky. This is not the case when we see irregular contours, which may build to peaking clusters. The diminishing width of spires and towers supports the same visual conception. The architecture diffuses gradually into the sky.

If one turns the shape of a skyline by 90° (Fig. 12), one is reminded that a similar gradual diffusion into the surrounding space is much less appropriate for the vertical boundaries of buildings. This is due to a basic difference between the vertical and the horizontal dimensions, to be discussed in the next chapter. But this difference is also symptomatic of what happens when fields of forces are not permitted to expand unchecked. In such cases, quite common in the horizontal relations between buildings, architectural structures control each other's outreach, the way countries stabilize their boundaries on the political map by power exerted from both sides.

As an example we may look at the size of open spaces bordering on buildings. The parvis in front of Notre-Dame de Paris was originally much smaller than it is now. Even so, it seems to me that the building is well served by the present, rather large, space in front of the façade. The space is large enough to let the structure exert its impact and confined enough to prevent dilution of its intensity. A building with a more open plan, for example, one with wings protruding beyond the center, calls for a more extended "doormat."

What I am describing here as the field of forces surrounding a building should not be taken to refer simply to the distance necessary for an observer to survey the shape of a building. Such proper viewing distances do exist, and I shall refer to them later, but what I am describing here affects the position of the observer in a different way, namely in the sense of "proxemics"—the proper distance prescribed by the nature of a thing or person one is facing. Buildings must maintain a proper distance from one another, and the same rule of conduct holds for an observer. Rembrandt is reported to have said, "You must not sniff at my paints"; and although there can be good reasons for someone to scrutinize a painting or sculpture from close by, there is always something disrespectful and inappropriate about it. The novelist Robert Musil has expressed this aspect of spatial response metaphorically: "Each thing or creature, if it wants to approach another one very closely, has

26

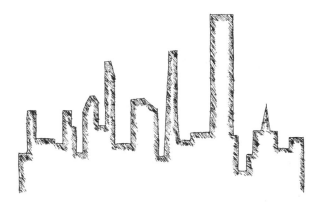

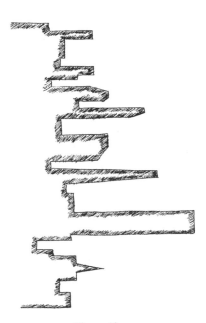

Figure 12

a rubber band tied to it, which tenses when stretched. Otherwise things might end up moving through one another. And so in every motion there is a rubber band that lets one never quite do all one wants to do."

In order for an object to be perceived appropriately, its field of forces must be respected by the viewer, who must stand at the proper distance from it. I would even venture to suggest that it is not only the bulk or height of the object that determines the range of the surrounding field of forces, but also the plainness or richness of its appearance. A very plain façade can be viewed from nearby without offense, whereas one rich in volumes and articulation has more expansive power and thereby asks the viewer to step farther back so that he may assume his proper position, prescribed by the reach of the building's visual dynamics.

As long as the base of a building is in contact with the ground, the need for visual breathing space does not apply to its bottom. However, when it is conceived as a mass suspended above the ground and resting on columns, piers, arches, or pilotis, a proper air space is required for this additional dimension as well. The particular size of such a ground space depends, of course, on the effect the architect intends. If the interspace above the ground level is large, the building may float like an anchored balloon and may even lose its connection with its base. If the space is too small, the visual forces issuing from the building toward the ground may seem constrained to occupy an area that is too small in relation to the building's mass. When Le Corbusier was designing the Carpenter Center for the Visual Arts at Harvard University, it was realized that the horizontal protrusion of the large curved North Studio on the second floor would lose much of its outward thrust unless a larger space beneath it rendered it more independent of the attraction exerted by the ground. For this reason an essentially unfunctional pit was dug beneath the studio area, which, resting on relatively slim pilotis, acquired thereby the necessary dynamic freedom (Fig. 13).

The preceding examples will have made it increasingly clear that in perceptual experience the spaces surrounding buildings and similar structures cannot be considered empty. Instead these spaces are pervaded by visual forces generated by the architectural structures and determined in their particular properties by the size and shape of their generators. Visual forces are not isolated vectors, but must be understood as components of perceptual fields that surround buildings and are also active in interior spaces. Among architects, the importance of these perceptual fields has been acknowledged explicitly by Paolo Portoghesi. Since the notion of

Figure 13. Carpenter Center for the Visual Arts. *Photo*, Harvard News Office.

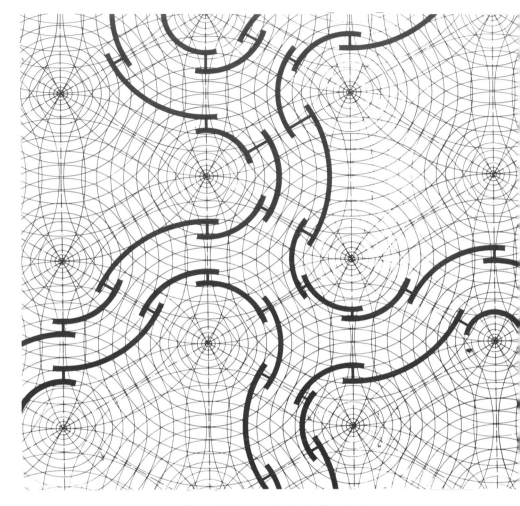

Figure 14. Drawing by Paolo Portoghesi.

perceptual and social fields has been adopted from physics, Portoghesi begins his discussion with a formulation of Albert Einstein's: "We speak of matter when the concentration of energy is high and of fields when the concentration is weaker. But in that case the difference between matter and field appears to be quantitative rather than qualitative." Conceiving of buildings as islands in space, Portoghesi is focusing upon those shapes that indicate the dynamics of fields most directly, namely on patterns of concentric circles, as they appear on the surface of a pond when a stone is dropped

30

into the water (Fig. 14). Just like its counterpart in hydrodynamics, a field of visual forces in architecture expands from the center and propagates its wave front as far into the surrounding environment as its strength permits. Portoghesi writes:

By emphasizing the generated field in addition to the architectural object, one raises once more the problem of space, but in different terms by giving the concept a different value. In traditional criticism space is a homogeneous structure, a kind of counterform to the mural envelope, indifferent to the lighting conditions and to its position in relation to the buildings, whereas the notion of field stresses the continuous variability of what surrounds the architectural structures.

Circular buildings expand into the environment, whereas concave walls "open the building toward the urban space." In the latter case the center of the generating field lies outside the architectural structure, which acknowledges the field's presence by yielding to its expansion. These observations go well with what is known about the dynamic effect of concavity and convexity in other perceptual situations, as I will point out later. What needs to be added here is that although circular fields are most easily recognized and described, a field theory of architectural spaces must acknowledge more generally that buildings of any shape create fields of forces around themselves, and that the particular configuration of such a field depends in every case on the form of the generating structure.

31

II. VERTICAL AND HORIZONTAL

I N THE preceding chapter I took some pains to show that space is created and structured by the objects that populate it. This means that the masses of buildings and the distances between them, as well as their shapes and boundaries and axes, organize the dwelling places of man outside and inside. At the same time, however, we must bear in mind that the spontaneously evident conception of space as an objectively existing framework is not simply a perceptual figment, but a reality supported by physical facts of fundamental importance. Among them are the effects of the sun and the moon and weather conditions. Yet even these objects and forces can be described as components of particular constellations that determine the structural skeleton of the particular space we experience. When the Japanese built homes with moonviewing terraces oriented toward the south, the moon and the house and the reflecting pool in the garden were almost tangibly united in a particular local configuration. But these cosmic elements reach so much further than the local relations discussed earlier, and they control our spatial environment as a whole to such an extent, that we can hardly be reproached for treating them as objective properties of space as such. This is particularly true for the influence of the force of gravity, discussed below.

ASYMMETRICAL SPACE

Man experiences the space he lives in as asymmetrical. Among the infinitely many directions of three-dimensional space along which he theoretically can move, one direction is distinguished by the pull of gravity: the vertical. The vertical acts as the axis and frame of reference for all other directions.

32

The asymmetry of perceived space is due to man's sensory limitations. If we were more discriminating, we would notice that verticals in different places do not run parallel but converge toward a common center, the center of the earth. A more comprehensive view, as might be enjoyed by St. Exupéry's Little Prince on his miniature planet, would make us see any particular vertical as one spoke of a wheel, as a single, undistinguished component of a centrically symmetrical system.

It is a matter of relative size. If a spherical object is small enough in relation to man's own size or if it is far enough away to appear sufficiently small, the parochial narrowness of sensory experience does not come into play because the system can be viewed as a whole. When astronauts are returning to Earth, there must be a transitional period when the spherical surface of the planet turns into the ground plane of terrestrial life. This is more than a straightening of curvature. It also means that the surface, once the mere outer skin of a solid, becomes instead the base of reference. Like the keynote or tonic in music, the ground plane now acts as the zero level for the gauging of all vertical distances. These distances are perceived as heights when they go upward and as depths when they go downward, and by digging into the ground one experiences moving not toward the center of the system but away from the base.

Geometrically there is no difference between going up and going down, but physically and perceptually the difference is fundamental. Anybody climbing a tree, a ladder, a staircase, feels he is striving to overcome a counterforce, which he locates in his own body as weight. Thus the gratification in climbing consists in the conquering of one's own inert heaviness for the purpose of attaining a high goal—an experience inevitably endowed with symbolic connotations. Climbing is a heroic liberating act; and height spontaneously symbolizes things of high value, be it the value of worldly power or of spirituality. To rise in an elevator, balloon, or airplane is to experience being liberated from weight, sublimated, invested with superhuman abilities. In addition, to rise from the earth is to approach the realm of light and overview. Therefore the negative overcoming of weight is at the same time the positive achievement of enlightenment and an unobstructed outlook. Digging below the surface, on the other hand, means becoming involved with matter rather than relinquishing it; it means proceeding from the everyday surface existence at "zero level," where matter abounds but leaves open spaces in between, to the compactness of the earth, through which openings must be bored. To dig is to explore the foundation on which all life rests and from which it sprouts. Digging creates an entrance to the realm of darkness, and therefore it stands symbolically for deepening, i.e., for exploring beyond the superficial. Whereas rising is the means of becoming enlightened, digging makes the light shine in darkness.

Thus all building shares the daring sin of hubris or encroachment, committed by the sons of Adam when they built the Tower of Babel, "whose top may reach unto heaven." It represents the intrusion of the realm of matter into that of empty space, the raising of the basis of human action beyond the safety of the common ground. It increases the load that must be sustained at ground level and, at the heights, exposes man and his work to the elements active in open space. The quest for the honor of scaling the heights, which made the noble families of medieval Italian towns vie with one another in the construction of tall towers, survives, for example, in the recent competition between two insurance companies in Boston to see which could erect the tallest building. Such episodes show the value spontaneously attributed to the purely symbolic quality of visual height and to the dignity that comes with being the tallest peak in the hierarchy of the cityscape. As an Italian writer of the sixteenth century, Lodovico Dolce, observed, the clock towers serve to hold bells, "but in some ways they also signify vanity, as the proverb says: *far campanili in aria.*"

Geometrically all three coordinates of the Cartesian system of space are equal in character and importance. Our earthly space, however, is pervaded by the pull of gravity, which distinguishes the vertical as the standard direction. Any other spatial orientation is perceived according to its relation to the vertical. By leaning physically, the campanile in Pisa deviates visually from the norm established by the surrounding buildings, a visual norm confirmed by the viewer's kinesthetic sense of equilibrium in his own body. The built-in standard of verticality is not easily overridden. It takes an environment of consistent visual tilt to mislead someone into believing that the pull in his body aims in an oblique direction. Off some American highways there used to be "mystery" houses in which, according to the advertising, the mineral core of a neighboring hill pulled visitors magnetically toward it. Actually, the small building was erected at a slant—a fact hidden from the eyes of the visitor by skillful landscaping (Fig. 15). Inside, the walls, ceiling, and floor were perceived as perfectly vertical and horizontal, but water ran at an oblique angle to the spout, and the visitor himself felt irresistibly pulled sideways and unable to stand straight, unless he closed his eyes and found that he *was* straight. York University in Toronto has an art building erected in

34

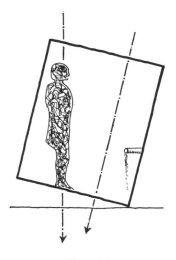

Figure 15

the form of a leaning slab. Some internal walls are accordingly tilted, and although the floors are fortunately horizontal, the objectively vertical piers supporting the building inside look diagonal and produce a bewildering disorientation in the viewer.

VISION TAKES TO THE UPRIGHT

In our spatial system, the vertical direction defines the horizontal plane as the only one for which the vertical serves as an axis of symmetry. It is the one plane on which one can move freely in any direction without the sensation of climbing or descending. Therefore no direction along the ground plane is spatially distinguished. Christian Norberg-Schulz has written that "the horizontal directions represent man's concrete world of action. In a certain sense, all horizontal directions are equal and form a plane of infinite extension. The simplest model of man's existential space is, therefore, a horizontal plane pierced by a vertical axis" (Fig. 16). And Frank Lloyd Wright has pointed to motorized transportation as having opened to Americans the unlimited freedom of the horizontal plane.

It follows from the asymmetry of space that being is experienced essentially as verticality. To come into existence means to detach oneself from the earth, be it by the organic growth of plants or the upward thrust of mountains or by their human equivalent, building. In daily visual experience, a thing or creature shows up by rising above the ground, and a vertical axis is a

35

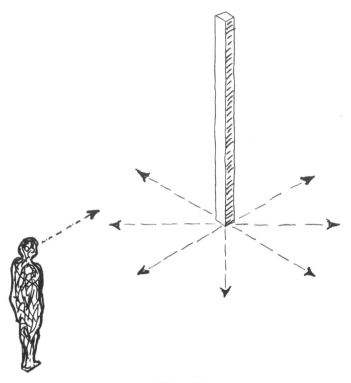

Figure 16

particularly characteristic aspect of its shape. Around the central stem of such an axis the mass of the object tends to arrange itself symmetrically, in accordance with the fact that in the horizontal plane all directions are equivalent. More will be said about symmetry later, but for now we should note that matter is grouped symmetrically around the vertical axis unless intervening forces modify this simple equilibrium. The cylinder of the tree trunk expanding by accretion in all directions is the prototype of shape in gravitational space. We may say that what requires explanation about any particular shape is not its symmetry but its asymmetry.

According to Gaston Bachelard, our image of a building is characterized by two qualities: we conceive of it as vertical and as centralized. This remark throws light on the particular nature of upright objects arranged like a set of organ pipes or like bottles on a table top in the still lifes of Giorgio Morandi (Fig. 17). The relations between erect objects are read as parallels; we do not make direct cross-connections between them as we do when we perceive

36

Figure 17. After a painting by Giorgio Morandi.

relations within a single object. Rows of windows in a building or the two eyes of a face are seen in direct horizontality. This holds true for the relations between different objects only to the extent that they add up to a single unit, for example, when a row of buildings in a street is seen as a continuous wall or when a hill town covers a crest.

This is not to say that in an arrangement of upright objects we fail to see cross-connections. However, in a predominantly vertical shape we see any horizontal element first of all at its place within the vertical order. Only in that context can it be compared with a similar detail in a neighboring object. For example, when details in two neighboring objects are located objectively at the same height, they cannot be appropriately perceived as so located if they occupy different places within each object's vertical pattern (Fig. 18). In fact, such a cross-connection between structurally disparate elements may come as a disturbing surprise in the visual relation between adjacent buildings.

In this connection compare the look of a symmetrical object, a violin, when it is placed first vertically, then horizontally (Fig. 19). We know from daily experience that symmetry is more readily observed in the upright position than in the reclining one. The vertical shape conforms to the dominant axis of space, and all elements of the symmetrical pattern are seen in the proper relation. But when the instrument is lying on its side, we may respond at first to the approximate upright symmetry suggested by the two lateral concavities

37

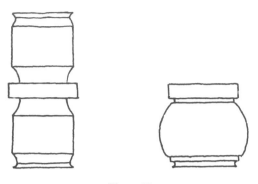

Figure 18

at the waist. The principal symmetry is inferred rather than truly perceived, unless one succeeds in viewing the object as though its axis were turned by 90°. Similarly if one turns a skyline on its side, as I did in the preceding chapter (Fig. 12), one sees an arrangement of horizontal layers, which does not respond to the viewer's spontaneous attempt to unify it along the vertical. The irregular relation among the shapes protruding from the profile boundary gives way to an acceptable array as soon as one sees it horizontally as a palisade of independently complete but coordinated vertical objects.

The stacking of floors, characteristic of most buildings, goes against the grain of our sense of sight when the dominant axis is vertical. The pile of horizontal layers resists the spontaneous visual tendency to integrate them in the upright dimension. This effect is frequently offset by buttresses, columns, vertically aligned windows, and other upright shapes, which counteract the slicing up of the building. Internally, staircases and ramps can fulfill the same function.

A more radical solution consists in emphasizing the horizontal as the building's dominant dimension. When that is done, the floors run along the direction prescribed by the low-slung structure as a whole, and the vertical integration, though indispensable as always, is subordinate. Easy mobility in the horizontal plane becomes the dominant characteristic of the entire building. The free expanse of the ground plane is repeated at each level, and the building conforms to what Frank Lloyd Wright called "the earth line of human life (the line of repose)." In many of Wright's one-family houses this horizontality dominates the outside and is enhanced by the scarcity of partitions indoors. The horizontal style of living promotes interaction, free mobility from place to place, and ease of progress, whereas vertically oriented

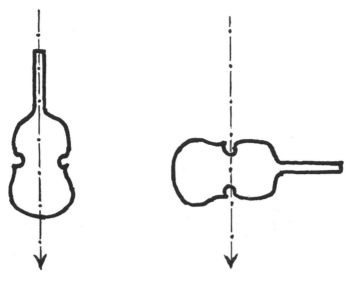

Figure 19

living stresses hierarchy, isolation, ambition, and competition. (Of course, other factors may override this purely spatial one. In a palace, for example, a horizontal arrangement may serve a functional hierarchy.)

PIERCING THE GROUND

The dominant axis of a prevalently vertical building meets the ground at a right angle, and since linear shapes have the dynamic property of continuing visually unless they are stopped, such a building tends to look as though it continues into the ground. This visual effect lends support to the biological metaphor of buildings growing from the soil like plants. Norberg-Schulz notes in this connection that the first permanent huts in Sumer were built by bending rushes without uprooting them. If we compare the look of buildings with that of plants, however, we observe a distinct difference. Plants present themselves as outgrowths of the earth. A tree trunk does not stand on a base but emerges from the ground. What is visible of the tree looks properly incomplete since a plant has its base in the root system underneath. A similar appearance is appropriate for a building intended to be seen as emerging from a subterranean structure, i.e., as incomplete. Commonly, of course, there is no such intention. Buildings aim at some ratio between being tied to the ground and being detached from it.

39

Figure 20. Baptistery, Pisa. *Photo*, Alinari.

Why does the baptistery of the cathedral in Pisa look as though it sprouted from the earth like the head of an asparagus? (Fig. 20) Partly, I suppose, because it reminds us somewhat of what we are accustomed to seeing as the crown of a building. But such reminiscence cannot wholly account for the effect. Aspects of the building's shape itself must be responsible. I mentioned a moment ago that, to the eye, linearly directed shapes tend to continue unless they are stopped. Why, then, does the extended horizontal ground around the baptistery fail to cut the building off at the ground? After all, there are two possible solutions to the encounter of two such shapes: either the ground is seen as continuing without interruption underneath the building, or the building is seen as piercing the ground. Penetration comes about when one of the shapes (Fig. 21a) looks incomplete, and when this incompleteness generates a sufficiently strong tendency toward completion. In such a case, shape *a* will take advantage of any available room for visual expansion and will be seen to penetrate shape *b* across the interface. Penetration is prevented when the shape looks complete (21c). The solids indicated in Fig. 21d—cylinders, pyramids, cones, etc.—are ambiguous in this respect: they can look either complete or incomplete, depending on the context.

This is one of the visual reasons why classical columns have bases and capitals. These terminal elements block the further expanse, upward and downward, of the columns. However, as will be seen from Figure 22, such buffers fulfill their function only if they are perceived as belonging to the column, not to the floor. The same is true at the other end: the capitals must be seen as parts of the columns, not of the architrave. Modern columns such as Le Corbusier's pilotis are unmitigated cylinders and run visually right into the floors and the ceilings, because they neither indicate completeness by their shape nor are supplied with buffers. Under certain conditions this effect may suit the architect's purpose; he may want the supports to be seen as rising through the building, unimpeded by the floors they cross.

Looking back at the Pisa baptistery we note that at the ground floor, only a few weak elements spell out the dividing line between building and ground. The openings of the four relatively small doors do so, as do the small bases of the half-columns supporting the arches. Taken as a whole, the ground floor looks like a shaft that announces no intention of stopping at ground level. Furthermore, the cylindrical building displays a definite center, which is perhaps mostly due to the Gothic ornamentation that was added in the fourteenth century. This central bulk establishes a kind of symmetry between the ground floor and the cupola which requires that the ground floor balance

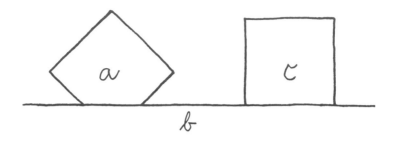

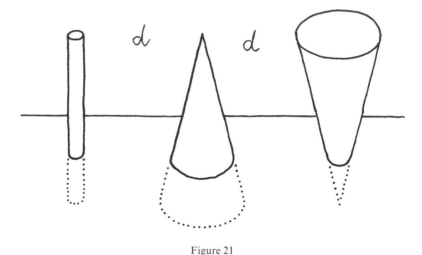

Figure 21

the substantial cupola with a sufficient counterweight—a requirement that could be met only by a greater mass, for example by increased height in the ground floor. Such additional height is potentially available under ground, and for this further reason the building seems to continue into the soil. One need only glance at Bramante's Tempietto in San Pietro in Montorio to see the difference: there the girdle of the gallery emphasizes the center, and the cupola is amply counterweighed by the tall columns of the peristyle on the ground floor, which stands on a base of steps (Fig. 23).

If my analysis of the Pisa baptistery is correct, it also shows what penetration of the ground does to a building's architectural design. Overall proportions and weight distribution are necessarily influenced by whether the

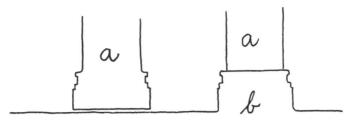

Figure 22

building above ground is seen as complete or incomplete. Any ambiguity in this respect creates an architectural problem.

It is a problem that presents itself when the architect insists, as Wright does, that buildings "belong to the ground." Such belonging is most effectively obtained when a building looks rooted in the soil. Physically, of course, most buildings are in fact so rooted, by means of their foundation, basements, etc. Visually, however, the balancing of the design reckons only with what is visible to the eye. The shape of the building must therefore assert its completeness, but—and here the architect is faced with the delicate task of satisfying two partly conflicting requirements—it must not lose contact with the ground.

Most buildings are bounded by straight walls and, for this reason, face the

Figure 23

problem indicated in Figure 21. They are ambiguous because on the one hand a cylinder, cube, or pyramid looks sufficiently complete to be seen as standing on the ground, while on the other hand its straight walls tend to continue into the ground unless something stops them. Although this latter effect is often undesirable, it is equally evident that an exhibition building shaped like a sphere or like a pyramid standing on its tip looks insufficiently anchored. It denies the pull of gravity and seems poised to take off in flight.

HORIZONTALITY

The difficulty illustrated by the Pisa baptistery can be avoided when the ground floor of a building is treated explicitly as a base. For example, on the façades of some of the eminently vertical Gothic churches the ground floor is set off from the upper body of the building by means of large, conspicuously protruding portals. This gives enough horizontality to express independence from the ground. The opposite problem arises for buildings whose main extension is along the horizontal. Here, "belonging to the ground" comes about not by penetration at right angles but by parallelism, which creates an easy harmony. The building hugs the soil and fits easily into the landscape. At the same time, it is rootless like a boat, it tends to float on the surface of the ground because parallels do not interlock. Contact is all the more tenuous because the shape of such a building undercuts the vertical dimension of gravitational pull. The building has little weight; it does not press down.

Distinctly horizontal buildings, such as some of Wright's prairie houses, give the impression of lying on the ground like a reclining animal. Most buildings, however, stand, and this effect can be obtained even when the overall width surpasses the height. Renaissance buildings offer many masterly solutions. A symmetrical façade, for example, strongly supports the vertical direction because it creates a central axis. Even when this axis is not spelled out explicitly, it may be indicated by a central portal, surmounted perhaps by a balcony, as in the Palazzo Farnese. Windows and doors tend to be upright rectangles, each of them a counterpoint to the horizontality of the whole building; and when the intervals between windows are kept large, the coherence of the horizontal rows is weakened. Sometimes a tower adds a vertical accent, such as that on Michelangelo's Palazzo del Senatore on the Capitol in Rome and the one on the Palazzo Venezia.

There is a sense of particular perfection in buildings of the early Renaissance whose façades approach the ratio of a square, or rather the equivalent

44

of the square appropriate to the asymmetry of gravitational space. (To the sense of sight, a vertical extension counts more than a horizontal one, so that an upright square must have slightly more width than height for the four sides to look equal.) When the articulation of windows, doors, columns, etc., helps carry out the effect, such buildings seem to strike a happy balance between self-contained completeness and due reliance on the supporting ground. However, it goes without saying that there is no one best solution, valid for everybody. The ratio between rising and reposing, lightness and weight, independence and dependence, is at the very core of the human sense of what life is and ought to be, and as such it is a principal variable of style.

In a more general sense, the relation between vertical and horizontal extension not only determines the particular shape of a wall, but establishes perceptually that it is indeed a wall. Every visual object comes about as a configuration of visual forces. This configuration *is* the visual object, and therefore what we call a wall is, as far as two-dimensional extension is concerned, the particular interplay of verticality and horizontality set off in our nervous system when an appropriate stimulus strikes the eye. The insensitivity of wall surfaces has occasionally been observed in the past and eyed with suspicion. In the eighteenth century, Marc-Antoine Laugier believed that walls should not be counted among the essentials of a building. They were added because they were needed to carry floors and roofs and because the inhabitants wanted protective shelter. But "believing in the precise presentation of static forces, [Laugier] was of the opinion that the wall had no aesthetic value, a logical deduction since by its very nature the wall tends to conceal or at least to blur over these forces" (Wolfgang Herrmann). And in our own time Paolo Portoghesi has written: "A wall can be an inert surface, the 'face' of a solid, but when it takes a part in architecture it absolutely must assume a direction, an orientation: it must become a part in a pattern of well-defined relations."

One can confirm the legitimacy of such a requirement by looking at large, empty walls, devoid of an explicit framework of horizontal and vertical articulation. They appear curiously insubstantial because the perceptual forces needed to establish their solidity are too weak. Without that solidity the wall fails to fulfill its eminently dynamic role as a barrier that blocks our path. As an obstacle to the visitor's progress, the wall displays its character in three-dimensional space, but it can do so only if its two-dimensionality is firmly established in the first place.

45

WEIGHT AND HEIGHT

The asymmetry of gravitational space not only influences the directional axes of buildings, but also affects the way we perceive the proper distance from the ground. An object moved to a different height changes in visual weight. The weight relations between different parts of a building depend on their height, and therefore the compositional place and function of any element of an architectural design cannot be described adequately unless one takes its height into account.

Three different factors govern this phenomenon: distance, load, and potential energy. (1) Physically, gravitational pull diminishes with increasing distance from the center of attraction, i.e., the object loses weight. Perceptually one cannot say that weight decreases with distance—in fact we shall see that the opposite is the case. At greater height, however, objects seem less subject to the pull from below. The upper parts of a high-rise building look as though they had been let off the leash.

This phenomenon comes about because the earth is not the only center of attraction: every object within a visual field constitutes a small gravitational center of its own. Depending on its visual weight it will be more or less powerful in attracting objects in the environment and also, as I shall observe later, in issuing directional vectors. The result is a very complex hierarchy of weights, each operating as the center of a field of its own, with the stronger ones out-pulling the weaker ones. The strongest of these centers of attraction is of course situated in the ground and brings gravitational pull to bear upon the entire building. Its influence is strongest near the ground. As distance from the ground increases, weaker centers of weight increase in power and independence. Thus, the upper parts of a high-rise building may exhibit conspicuous freedom as architectural centers of their own; they cease to seem merely the most remote outreaches of the earthbound structure. They are perceived as pressing down less forcefully than they do physically. They seem loftier, easier to carry. There is no reason to assume, by the way, that the physicist's or engineer's formula for the lessening of weight with increasing distance from the center precisely accords with the corresponding perceptual effect. We know very little about the experience of visual weight. It may be a direct carry-over from the kinesthetic sensations in our own bodies; it may be due to a physiological asymmetry in the brain field that organizes incoming visual stimuli; perhaps also we attribute to all perceived objects empathically what we observe about the behavior of things not bound to the earth,

46

such as birds, airplanes, and clouds, and the proud independence of the sun and the moon.

(2) The weight of a visual mass may also be influenced by the distribution of loads within a building. Physically, the ground floor is the low man on the totem pole, carrying the greatest load. With increasing height the load decreases. The visual effect of this physical asymmetry is to make the top floors of buildings look lighter than those at the bottom—a compositional factor that the architect may accept, may offset by adding visual weight to the higher levels, or may emphasize and strengthen. In designing the Northwick Park Hospital in England, the architects Llewelyn Davies and John Weeks determined the number of structural uprights on each floor in accordance with the physical load to be carried (Fig. 24). They may have meant this device to be a visual reflection of the physical distribution of weight. Here again, however, there can be no assurance that the physical formula automatically corresponds to the visual effect, that is, that the load looks the way it "is."

(3) The two factors so far discussed tend to lighten visual load with increasing height. The third factor works in the opposite direction. Physically, elevation adds to an object's potential energy. This seems to be reflected perceptually by an increase in visual weight. In framed paintings, which look less tied to the ground than buildings, and to some extent also in sculpture, one observes that the higher a compositional element is, the more its visual weight counts. The same black square looks heavier in the upper region of a picture than at the bottom.

In architecture all three factors are simultaneously at work, and the net result depends on complex configurations of conditions in the individual case. A rose window, for example, looks relatively light because its independence from the ground and the strong autonomy of its round shape loosen its

Figure 24

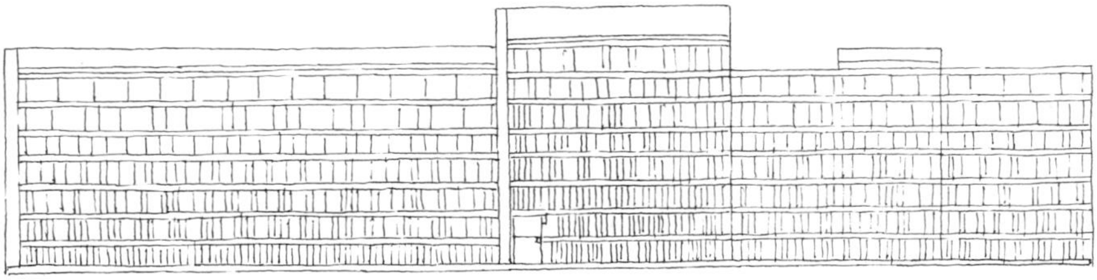

47

tie to the gravitational base. It is also seen to carry a smaller load than it would if placed lower down. (I am not considering here that for reasons of optical projection, the window may look smaller when seen at greater distance—another factor that diminishes visual weight.) On the other hand, because of its high location the window may be charged visually with more potential energy and therefore look heavier. The cumulative effect of these various factors is gauged intuitively by the sense of sight. The architect must decide how much weight he wants his building to carry and where he wants to put it. It is a matter of style.

DYNAMICS OF THE COLUMN

The location of an architectural element influences not only its visual weight, but also the attractions and repulsions exerted by the element on surrounding features of the architectural design. I will now discuss these dynamic effects more particularly, restricting myself for the moment to the upward and downward directions along the vertical. In principle, all such effects of visual direction are ambiguous: they read both ways, which means in the present instance upward as well as downward. In a simple straight line drawn on paper the movement will go in either direction, as long as the line is not anchored at either end. But arms attached to the body or branches attached to a tree trunk are seen as issuing from their base and moving toward the extremity. To see an arm governed by the opposite dynamics, running from the finger tips to the shoulder, one has to read the movement against the natural grain.

Similarly, the dynamics of a building operates in both directions. Upward movement is favored because the building is anchored in the ground and has a free end on top. But there are powerful incentives in the opposite direction as well, the preeminent one being the visual weight of the total building pressing downward toward the center of gravity. This interplay repeats itself in the components of the building, adding up to a complex dynamic situation. I shall illustrate this with a few notes on one of the simplest architectural elements, the column. One reason I have chosen this particular example is that it was used as his prime exhibit by Theodor Lipps, the only earlier theorist to have acknowledged and systematically described the dynamics of visual perception. The best formulation of his observations appears in the first part of his book of 1897 on the aesthetics of space and the geometric-optical illusions.

Since a column is an essentially linear object, the dynamic vectors per-

48

vading it run for the most part along the vertical in both directions, upward and downward. The particular nature of this interplay depends in every case on the shape and proportions of the column itself and on the architectural elements surrounding it. One obvious determinant is the height of the column in relation to the building's other dimensions. Short columns are the relatively passive recipients of the pressures exerted from above by the load of the roof and from below by the resistance and upward push of the base. Such columns seem squeezed between the two principal powers, and as such they are not perceived as static cylinders of stone but as conduits for antagonistic forces issuing from above and below.

Longer columns have enough visual weight to establish a center of their own. From that center, vectors issue in both directions, pushing against the weighty roof, which presses downward, and against the base, which surges upward. This active challenging of the superior powers gives the tall column an elating sense of freedom, of victory over oppressors.

All visual dimensions being relative, the dynamic effect of column height depends on the relation between height and thickness. Thickness increases the visual mass and therefore the weightiness of the column, but it also weakens vertical linearity and thereby decreases the dynamic impact in both directions. The thicker the column, the more inertly it reposes in itself. In a broader context, the length of a row of columns strongly controls the effect, because although the single column may be slim in itself, it is seen as part of the framework of the entire colonnade, which generally has more breadth than height. The frontal row of columns in the façade of the Parthenon forms a horizontal rectangle of about 3:1, which diminishes the vertical thrust considerably. By the same token, the eight frontal columns have much more verticality than the seventeen on the sides.

The dynamic effect depends not only on proportion but also on shape. I have already referred to the strictly cylindrical pilotis of modern architecture, which rely for their dynamics exclusively on vertical extension and the relation between length and girth. The neutrality of their shape makes them depend strongly on the forces acting upon them from above and below. At the same time, the dynamic encounter with ceiling and floor is weakened by the impression that these straight-shaped elements pierce the surfaces they meet and therefore largely bypass the confrontation.

In traditional columns, as I pointed out earlier, the bases and capitals prevent the vertical movement from seeming to continue visually beyond the interface with ground and ceiling. But these buffers can also act as barriers to

49

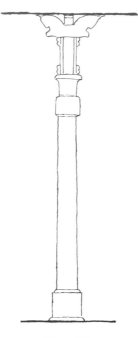

Figure 25

dynamic interaction, as can be seen from what happens when these elements are unusually heavy and sharply detached from the shaft of the column. In viewing the reconstruction of Xerxes's Hall of the Hundred Columns in Persepolis, one observes that the heavy drums at the bottom and top and the further elaboration of the capitals isolate the columns almost completely from their environment (Fig. 25). Greek and Roman columns avoid this effect by reserving brusque interruption for the interface, whereas the base and especially the capital grow smoothly from the shaft by shapes that are most compact in the Doric style, disperse into a branching pattern in the Corinthian, and curl back after impact in the Ionian.

The classical column is broadest at the bottom and thereby establishes a weight center, from which it tapers toward the top. This shape creates a strong connection with the ground and favors the upward thrust of rising toward a relatively freer end. In the opposite case, when the shaft is broadest at the top and tapers toward the bottom, the dynamics is likely to read downward. This is especially true when such columns carry a visually heavy

50

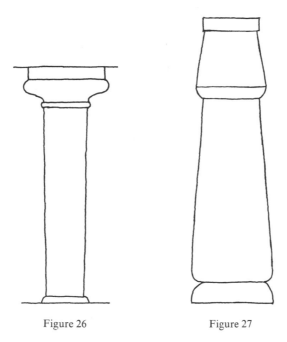

Figure 26   Figure 27

weight, which is seen to press through the columns toward the ground. It should be kept in mind, however, that, as I pointed out earlier, all dynamics can be perceived in both directions. If the downward-tapering column is viewed inversely as rising from the base of the ground, it may look slight at the bottom and gain weight as it grows. Examples are found in the Minoan columns of the palace of Knossos on Crete (Fig. 26) or in modern architecture, e.g., in Le Corbusier's Unité d'Habitation in Marseilles and in buildings by Nervi. When in such buildings the supports are seen to point downward like legs growing from the mass they carry, they counter the normally strong connection between column and ground.

The dynamics animating a column, however, does not issue entirely from its extremities. The weight center established by the column itself is sometimes made explicit by a swelling. Examples are the so-called bud-and-bell columns, imitating bundles of papyrus reeds, in Egyptian architecture (Fig. 27). The swelling is greatest well below the column's center and thereby emphasizes upward movement. The same is true for the entasis of classical columns, which departs farthest from the straight line about one-third of the way from the base.

51

Entasis represents a special case in that the curvature is perceived only by its effect, not as an explicit geometric property of the profile. It is one of the so-called architectural refinements, which are generally explained as optical corrections of the apparent hollowing of uprights and sagging of horizontals. If there is any reliable experimental evidence for these psychological effects, I have not come across it, which does not mean the explanation is wrong. It seems quite possible, however, that one main function of these slight curvatures is to relieve the rigidity of straight lines, which are least congenial to the visual expression of dynamic action. If that is so, the dynamics created by the swelling would not merely compensate for an optical illusion in order to re-establish straightness but would create a visual expression of its own. In keeping with the ambiguity of dynamic effects, that expression could be mainly passive or active. According to Lipps, the Greek column expands, "as though it were held back and pressed outward by its own weight or by the load." Similarly the architect Richard Neutra surmises that Greek columns "showed a pronounced swelling at the lower part of their shaft to indicate something like a visible capacity of elastic compression under load." This effect would be one of pure passivity. In more active terms, the swelling can be likened to that of a muscle. It helps create a center of energy from which forces issue upward and downward.

Any change of shape contributes to dynamics. The change may be a simple gradient of increasing or decreasing girth as in the tapering of columns, or a curvature involving a change of direction as in swellings. The most imaginative demonstrations of the effect of gradual change come from the supports designed by Pier Luigi Nervi. On the ground floor of the Unesco building in Paris, for example, Nervi's pilotis start at the base as an oval shape whose major axis parallels that of the building; as the pier rises, that axis gradually changes into one oriented at right angles to the first (Fig. 28). Simultaneously the originally round shape of the oval turns into an elongated rectangle. These transformations add secondary visual stresses to the overall gradient of the piers, which grow in girth as they rise toward the bulk of the building and also, looked at the other way, descend from the building like legs standing on the ground. The piers are not vertical but incline toward the inside and form symmetrical pairs, each of which represents a base, broad at the bottom and tapering as it rises (Fig. 29). Thus Nervi achieves a counterpoint between the crescendo of the single shapes and the decrescendo of each pair of pilotis rising from the ground. Only by describing such patterns in terms of their dynamics can one do justice to their expressive richness.

52

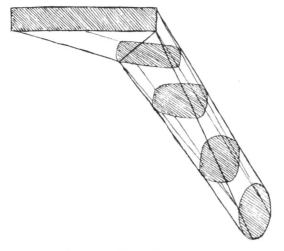

Figure 28

THE PLAN AND THE SECTION

The asymmetry of terrestrial space also affects the various means drafts-men adopt to represent a building in two-dimensional drawings. We compare here the plan, which is a map of a horizontal level, with a section, which cuts through the building vertically. Immediately we run into a curious paradox. As a visual image, a building presents itself to us in the vertical dimension. Think of Notre-Dame de Paris, and you see it rising from the ground, with its two cubic towers sitting like ears on its head and its body extending behind it in the couchant position of a sphinx. The building's image is given to us by what stands up on the ground, and we like to think that we come to know it well. And yet it is an equally common experience that after looking at good photographs of a buildings or even walking around

Figure 29

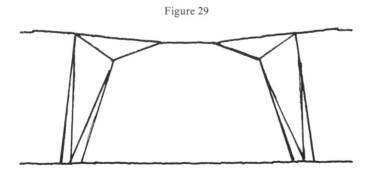

it, when we are shown a plan of it, we exclaim: "Oh, I see! That's the way it is!" At a glance, we have grasped its essence, its way of serving its function. This is less true for buildings like Notre-Dame, intended mostly as a visual monument and showpiece. Its essentials are contained in its appearance, and the plan does little to prepare us for what we see when we approach or enter the church. The opposite is true for buildings whose overall form is less simply surveyable and less determined by convention.

It seems remarkable that the true nature of a building should be revealed by its plan, that is, by a view not available to anybody once the building is standing. Only when it is demolished, burned to the ground, or revealed in its foundations by archeologists can a comprehensive glimpse of it be obtained from a helicopter. But when we walk through the intact building, its plan is distorted by perspective and broken up by partitions, and the simultaneity of the overall pattern is replaced by a sequence of vistas. Yet almost inevitably do we try to reconstruct mentally the plan of the whole from the partial glimpses we receive. When we succeed, the flash of insight is a genuine *Aha*-experience, as psychologists call it. And only after this has happened do we feel confident that we know where we are.

The paradox derives from a fundamental difference between the world of action and the world of vision. The principal dimension of action is the horizontal surface, and whatever is relevant to action tends to be revealed by the plan. The principal terrain of vision, however, is the vertical. Only a small range of things can be surveyed as we cast our glance downward, certainly not a building. If we want to see a large expanse without constraint or excessive foreshortening, it has to face us in the vertical, where it meets our line of sight perpendicularly. Therefore a building intended essentially as a visual monument, such as a cathedral, displays its character in the vertical dimension and declares by its emphasis on the upright that it is not made for human habitation but as a superhuman image for dwarfs who are endowed with the sense of sight.

Since the arena of action is the horizontal dimension, the ground plan tells us how a building serves as the object and organizer of human activity. The plan tells us where to go to do what. Take the simple example of the plan in Figure 30. Only when the visitor realizes that he can reach his goal (A) equally well by turning to the left and to the right can he decide sensibly how to proceed. Even though the symmetry of the two paths can never be directly seen, grasping it is a prerequisite for understanding the building's structure and for making proper use of it.

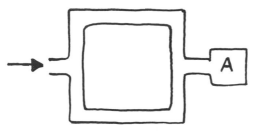

Figure 30

The same pattern can also exist vertically. There are buildings, or combinations of adjacent buildings, in which one can get around an obstacle, perhaps an auditorium, only by climbing up one floor and crossing above it or by going down one floor and crossing underneath. Here again it is useful for the visitor to know the alternative exists, but the pattern is not experienced as symmetrical because, as I mentioned earlier, symmetry along a horizontal axis contradicts our intuitive system of spatial relations. In fact, such symmetry is not even perceived as a genuine part of the building. In making use of it, the visitor feels he is taking cunning advantage of a possibility that the architectural configuration permits but does not really intend.

In its plan, a building reveals itself as an instrument for human activity. Accordingly, the plan displays the principal dimension of those buildings whose main thrust symbolizes human behavior. For example, the theme of Le Corbusier's Carpenter Center for the Visual Arts at Harvard University can be understood only by a look at the plan (Fig. 31). The plan reveals a combination of two similar kidney-shaped studios, whose curvature pushes aggressively into two directions of the environment. From the outside, only partial features of this scheme can be seen. Eduard Sekler has pointed out that the torque of the two corresponding shapes "remains a phenomenon only perceived in plan, or by looking at the building from a high vantage point. It does not affect the experience of space inside the building, since the two free-form studios are on different levels."

As this statement suggests, in a strict sense Le Corbusier's theme cannot be shown even in plan, unless the plan combined the ceiling of the second-story studio with the floor of the third—surely a confusing procedure. Instead what is needed here is a synthesis of two plans taken from different levels with certain features selected from each. When a plan is confined to a single level, it will be representative of the entire building only if no relevant change

55

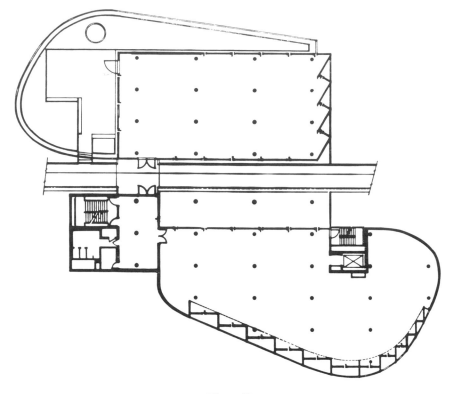

Figure 31

occurs in the vertical, as for instance in an apartment house having the same floor plan on every story, except for the lobby and the basement. Of course, the vertical dimension is never altogether irrelevant. To use the simplest example, when an architect prepares a technical floor plan, he selects the horizontal level in such a way that windows, doors, etc., show up.

It is true that not much happens architecturally between floor and ceiling in most buildings. The walls can be collapsed into the outlines shown on a plan without any essential information being lost. To be sure, if the plan is to show the furnishings of a bathroom or office, it must synthesize the boundaries of objects regardless of the height at which they attain their principal range. But no such integration in the vertical dimension is required for relations between different floors in an office or apartment building. Tenants live their lives in independent layers, often unknown to one another.

Even the upright human body is a small model of such functioning in parallel layers: at the level of the head the central nervous system perceives and processes information, makes decisions, and directs action; at the level of the arms is the sphere of work; and at the level of the legs, we have the sphere of locomotion (Fig. 35).

It is risky, however, to ignore the interconnections, and the architect constantly weighs the relations between different heights. If a road crosses on the ground level at right angles to the main thrust of the building, road and building have to be thought of in interrelation. If a protruding studio on the second floor yields an open terrace for the inhabitants of the third floor, the two levels have to be designed together. Nor can the problem be limited to such piecemeal connections between parts. If the building is to be architecture, i.e., a product of the form-creating mind, it must meet the general standards of the mind, and therefore it must be conceived as a whole, regardless of how useful this overall unity may be to the inhabitants or even how accessible or knowable it is to them. Such unity requires integration along all relevant dimensions.

THE SECOND AND THIRD DIMENSIONS

Even though a building's total design requires three-dimensional integration, its reduction to flat plans and sections is more than a mere technical convenience. The practical advantages are considerable. Within the two dimensions extracted from the whole, all sizes and relations can be rendered correctly. Nothing is hidden, everything can be reached by the eye. As representations of a three-dimensional object, however, these flat slices are severely deficient. And yet, there is a psychological reason why plans and sections cannot simply be replaced by three-dimensional models. The history of sculpture, phylogenetic as well as ontogenetic, tells us that a truly three-dimensional conception is so intricate that it is attained by the human mind only step by step. In early sculpture a three-dimensional object is composed from a set of planes, related to one another at right angles (Fig. 32). There is a front face, a top face, and a back face, and there are two similar side faces. The symmetrically conceived seated figures and sphinxes of ancient Egypt are well known as prototypes of this method. The connections between the two-dimensional projections are made secondarily, and even the completed work retains a basic cubic structure, made up of self-contained two-dimensional views. Only under special historical conditions does the sculptor's spatial conception overcome this basic Cartesian framework and invent freely

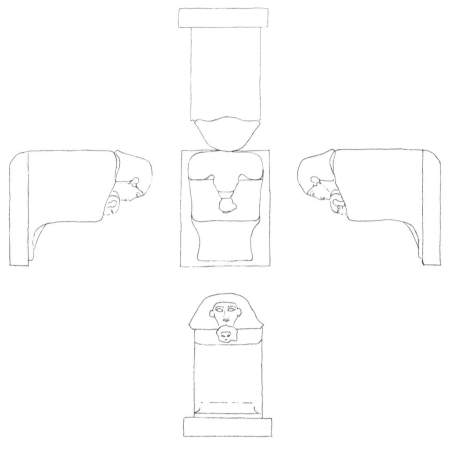

Figure 32

in all directions—a development that can be studied, for example, in the history of classical Greek sculpture from the archaic early figures to the complicated twists and obliquities of the Hellenistic period.

These same psychological constraints exist in architecture, with the difference that only in certain extreme examples of our own time can the architect be said to have left the Cartesian framework behind in a truly sculptural sense. In such cases the dimensions of the horizontal and the vertical are nowhere explicitly visible, except perhaps on the floor. They are only implied as the spatial norms from which leaning curvatures deviate. The prime example of such liberated architecture is Eero Saarinen's air terminal at

Kennedy airport, built in the early nineteen-sixties for Trans World Airlines. Most people have difficulty maintaining their inner sense of the spatial framework if it is visually supported by nothing but the floor and the upright bodies of their fellow travelers, who, not having been designed by the architect, introduce a discordant element of sanity. Sculpture, on the other hand, can afford such freedom for two reasons. Since in itself it is not a spatial environment but in most cases only a part of one, the sculpture's framework comes from its natural or man-made setting. In fact, in deviating from the explicit coordinates of the setting, sculpture fulfills an important aspect of its function. Furthermore, a sculpture is not a vehicle of human habitation. It serves purely visual, not physical, purposes. Therefore it is free from the obligation to satisfy the gravitational needs of human bodies and to assure the eyes that those needs are being met. In the film *The Cabinet of Doctor Caligari*, the "Expressionist" architecture and furniture created an unintentionally hilarious discrepancy between the crookedness of the setting and the organic shape of the actors.

Even when the architect eschews eccentric deviations from the basic three-dimensional framework, the task of visualizing a three-dimensional structure remains a formidable one. The human mind receives all its visual information about physical space from two-dimensional projections on the retinae, and the flat images of plan and vertical section in architectural drawings conform nicely to that limitation of our sense of sight. In Chapter IV, I shall deal more explicitly with the relation between the objective shape of buildings and their perceptual appearance. For the moment it suffices to emphasize that genuine three-dimensional conception is essential and that psychologically it is feasible within certain limits, not only in direct perception but also in mental images.

It would be impossible to grasp even the most elementary scheme of Le Corbusier's Carpenter Center of the Visual Arts if one visualized nothing but the horizontal motif of the two kidney-shaped studios (Fig. 31). A vertical section through the center is even less revealing (Fig. 33). A good photograph of the building's external appearance certainly gives us much to look at, but allows only the merest guess at the building's basic structural skeleton (Fig. 13). In order to grasp that basic scheme one must realize that a central cubic core, externally reflected by the equally cubic staircase tower, constitutes the spine of the building and bears the horizontal wings as a tree trunk bears its branches. One can think of this theme as a variation on the even simpler shape of a spinning top (Fig. 34). Some such image of the interrelation of vertical

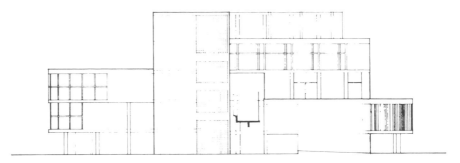

Figure 33

and horizontal elements is indispensable for the most basic understanding of what faces the visitor when he approaches Le Corbusier's creation.

The usefulness of horizontal plans for a viewer's orientation depends, as I mentioned before, on how much happens in the vertical dimension. We have seen that a plan is not simply a footprint, but synthesizes the building's decisive features within a given height range. This can be rather useful as long as the building can be reduced to a number of transversal cross-sections, each of which describes a significantly different level. A set of such horizontal sections from a Gothic church may give us one plan at the level of the nave and lateral aisles, another of the clerestory, and finally one showing the shape and location of the towers on the roof. By superposing these plans, the architect can discover the relations between shapes situated at different levels—an awareness indispensable to the unity of the whole.

Figure 34

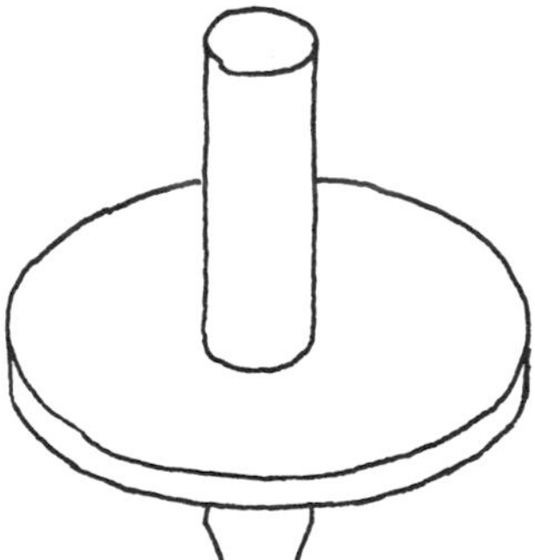

60

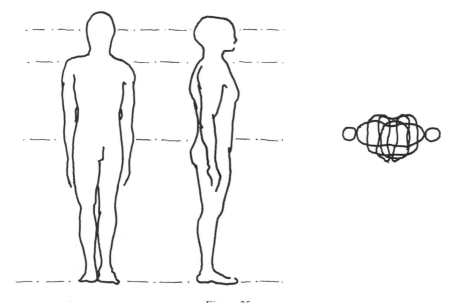

Figure 35

The advantages and limitations of this approach can be illustrated by superposing various cross-sections of the standing human body (Fig. 35). Such a composite of plans can show compellingly how the feet are placed in relation to the head and how the pelvis matches the shoulders. At the same time, the complete exclusion of the vertical dimension falsifies the relations between levels since these depend considerably on the distances in between.

In addition, this collapsing of the vertical becomes quite unsatisfactory as soon as the changes within the upright direction create characteristic shapes. It is evident that a set of hypsographic contours indicating the shape of a cupola or a pyramid at various height levels will give us sufficient data to construct it, but very little toward a synoptic view. The problem has become urgent in modern architecture. The German poet Paul Scheerbart wrote prophetically in his whimsical little treatise on *Glass Architecture* in 1914:

Steel construction makes it possible to give any desired shape to the walls . . . ; one can shift the cupolas from the top to the sides, which will enable us to observe their effect by looking sideways and up while sitting at the table. Curved surfaces are effective also at the lower levels of walls, especially in smaller rooms, which in no way remain committed to the vertical. The significance of the plan in architecture is thereby strongly reduced; the profile of the building gains new importance.

And indeed, the swinging shells and slanting walls that modern builders

61

Figure 36

are now free to use, by pouring concrete rather than piling bricks or stones, cannot be inferred from horizontal cross-sections. Profiles do show up in vertical sections. A cupola reveals its nature to the eye when seen from the side, but we must add immediately that this is so only because any vertical cut through the top of a cupola is identical with any other. Similarly, a frontal elevation of a Gothic church tells us a great deal, in this case because the building has a façade that is not only prominent among the building's vertical aspects but also representative of the sections all along the nave (Fig. 36). To oversimplify, one can say that for such a building, the volume is an extension of the shape of the frontal plane, or conversely that the building's relatively constant cross-section manifests itself in the façade.

Such dependence on an elevation, however, is rarely possible; the Parthenon, for example, which is quite basically a cube, can be understood only by the relation between front and sides. The Parthenon's front face, taken by itself, gives the misleading impression of a flat, self-contained portico. The ratio between height and width in the frontal rectangle has to be perceived in relation to that of the sides; the colonnade does not stop at left and right but wraps around the corners and continues uninterrupted all the way around; the pediment is only the terminal surface of a long pitched roof. In keeping with this three-dimensionality, the building is placed on its site in such a way that the visitor entering the Acropolis from the Propylaea faces it not head on but at an angle. By this means the foreceful completeness of the symmetrical façade loses some of its power to mislead. The view presented to the approaching visitor invites him not to enter the building, but to walk around it.

Such are the limitations of any single upright projection of a building. An orthogonal elevation compresses all shapes running into depth. An angular view distorts proportions, angles, and symmetry. The so-called axonometric projections, drawn in isometric perspective, offer the most successful way of combining minimal distortion with the best overview of a building as a three-dimensional solid.

I shall limit the discussion of this intricate problem to one more remark on the difference between horizontal and vertical sections, which will refocus our attention on the guiding theme of this chapter, the asymmetry of experiential space. A ground plan, whatever its limitation, has a completeness that no upright section can boast. Although a ground plan withholds information about the superstructure, it covers the total range of the space in which man moves. It depicts the whole story of how the building reaches into the surrounding world and how it can be entered, traversed, and occupied. It enumerates the accesses and the barriers. Because the plan locates the building in its setting, it shows its closeness to, or remoteness from, its neighbors, its relations to them, its particular place in the environment. The space represented on a plan is complete in the sense that the absent third dimension is not experienced as a missing component of what is shown. The vertical structure of the building above ground as well as the underground stories are additions to the plan, not completions of an incomplete presentation.

An elevation can never have that same completeness. Whereas a plan, like a map, can be looked at from any direction, the elevation has a built-in distinction between up and down and sideways, and of its two dimensions only the vertical offers completeness. The horizontal gives full information only in those rare cases in which the represented shape is centrically symmetrical. All sections of a circular tower are equivalent, and other centralized buildings have at least two exchangeable sections. But even in these instances the section is a perceptibly two-dimensional image of an essentially three-dimensional structure. Although, as I said earlier, the traditional basilica is essentially a two-dimensional theme extended longitudinally, a vertical section, slicing through it, fails to predict, for example, the presence of a transept.

In the last analysis, this deficiency of any vertical section comes about because the plane it represents is only one among the infinite number of basically equivalent sections available in the 360° range of horizontal space. And although at any one moment a visitor views only one of these sections, he does so with an awareness of this section's place and function among all the other possible ones. Only by knowing of this spatial context can he truly understand the nature of the path he is pursuing. Accordingly, a building will make sense to him only if he can visualize any one of its dimensions in relation to all the others.

THE MIND ADDS THE MEANING

The psychological properties of verticality and horizontality would hardly be worth our attention if their dynamics did not greatly contribute to making buildings into symbolic images, in which man sees fundamental conditions of his own existence. Although a discussion of this final purpose of architecture properly belongs later in our survey, allow me to insert here the visions of a novelist who captures the symbolism of the upright by a powerful religious example. William Golding's novel *The Spire* tells the story of a medieval churchman who adds a spired tower to his cathedral as a perilous monument to his devotion and ambition. The book evokes the state of mind that gave meaning to the great churches, but it supplements it with the more personal images and motives of the kind brought to consciousness only in our own time, although attributable to a man of the past as well. By this fusion of past experience and present discernment Golding's description comes close to adumbrating the full range of meaning arising from the fundamental spatial dimensions.

Golding's story shows, first of all, the dimension of verticality still intact, visually as well as ideally. Only because the tower alone reaches beyond its environment into virgin space can it serve as the architectural fulfillment of a climactic aspiration. The same building in a modern city, surrounded by other buildings reaching much higher for a much lower goal, would look like a pathetic parody of vanished power. Above the roofs of the old town, the great gesture impresses its meaning upon the undistracted minds of clergy and parishioners. Yet this meaning is not limited to a single aspect. In addition to the dynamics of yearning for what is beyond human reach, the tower embodies the attainment of height, which stands for worldly power but is also a pinnacle of virtue. High up is furthermore the position of the watchman, of the custodian and the judge, surveying good and evil deeds. Looked at from below, the tower is an admonition, a center of orientation. "The countryside was shrugging itself obediently into a new shape. Presently, with this great finger sticking up, the city would lie like the hub at the center of a predestined wheel."

A wealth of connotations thus adheres to a simple shape of correspondingly simple visual expression. A family of meanings is ordered into a hierarchy by the town's religious climate; but the conspicuous monument also offers a play of facets, which interact in an overall meaning of considerable intricacy. The vertical dimension is defined only by its contrast with the horizontal, which is equally embodied in the building. Safely reposing on the ground, the church is "the great house, the ark, the refuge, a ship to contain all these people and now fitted with a mast."

The ground plan introduces the element of man. The traditional shape of this plan recalls not only the cross, but also the human figure. This equation between building and man is used by Golding, quite convincingly, in a modern, psychological sense, rather than as the more academic philosophical parallel offered, for example, in the writings and architectural drawings of Francesco di Giorgio (Fig. 51). Here the horizontal position is taken more literally: the human figure with its extended arms lies prostrate on its back, thereby giving the building itself the sense of being tied to the ground. From this condition of weakness the spired tower rises all the more dramatically—as an aspiration, a yearning, an appeal, but also a dangerous insolence. Dean Jocelin, the prime mover of the project, dies from a mysterious back ailment, stretched out helplessly in the image of his church.

The sexual element enters the story quite naturally. The erection of the tower in the virgin sky is also a vulgarity and a sin. Golding introduces this theme explicitly through an episode in which a man on the building crew mockingly takes hold of the small model of the church and dances forward, the spire projecting obscenely from between his legs. And since Dean Jocelin is also an unfulfilled man, haunted by the vision of a woman, we are told that on his deathbed "he looked up experimentally to see if at this late hour the witchcraft had left him; and there was a tangle of hair, blazing among the stars; and the great club of his spire lifted towards it."

65

The complexity of the human connotations—religious, social, and sexual—contrasts significantly with the simplicity of the architectural theme that generates them. It is precisely the stark visibility of basic conditions that makes artistic statements so indispensable to the human mind as it struggles to find the theme underlying the bewildering multitude of individual experiences.

III. SOLIDS AND HOLLOWS

I T IS tempting to deal with buildings as isolated objects as though they were paintings or sculpture. The human mind finds it easier to handle one thing at a time; this holds true for the architect who conceives the building, as well as for the critic or theorist who describes it. The inclination toward piecemeal treatment is reinforced by an individualistic civilization, in which the community has been replaced with agglomerations of single elements, ignoring one another, fighting, competing, or at best trying to get along with the neighbors. Yet even the chaos of our present way of life can be understood only if we view it "from above"—to adopt Max Wertheimer's terminology—that is, by starting from the whole and considering individual elements in their context. Chaos cannot be seen as long as we look at the world "from below," bit by bit. And surely order remains hidden from such an approach.

BUILDINGS IN CONTEXT

Some rudiment of order, of course, is always present, and to some extent any object is governed by its immediate surroundings. Even paintings and statues have acquired their present movability, that is, their insensitivity to place, only in the centuries after the Renaissance. A painting used to be made for a particular wall of a particular building, and the meaning and function of a statue, too, was controlled by the context. A building certainly stands in an environment, and for better or worse the two depend on each other.

But physically the environment is endless, and we find it by no means easy to decide how much of the context we must consider to do justice to a particular building. How should we subdivide the environment and thereby isolate one complex of things from its surroundings, so that we can treat it by

67

itself? Can we deal with Wright's Guggenheim Museum in New York without considering the row of patrician mansions it interrupts? Can we ignore the expanse of Central Park supplying that building with *respiro* and vista, or the high-risers at the horizon staking out the boundary on the far side of the park? Can we view punctured Fifth Avenue by itself without keeping in mind the irregular assortment of traditional and boldly modern buildings that characterizes the entire Upper East Side? And how does a building in Manhattan look at first sight to someone arriving from a different land- or cityscape?

Clearly, there are no fixed bounds in either space or time for any object. But relativity should not deter us from attempting to describe architectural objects with some precision. On the contrary, given a defined framework, the interaction between the object and its context has objectively establishable effects. This framework must include not only the conditions outwardly presented to the perceiving mind but also those prevailing in the viewer himself: his mental preparation, his intentions and goals, his ways of looking at things, and so on. For a valid analysis one has to make explicit both the framework that is being considered and those potential influences which are being bracketed out.

These principles guide us throughout the present investigation. They lead us to consider here what psychologists call the relations between "figure" and "ground." These terms are not self-explanatory. They refer to specific perceptual phenomena, susceptible of clear-cut definition. They are not what a sculptor calls a figure nor what a builder calls the ground, although they can be applied to both.

BOUNDLESS GROUND

Admittedly, psychologists themselves have not done all they could to sharpen the meaning of these concepts and to protect them from loose generalization by analogy and metaphor. In perceptual studies particularly, psychologists have limited their attention mostly to the simplest case of the figure-ground relationship, in which the ground appears as endless and shapeless. When a single shape, e.g., a black square, is placed on an undefined and potentially unlimited ground, only one relation between the two surfaces is considered relevant: one visual object lies in front ("figure"), the other behind ("ground"). The figure has an articulate shape, from which the active properties of the percept derive. Its shape is the sole determinant of the relation between the two partners in the situation. The ground is induced by

68

the figure to lie behind, and it lacks boundaries even in relation to the figure since it continues beneath the figure without interruption. Having no boundaries, the ground has no shape, only some general spatial or textural properties such as low density.

This simplest way of viewing figure and ground accords with what I described earlier as the elementary and spontaneous way of perceiving space. According to that view, space exists as a container, like a huge terrarium into which one can put soil and rocks, plants and creatures. Space is empty and does not generate action or exert any influence of its own. It may be thought of as having boundaries, but they simply constitute an additional object, the glass box of the terrarium; they do not alter the nature of space as an empty medium.

The conception does not basically change when the simple and static distinction between substantial objects and empty space is replaced with the more sophisticated notion of objects as generators of fields of forces that spread through the surrounding space. Space is now pervaded by vectors, but although the behavior of these vectors is modified by the available distances and expanses, they are generated exclusively by the objects and interact with similar forces issuing from neighboring objects. The discussion in the first chapter was limited to this preliminary approach.

THE INTERPLAY OF SPACES

It is necessary, however, to go beyond this special case and consider the very frequent instances in which adjacent areas are all potentially able to assume the role of figure, although they may not all have equal qualifications for that role. In a two-dimensional surface, when adjoining areas are equally qualified to act as figure, a rivalry ensues. They cannot both be figure at the same time. This rivalry is spectacularly evident in the bravura drawings of M.C. Escher and the works of other surrealists, such as Dali, Magritte, and Tchelitchew. Reversible patterns of this kind exhibit an unstable equilibrium and oscillate erratically between the competing versions.

More common, and certainly more useful for the artist's purposes, are situations in which all areas have properties enabling them to be perceived as figure, although some are so clearly dominant in this respect that ambiguity is avoided. Under such conditions, the subordinate areas are seen as ground in the total context, but they are not simply endless and without formative powers of their own. They rather act as "negative" spaces. They have a shape of their own, which contributes to the total pattern. But these negative

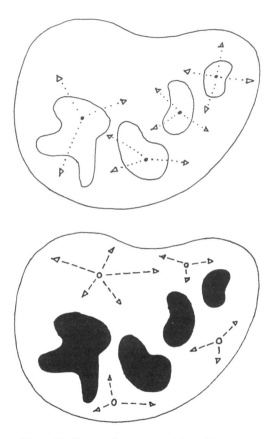

Figure 37. Shapes after a composition of Jean Arp.

shapes can be consciously perceived only if by a subjective effort one forces the structure to invert itself. When this is done the ground can become figure for a moment. Artists do this in order to appraise and control the influence of these negative spaces, which counterbalance the positive ones like a sort of perceptual antimatter (Fig. 37). We shall see that without the counterforce of these negative spaces, the positive ones would be shorn of an essential means of holding together.

As long as the ground is shapeless and endless and therefore devoid of its own structure, the contours are controlled only by the positive figures. But as soon as the negative spaces have any figure power at all, they too influence the contours, although when the pattern is viewed as a whole, they do not possess or share them. Dynamically, the vectors issuing from the inside of the dom-

70

inant figures press upon the contours and try to make them expand into the surrounding space. If this expansive power goes unchecked, the figure lacks definition and floats. Its boundaries acquire perceptual stability only when the internal pressure is balanced by a counterpressure from the outside, that is, by vectors issuing from the negative interspaces. The apparent stillness of the contours reveals itself to the more sensitive eye as the resultant of pressure and counterpressure.

In successful paintings, truly empty spaces, devoid of such countervailing forces, are quite rare. The shapes perceived as figure are held in place, and the range of their influence is defined, by the forces issuing from the ground, and the interplay of all these forces constitutes the pictorial balance, without which a visual statement remains unreadable. It is also true that the figure forces acquire their true vigor only through the resistance of their environmental antagonists. A punch into empty space evaporates.

Our view curiously echoes assertions attributed to the Pythagorean philosopher Archytas. According to Max Jammer, Archytas held that

space has the property of setting frontiers or limits to bodies in it and of preventing these bodies from becoming indefinitely large or small. It is also owing to this constraining power of space that the universe as a whole occupies a finite space. To Archytas, space is therefore not some pure extension, lacking all qualities or force, but is rather a kind of primordial atmosphere, endowed with pressure and tension and bounded by the infinite void.

Theodor Lipps has made the same point very clearly: "To every activity effective in any shape there is a corresponding countertendency or, if you prefer, counteractivity. Shape exists and can only exist by virtue of the equilibrium between the two."

Boundaries turn out not to be the kind of inert delimitation they seem when looked at as properties of physical objects. Physically, a line on paper is indeed a dead thing, and so is the edge, profile, or surface separating a building from the surrounding space. The perceptual images of these lines, edges, or surfaces, however, are products of the nervous system, and as such are the highly dynamic resultants of the antagonistic forces I am trying to describe. The psychological effect is elementary and universal, but only the artist sharpens his intuition to the point of using this effect in his work, and even he may not be explicitly conscious of what he experiences. The man in the street is even less likely to be aware of the dynamism of perceptual objects, although it always has some influence on his visual world.

The basic premise of this approach is the recognition that interspaces can

71

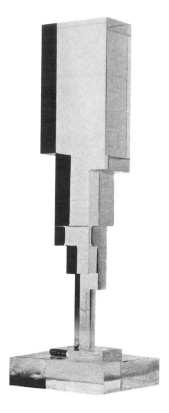

Figure 38. Sculpture by David Carr.

be, and often are, visual objects in their own right. Some years ago, the British artist David Carr exhibited sculptures derived from the interstices between New York's skyscrapers. The steplike setbacks of the buildings yielded a kind of hanging stalactite (Fig. 38). Such sophisticated reversal of figure and ground is, as I said, not characteristic of common perception. But it did not escape the attention of Aristotle, who defined space as what is bounded by the interfaces between physical objects and the open areas around them:

Space and time also belong to this class of quantities. Time, past, present, and future, forms a continuous whole. Space, likewise, is a continuous quantity: for the parts of a solid occupy a certain space, and these have a common boundary; it follows that the parts of space also, which are occupied by the parts of the solid, have the same common boundary as the parts of the solid. Thus, not only time, but space also, is a continuous quantity, for its parts have a common boundary.

72

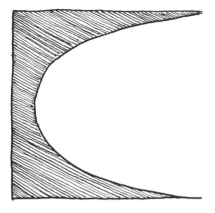

Figure 39

Aristotle thus overrides the ordinary psychological distinction between bounded solids and boundless space; he envisages the physical world as a tightly filled continuum, in which object borders on object as in a jigsaw puzzle. In this he closely approaches the world of the painter and also of the architect, who must cultivate his sense of when open space is empty and when it is not.

In Aristotle's presentation, neighboring objects share their borders peacefully. In perception, however, boundaries are the precarious products of opposing forces. Psychologists speak of "contour rivalry," which comes about in the two-dimensional plane when two adjacent surfaces each attempt to annex the common contour as its own boundary. The contour cannot serve both at once (Fig. 39). In the extreme case, when all the factors determining the distinction between figure and ground favor the same party as the figure, the victor snatches the contour, and the other surface becomes borderless ground. When the predominance of one party is not absolute but only relative, that party has the stronger, although not an uncontested, claim to the boundary. Some contour rivalry prevails.

This contention may seem to be contradicted by common experience. The architect in particular seems to be surrounded by examples of shapes bordering on each other without any indication of a perceptual power struggle. On any brick wall the rectangular units share their seams peacefully (Fig. 40). This is so, however, only because the contours between the bricks are straight lines. The straight-line contour is the exception that confirms the rule, because it happens to be the only possible symmetrical boundary between two

73

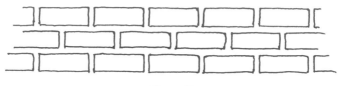

Figure 40

surfaces—symmetrical, that is, not only as a whole but in all its parts as well. It creates exactly the same shape conditions on both sides, and for this reason the antagonistic vectors evoked by the boundary balance each other at every point along the way. Equilibrium is the closest a dynamic interplay of forces can come to reaching a standstill; but by no means is it static inertia.

All other boundary shapes create unequal conditions in the contiguous surfaces or volumes and therefore also different dynamics. The reason why boundaries cannot be shared comfortably is that they fulfill different functions in the two adjacent areas and therefore cannot be seen as one and the same thing. When Aristotle said that adjoining units have a common boundary, he was correct physically but not psychologically. Perceptually a disturbing contradiction is created when an interface belongs to two different boundaries but is only one thing nevertheless. In such a case the interface is related dynamically to two different vectorial centers and is therefore torn in opposite directions. While these antagonistic pulls and pushes make for balanced borderline conditions when the interface is a straight line, they create asymmetries in all other cases—for example, when curves generate convexity on the one side, concavity on the other. The resulting difference is so strong that the identity of the common shape is not recognized perceptually.

More will be said in a moment about the shape of boundaries. But they are only one of the factors governing the spatial relations between contiguous visual areas. For our particular purpose the situation is complicated by the fact that architecture does not primarily deal with flat surfaces bordering on each other in a plane, but with volumes in three-dimensional space.

The rules that have been explored by psychologists for conditions in the plane would make us expect to see buildings as figure and the surrounding space as ground. One of those rules predicts that surrounded shapes are seen as figure unless other factors intervene. In three-dimensional space, an object can be surrounded even more completely than a shape in the plane. An isolated building reveals the solidity of its volume as we walk around it and see its side-faces, its front and back (Fig. 41). It is closed off everywhere, not only

74

Figure 41. Apartment houses in Islington. *Architects*, McMorran and Whitby.
Photo, John Gay.

along the contour of one profile. With this overwhelming closedness the building forcefully asserts itself as the figure, the possessor of the boundary—that is, of its own outer surface. And as the visitor walks toward it, the arrow of his intention singles it out all the more clearly.

In fact the all-around completeness and detachedness of a building can be essential in giving its owner the conviction that he possesses his own home. Lenelis Kruse, in a phenomenological study of the spatial enviroment, reports from Germany that during the planning of a housing development, potential purchasers protested against a proposal to have houses "semi-attached" by adjoining walls, even though this would have given the occupants more garden space. They maintained that one's own home is a home only if one can walk around it.

THE STREET AS FIGURE

This, however, is not the whole story. In cities especially, buildings rarely stand alone. They are parts of rows, and as such they hardly exhibit their three-dimensionality. They fit inseparably into two-dimensional walls, and the walls are experienced as the sides of urban canyons. Besides, the street-dweller is oriented toward the street, not toward any one of the buildings, as long as he has not reached his destination. His eyes direct his course through the open channel. Clearly, this channel is the dominant feature of the urban traveler's spatial experience; it has figure character (Fig. 42). But does this mean that the figure-ground situation is simply reversed: as the empty space becomes figure, do the solid buildings become ground?

"To become a true form, the street has to possess 'figural character,'" writes Christian Norberg-Schulz. What is meant here by true form? Clearly we are being reminded that in order to fulfill its function, the street must offer more than the technical means for pedestrians and cars to reach their destinations. If streets are to serve man as a whole human being, they cannot treat him simply as a vehicle of locomotion. Man is the possessor of a mind, which steers him, anticipates what lies ahead, and distinguishes between obstacle and path. Therefore, the sight presented by the street must let the visitor know that the path he has chosen is the appropriate one for his purpose. What is more, the sight must not only provide the practical information required for spatial orientation; it must also have the expressive qualities that convey the "feeling" of a street: a sense of ready access, of clear direction, of well-defined boundaries for safe progress, etc.

Visually, first of all, a street is more than a path on the ground. Legs and

76

Figure 42. Rue de Furstenberg, Paris. *Photo*, John Gay.

wheels need only a strip of cleared surface to move along, but even on country roads there are ditches and shoulders and trees to direct the eyes on their way. In town, a street is visually a three-dimensional canyon, an elongated duct, formed by the buildings and the ground. To some extent, the façades do not even end at street level but fold at a right angle and continue across the pavement to rise again on the opposite side—the street is an unbroken container. Remember here the earlier observation that the horizontal plane is man's field of action, whereas the primary dimension of vision is the vertical. The street adds an upright dimension to the path and thereby makes it visible as a three-dimensional duct.

The hollow of the street canyon also accomplishes something that I shall soon describe as a prime quality of interiors, namely it acts as an exhilarating extension of man into surrounding space. Although man is only a small creature in comparison with the openness around him, he generates perceptual forces that permeate the environment. This enables him to experience the street channel as filled by a blown-up self-image, which invades space in all directions and also anticipates forward movement.

The street canyon is the realm of man's amplified presence and is therefore perceived as figure. This is all the more evident when one drives, rather than walks. The increased speed emphasizes the penetration of empty space and centers one's attention even more clearly on what is happening within that space. Even physically, the growth of vehicular traffic has greatly enhanced the dominance of the street. Heide Berndt points out that the map of pre-industrial towns testifies to the dominance of the pedestrian:

The narrow and partly confused network of streets was functionally appropriate to streets that served only as access to buildings. Few streets were broad enough to permit the passage of vehicles. The basic element of a town plan was not the street or road, but the dwelling units and public squares. The narrow lanes were determined by the spatial arrangement of the entrance doors.

In the industrial age, the spatial relation between buildings and streets changes. With the increased demands of the transportation system, streets have become more important than the arrangement of buildings in determining the layout of town and city. "The city map shows rectilinear streets that cross at right angles. This opens up the view for perspective vision and reveals vanishing points."

Such a shift in emphasis, however, does not make the buildings and the street floor assume the role of empty, nondescript "ground." To be sure, the buildings provide an enclosure, which gives the channel its shape. The street front hides the cubic volume of the buildings, which would claim the façade as their outer surface. Their flatness enables the façades to serve as boundaries for the hollow channel. The integration of a building's front into the continuous wall of the street can submerge the identity of an individual building. Paolo Portoghesi recalls that as a boy he could not reconcile the building housing his family's apartment, which for him was epitomized by the animated life of the inner courtyards, with the anonymity of the street front:

I left that house at the age of nine without being able to understand the physical relation between what I saw every day from our windows and what I saw outside, in the adjoining streets. The streets were straight like corridors, and instead of the complexity and vivacity of the big courtyard, the severe Renaissance façades ran their course with their constant rhythm and inert opacity.

The continuous flatness of the façades is enhanced in tall buildings by the lack of visible rooflines. Tall buildings reach beyond the pedestrian's visual field and thus hide setbacks and slanted roofs from immediate observation. One sees no tops turning away and opening the channel overhead. Hence the sometimes frightening enclosedness of streets in the high-rise districts.

Even though their autonomy is eclipsed as long as the street channel dominates, the buildings remain positive figures in their own right. A change of attitude can rescue the buildings from the subordinate role of canyon walls and allow their own figure character to come to the fore. The philosopher Heidegger made an analogous observation about bridges. He points out that a bridge traversing a river causes the banks of the river to change character. The bridge makes the banks face each other. Without it, they would "trail along the river as indifferent border strips of land." The bridge accomplishes the transformation by meeting the banks perpendicularly. This is also what happens when a pedestrian or driver turns sideways and focuses on the entrance of a building as a target. Now the "indifferent" wall of masonry is revealed as a face. If I may resort to still another analogy: it is as though a dignitary reviewing an honor guard turns to address one of the anonymous soldiers as an individual person. At that moment the soldier, having been an undifferentiated segment of a running ornament lining the path, turns into a positive figure.

Architecturally, this change in function points to the delicate problem of reconciling the form of a continuous, longitudinally oriented street with that of an array of façades, each complete and frontal, each independent enough to qualify as the sole objective of a journey. It is one of the many instances in which the architect is called upon—when, indeed, he has a say in the matter—to reconcile the independence of the parts with the coherent sweep of the whole. The rows of innumerable small houses lining the canals of Amsterdam, each particular in its design and character but all fitting into a continuous lace pattern of gabled elements, are the prime example of a perfect solution; whereas many of our modern city streets defeat orientation by throwing together buildings that have been designed (if that is the appropriate word) without any regard for one another. The intended and requisite functional unity of the street is lost amidst the discontinuous boundaries.

The height of the buildings that form a street influences the canyon effect we are discussing. Height, however, depends on width, and width also contributes strongly to a street's character. Architecture needs breathing space. If the street is too narrow, buildings facing each other will step on the toes of their opposite number and squeeze the interspace unpleasantly. But the street must not be too broad either. Visual centers can be created only by visual objects, and since the street channel exists only by virtue of the surrounding walls, it cannot establish a vectorial center of its own without proper architectural boundaries. When the width of the street extends beyond the visual fields created by the buildings, there will be "emptiness," in my sense of the term, that is, an area devoid of structure. Unless auxiliary shapes, such as flower beds or trees articulating the central strip of the street, compensate for the deprivation, the visitor will experience forlornness. He will receive no clear guidance on the direction he should take, nor will he be able to gauge his distance from buildings adequately. He will have to muster whatever spatial control he can from within himself, just as one steers a course through a dark corridor. He would be better off walking in an open field or flying in the sky, where the perceptual situation would serve clear notice that he is on his own. What is disconcerting about an overbroad street is that boundaries do visibly exist, but the visitor cannot grasp the aid they dangle just outside his reach. This makes him feel not just alone, but abandoned.

Under what conditions, then, does the street assume figure character? We recall here the analogous situation of columns, which seem squeezed between the jaws of architrave and base when they are too short, but do not meet enough resistance to establish a vectorial center of their own when they are too long. Something similar happens in the relation between buildings and street. Only when the street has just the right breadth can it establish

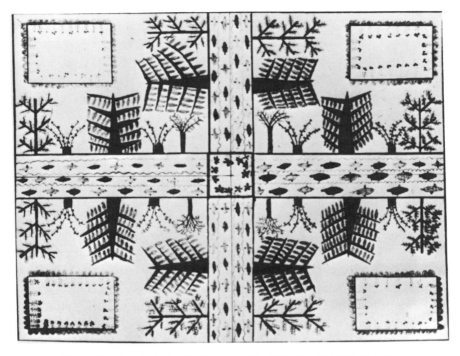

Figure 43. From H. Schaefer-Simmern, *The Unfolding of Artistic Activity.*

itself as a visual object with a vectorial field of its own, which actively resists the forces issuing from the buildings on either side.

CROSSINGS AND SQUARES

What has been said about streets can be applied more generally to all open spaces between buildings. When two streets cross at right angles, the area of overlap is spatially ambiguous. The alternating right-of-way imposed by traffic regulations at such a crossing is a social compromise, designed to cope with the dilemma that two things cannot be in the same place at the same time. I am reminded here of an episode reported by the art educator Henry Schaefer-Simmern from his work with mentally retarded persons. A group of women had designed a landscape in which rivers crossed at right angles, and they puzzled over how to treat the crossing. The lines of fishes swimming along the two streams got into a traffic jam where they met in the center. Eventually one of the participants hit upon a solution: the crossing was made into an island (Fig. 43).

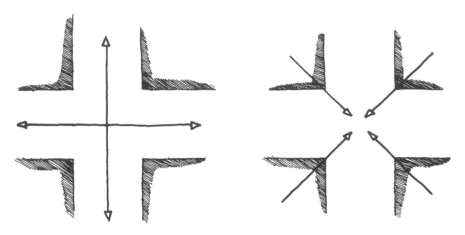

Figure 44

In practice such problem situations can be fruitfully restructured when the two independent thoroughfares are unified in a cross pattern, which defines the area of overlap as a symmetrical centerpiece (Fig. 44). This structural change reorganizes the visual character of the four corner buildings, each of which was split into two essentially independent and two-dimensional façades as long as they were conceived only in relation to the linear streets. The meeting of two flat fronts is now replaced by a three-dimensional conception, in which the corner buildings are seen as cubic solids, symmetrical in relation to their protruding edges and to both streets. This spatial restructuring vastly increases the figure power of the corner buildings. An architect who understands the possibilities of such an integrated conception will design a corner building around a prow pointing toward the center of the square.

What is the dynamic character of the space created by a crossing? Certainly it is not simply empty. Each of the corner buildings generates a field of forces that advances along the building's axis of symmetry toward the center of the crossing. If these four fields were the only dynamic factors in the situation, the buildings would give the impression of advancing toward the center until checked by the impact of the others. The crossing would be a configuration of four centripetal vectors, formed by the buildings as figure and the center space as ground. As befits a ground, the central area would have no boundaries and therefore no shape of its own.

This one-sided solution is overcome when the central area acquires some figure character, that is, when it establishes itself as a structural center in its

82

own right by sending out vectorial counterforces, which balance those advancing from the four prows. When this is accomplished, the location of the buildings can be viewed dynamically as resulting from the interplay between their own outgoing forces and the counterpressure meeting them from the center.

How does the open space of a crossing acquire the figure character of a "square"? We anticipate that relative size is a factor. When the area is too small, it has insufficient space to respond to the pressure of the buildings by generating a vectorial center of its own. If it is too large, the dynamic fields of the buildings do not extend far enough toward the center; and by the same token, whatever focus develops at the center cannot spread far enough to engage the boundary forces and thereby establish a structural organization throughout the square. An example might be the Place des Vosges in Paris, which is more a frame than a square. This example also shows that horizontal distance is relative to the height of the boundary buildings. The buildings are only three stories, which makes the horizontal expanse larger.

On the other hand, the closed shape of the Place des Vosges strengthens its character as a square, as opposed to a crossing, which has no such complete boundaries. It stands to reason that the more explicit the contour, the more prominent the square will be. Compare the crossing of two streets with that of four streets (Fig. 45). Other factors being equal, the square has a much greater chance to establish its identity in the latter case.

Figure 45

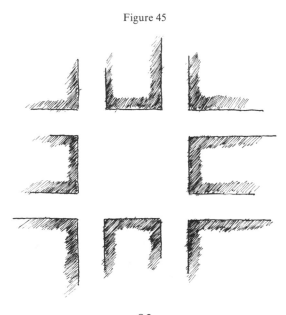

83

Figure 46

At best, however, straight-line boundaries do not close a square compellingly. They stop at the corners, but their very straightness impels them to continue rather than to terminate. This ambiguity of rectangular corners was welcomed by Piet Mondrian, who in his later years endeavored to eliminate in his abstract paintings the "realistic" difference between solid visual objects and empty space. In a letter written to James Johnson Sweeney in 1943 he explained:

You know that the intention of cubism—in any case at the beginning—was to express volume. . . . This was opposed to my conception of abstraction, which is that this space just has to be destroyed. In consequence I came to destroy volume by using the plane—then the problem was to destroy the plane also. This I did by means of lines cutting the planes. But still the plane remained too much intact. So I came only to lines and brought the color in to those.

Mondrian dissolved the closure of his rectangles by transforming the contours into what I call object lines. He made the corners into crossings (Fig. 46). He was aided by the tendency of straight lines to continue in their own direction rather than break around a corner. This tendency is equally strong in architectural crossroads. The outlines of the square are temptingly aligned with the crossing streets, and the visitor is all the more inclined to treat them as parts of the streets when he himself proceeds on a linear, one-dimensional path.

84

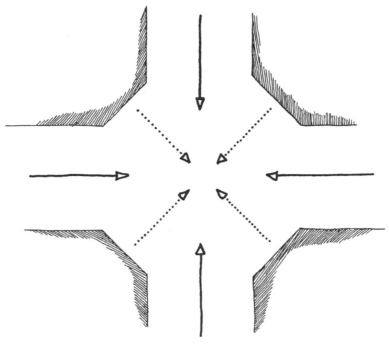

Figure 47

Although a rectilinear square has difficulty asserting its identity, it is ideally suited to making the open space fit smoothly into the street grid. This advantage diminishes as the square becomes more self-contained. A more distinct closure can be obtained by a change of shape. The English word *square* implies right-angular shape; *piazza*, *place*, or *Platz* do not commit the opening to any particular contour. If, for example, the protruding corners of the four buildings at a crossing of two streets are truncated, as they are at the Quadrivio delle Quattro Fontane in Rome, one obtains, in the words of Paul Zucker, "a miniature octagonal square" (Fig. 47). Each corner is blunted by a narrow façade, which is decorated with an inset fountain. These four decorative panels look orthogonally toward the center, creating a centric symmetry. The two streets, the Via del Quirinale and the Via delle Quattro Fontane, no longer form a crossing but constitute the four beams of a star.

The more circular a square, the more self-contained it is. To relate a circular square to its surroundings is as difficult a task in the horizontal dimension as that of fitting a rose window into a façade is in the vertical. The round shape has to be accepted as the dominant focus. A circular square not only stresses its identity by the unbreakable coherence of its contour, it also establishes its center with compelling precision and thereby marks the hub of the square's own vectorial system. From the center, the square's field of forces expands in all directions and is confirmed by the concavity of the boundary façades. The convexity of the square's shape designates it as the dominant figure, whereas the concave buildings recede under the impact of the forces advancing from the center.

But again, as in the case of the street, the surrounding buildings are not simply neutral ground. However dominant the square may be, it cannot annex the surfaces of the buildings as its own boundaries. After all, the square is but hollow space, whereas the buildings are solidly opaque. Under any circumstances, therefore, it is to the buildings that the boundaries belong. In the case of a circular square, these boundaries express by their concavity a strong passivity and subservience. The buildings are seen as being squeezed, pressed back by an external, invisible force. Thus figure borders on figure, but no contour rivalry results because only one of the contending parties is visible as an object or a group of objects.

"Alles Räumliche dehnt sich aus," says Lipps in one of his decisive statements. Everything spatial expands. The hollow space of the square expands with the strength of its vectorial powers, but the surrounding buildings, possessing an expansive power of their own, hold the square in check. Dynamically, therefore, the reach of the square is determined not simply by its geometrical area but by the interplay between centrifugal expansion and surrounding constraint. The resulting equilibrium reflects the precise ratio between the powers of the contending parties.

In the case of the circular square, the dominance of the open area is indicated by the concavity of the walls. A more active counterthrust on the part of the adjoining buildings will enrich the dynamics. For example, one of the buildings may invade the open space with a convexity of its own, as does the church of Santa Maria della Pace in Rome, with its semicircular porch protruding into the square (Fig. 48). This porch was added to the quattrocento church in the seventeenth century by Pietro da Cortona, and the highly dynamic interplay between buildings and square therefore is a reflection of the Baroque spirit. The small square, the Vicolo della Pace, does not simply serve as a parvis for the church by providing space for its vigorous advance. The square's pronounced symmetrical plan also gives it a positive character of its own. In fact, as Hans Ost has pointed out, the square has the intimate closure of an architectural interior, which contains the church, just as the courtyard of San Pietro in Montorio in Rome contains Bramante's Tem-

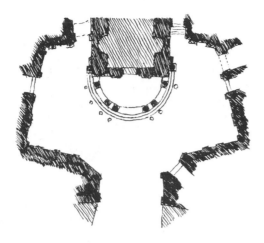

Figure 48

pietto; and it is the Tempietto that inspired Cortona's conception of the semicylindrical porch. Thus the strongly positive shape of the square is qualified to oppose the thrust of the principal building. A dynamic equilibrium is established.

The center or focal point of a square is often explicitly marked by a fountain, obelisk, or monumental sculpture. Such an accent not only confirms the geometrical form of the symmetrical square, it also supplies a tangible site for the square's vectorial center. And while the centrally based field of forces helps actualize the square as an autonomous visual object, it also provides an architectural counterpart to the human occupant's presence. Antlike in relation to the dimensions of buildings and square, man could never assert the right of his presence by his own power. Only a crowd, such as the one filling St. Peter's Square on Easter Sunday, can possibly do that. But a crowd is a very particular manifestation of man; he gives symbolic expression to his special nature mainly by appearing as an individual. Singly, the human visitor must rely on being amplified by visual forces of architectural magnitude. Thus strengthened, he can perform his role as a well endowed partner in the encounter between man and the world he has built for himself.

CROSSINGS IN CHURCHES

A discussion of crossings can profit from some reference to its prominent architectural application in the design of traditional churches. I implied earlier that a street crossing is not really visible, in the sense of being appre-

Figure 49

hended at a single glance, unless one happens to look down on it from a helicopter. The various perspective views available to the pedestrian or driver allow him to infer the objective cross shape of the configuration; but none of these partial vistas contains, or is contained in, that objective image. The same is true, with more weighty consequences, for the design of churches. As the medieval architect laid out the design of a church in which the longitudinal nave was crossed by a shorter transept, he was conscious of creating a building in the image of the cross; and of this symbolic shape some of the building's users were certainly aware. But this underlying design is not immediately evident to the person entering the church through its main portal (Fig. 49). The visitor is presented with a linear vista, a path for his

88

pilgrimage to the sanctuary at the altar, which is located at the opposite end of the channel created by converging perspectives.

Perceived in that way, the church is the architectural embodiment of a path, but not really of a dwelling place. And whereas it assigns a location for the divine being to be worshiped, the altar, it does not similarly acknowledge the presence of man, except by offering him passage. Here the transept provides an essential modification. For one thing, it transforms the building from a channel into a place because any crossing marks a place. Mere passage gives way to stable position. A building can be said to become a "place"—as distinguished, for example, from a covered bridge, which is a passage—when its basic pattern occupies both horizontal dimensions, not just one. The building makes its mark.

The crossing also establishes a dwelling place for the worshiper on his way to the altar. It creates a second center, rivaling the first in importance (Fig. 50). This ambiguity in the basic arrangement, the presence of two competing centers, enables the layout of the Latin cross to function as a highly dynamic image of the meeting of man and God. As the approaching worshiper reaches

Figure 50

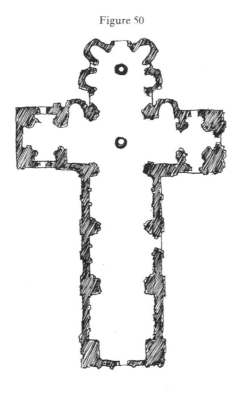

89

Figure 51. After Francesco di Giorgio.

the crossing he is stopped at the sight of the transept, and he may also discover that he stands under a cupola. The cupola is an image of the sky and as such points to the dwelling place of the divine power, whose terrestrial representation at the human level is the altar. The height of the cupola reinforces the remoteness of the altar. At the same time, however, the cupola is certainly a canopy for man, since it is he who stands below it, protected and thereby exalted. It may be worth noting in this connection that in Francesco di Giorgio's well-known imposition of the human figure upon the Latin cross of the church plan, the head, that is, the seat of intellectual and sensory power, fills the choir, whereas the crossing as the center of a circular pattern, establishes another focus in the figure's chest—where its heart is (Fig. 51).

Thus the crossing stakes out an architectural place of sufficient weight for the worshiper, and confirms him in his identity before he proceeds further to pay homage at the altar. When the center of the crossing is emphasized by a special marker, as in the case of the huge baldachin erected by Bernini in the basilica of San Pietro, this explicit accent bestows increased weight upon the secondary center and therefore cannot but carry considerable significance. It is a move toward diminishing the importance of the high altar and toward a centralized plan for the church.

Rudolf Wittkower has drawn attention to the revived popularity of centrally planned churches in the Renaissance. These highly unified and symmetrical buildings replace the ambiguity of the two competing centers with a strictly unitary concept, and in doing so return, consciously or not, to the similarly symmetrical form of the Greek cross in early Christian architecture. Like the centralized squares I discussed earlier, these buildings eliminate the sense of the linear path and also of the crossing, and offer instead a self-contained, closed-off dwelling place. In a partly classical, partly Christian sense, the centralized church is an image of the cosmos and of God. "For the men of the Renaissance," writes Wittkower, "this architecture with its strict geometry, the equipoise of its harmonic order, its formal serenity, and, above all, with the sphere of the dome, echoed and at the same time revealed the perfection, omnipotence, truth and goodness of God." This observation is surely correct. However, when we consider the historical shift by which the double-centered ambiguity of the Latin cross was collapsed, as it were, into the simple unity of the centralized plan, we may conclude that by the bold coincidence of the two centers, the duality of man and God was being fused into a single power, to the major glory of both.

INSIDE AND OUTSIDE

A visual relationship can be directly perceived only when the two parties to it are present in the same image. The image may be provided by a configuration observed in physical space or by a picture or schematic drawing, or it may be visualized in the imagination. The relation may be spatial or temporal, but unless the coherence of the image is safeguarded, the perceptual interplay of the components cannot be grasped. At best, they may be understood singly and connected intellectually.

No spatial problem is more characteristic of the architect's work than the need to see outside and inside in relation—that is, synoptically, as elements of the same conception. To what extent and how is this possible? The challenge is not unfamiliar to the biologist, physiologist, or engineer, but it exists for neither the painter, the filmmaker, nor the sculptor. The painter can show either an exterior or an interior, but he cannot integrate both aspects of the same thing in the same image. The filmmaker can let exterior and interior follow each other in counterpoint, but only one of them can be presented as a unitary image on the screen at any one time. Traditionally sculpture has limited itself to making objects of a coherent, closed surface, having no inside. In the nineteen-fifties, Henry Moore experimented with hollow containers carved of wood, in which he placed a second, human-like figure. These sculptures, recalling a chrysalis in its cocoon, did attack the inside-outside problem, but it is essential for our purpose to realize that to look through an opening into an interior is different in principle from being inside and surrounded by boundaries. When one looks into windows from the outside, one sees the offices or living rooms within as recesses or pockets in the building's outer surface. They form concavities within the building's relief. An interior is something else.

Architecture as we know it combines two not easily reconciled tasks. On the one hand, it has to provide a shelter that protects its inhabitants against unwelcome outside forces and offers them a congenial internal environment. On the other hand, it must create an exterior physically adapted to its functions and visually impressive, inviting or deterring, informative, etc. Perceptually and practically, the worlds of outside and inside are mutually exclusive. One cannot be in both at the same time. And yet they border directly on each other. One need only pass through the thinnest of doors to leave the one world and enter the other. On the architect's ground plan, which describes the arena of human action, the partitions between the two worlds are nothing but lines or thin strips, constantly pierced by the continuity of our daily locomotions, which cross back and forth without much effort. The great challenge to the architect, then, derives from the paradoxical contradiction between (1) the mutual exclusiveness of autonomous, self-contained interior spaces and an equally complete outer world, and (2) the necessary coherence of the two as parts of the indivisible human environment. This justifies Wolfgang Zucker's statement that the erection of a boundary separating inside from outside is the primeval architectural act.

A Swiss zoologist, Adolf Portmann, has pointed to a characteristic difference between the interior and exterior formations of organic bodies, especially animals. Inside, what governs is the need for space. "The organs abandon their symmetry; they are twisted, as for example in the alimentary canal, or bunched like grapes, as in the lungs or kidneys. Every means of enlarging the surface is seized upon, and the interior space is used to best advantage, the way we pack a suitcase for travel, without regard for aesthetic considerations or concern for its effect on any sense organ." The exterior follows different principles. It creates symmetry. Geometrical shapes appear in surface ornaments and give form to external organs. In ways that cannot be explained by practical utility, the organism manifests its particular self in the space around it, which is exposed to the light ("Selbstdarstellung im Lichtraum"). This basic difference between outer and inner structure is evident, for example, in the human body, which is symmetrical on the outside but closely packed inside. Only in very simple organisms, notably transparent ones, does one principle of formation govern the body throughout.

These observations are suggestive for the architect, although buildings differ from organic bodies—among other ways, in containing illuminated spaces, filled with traffic, in their interior. Even in biology, however, the contrast is less extreme than Portmann implies; internal organs and structural elements are not altogether lacking in aesthetic beauty. What matters in architecture is that the outer shell of a building and also, to a more limited extent, the interior surfaces of walls and ceiling inform and gratify the eyes by their appearance. They carry elements of decorative display. Close packing is most clearly reflected in a building's plan, which tends to show intricate patterns of practical necessities and is much less readable to the casual viewer than, say, the design of a façade.

From the outside, architecture is never alone. Surrounded by other buildings, by landscape, or by unoccupied space, a work of architecture depends in all its visual dimensions—size, shape, texture, color, spatial orientation, etc. —upon its environment. The surroundings decide whether a building appears as a pinnacle or an inconspicuous attendant, whether it is large or small, harmonious or out of step. At the same time, however, a building or complex of buildings seen from the outside has the all-around completeness of solids. Dynamically it displaces space, as an object displaced water in the bathtub of Archimedes. It expands radially from its center.

An interior, on the other hand, is a closed world of its own. Even when an oculus in the roof reveals a bit of sky, we do not really acknowledge another space but perceive it as a recessed portion of the room's boundary. Similarly, a landscape seen through a window is essentially a backdrop, parallel to the wall, unless we step close to the window and thus leave the room visually to enter the outside space. An interior permits comparison with other places only through the visitor's memory or anticipation. He can perceive its size or shape in relation to what he has seen before or expects to see later. But in its immediate impact, the interior is essentially without relation to anything elsewhere. For this reason, its size tends to be curiously vague and unstable. One cannot quite tell whether an interior is large or small. What looks huge at first may shrink to more ordinary size after a while. In being to some extent spatially unfathomable, an interior like that of the Pantheon strengthens its mysterious, unworldly character.

Instead of leaving the occupant in a boundless world, an interior encloses him like a womb—an experience that can be reassuring or oppressive. The world of the interior can be totally encompassed; it is surveyable, more nearly relatable than the outside to the size and power of a human being, and is therefore susceptible to his domination. He is taller than many of the furnishings, and can reach most of the rest. Made for him and at his service, the interior surrounds its occupant as courtiers surround their king. Gaston Bachelard, in commenting on this subject, observes: "Seen from the inside, without exteriority, being can only be round."

Consequently, an interior reveals its typical character most clearly when its walls or ceilings, or both, are concavely rounded. Since convexity enhances figure character, concave boundaries define the hollow of the room as the dominant volume. They give visual expression to the fact that in an interior, the hollow matters more than the material walls. Inevitably one is reminded of what the Tao Tê Ching says about the value of "nothing":

> We put thirty spokes together and call it a wheel;
> But it is on the space where there is nothing that
>   the usefulness of the wheel depends.
> We turn clay to make a vessel;
> But it is on the space where there is nothing that
>   the usefulness of the vessel depends.
> We pierce doors and windows to make a house;
> And it is on these spaces where there is nothing
>   that the usefulness of the house depends.
> Therefore just as we take advantage of what is
>   we should recognize the usefulness of what is not.

CONCAVITY AND CONVEXITY

Earlier, in reference to circular squares, I observed that although the hollow space acts as the dominant figure it does not annex the façades that form its boundaries. The viewer, surrounded by the hollow space and looking at it from the inside, perceives the square's expansive power only indirectly, by its effect upon the surrounding façades, which recede concavely. This experience is even more compelling in a round interior.

In the Pantheon, the cupola is seen as concave, and the same is true for its cylindrical wall at ground level. This accounts for the curious effect obtained when one uses a model of an interior space as a mold and makes a cast of it. A.E. Brinckmann has recommended this procedure for study purposes; but whatever its virtues, it certainly can be used only with caution in determining the visual character or the aesthetic excellence of the hollow form. Often there is little similarity between the perceptual characteristics of the two shapes. The architect Joseph Watterson has referred to a plaster model made by William L. MacDonald to show the interior space of Hagia Sophia as a solid (Fig. 52). "As a solid, it is an awkward, bulbous form that no sane architect would ever conceive for the mass of the building." Be this as it may, the striking discrepancy comes about because in the cast the interface belongs to the surrounded volume, whereas in the actual building it belongs to the

Figure 52. From W. MacDonald, *Early Christian and Byzantine Architecture.*

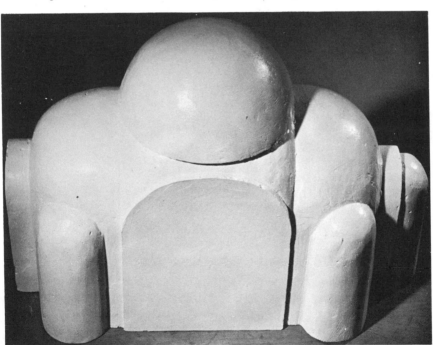

95

Figure 53

surrounding shell (Fig. 53). The two resulting shapes bear little resemblance to each other.

As in the case of circular squares, the hollow space of an interior can serve as the architectural representative of man, the occupant. Here again the occupant can assume this role because he constitutes a focal center from which vectors issue radially and fill the empty space with his presence. The hollow volume is perceived as an amplification and extension of the human

96

focus. The concavities of cupolas or curved walls look as though they had acquired their passive shape by yielding to the invading possessor. One thinks of birds shaping their nests by sitting inside and pressing their bodies against the walls. "When the first pieces of grass and stalks have been collected," writes Karl von Frisch in his book on animal architecture,

the bird sits down and makes rotating movements with its body. These are the same kind of "cup-molding" movements which the male ostrich makes in the sand of the desert—with the difference that this is all the nest-building he does. *Sylvia* warblers sometimes make these molding movements even before they have collected a single straw, thereby taking possession, symbolically, of the site of their choice.

Although man does not commonly shape his abode by creating a hollow with his own body, a strongly concave interior behaves as though he wielded some such power. The occupant feels elevated and expanded as he reaches out to the confines of the room. Compare this with the experience of coming to a building from the outside. In that case, it is the building that possesses all the elevation, and man approaches it in his smallness.

Standing in the Pantheon in Rome, one feels stretched vertically toward the upper limits of the cupola and through the oculus into the sky; horizontally the expansion is radial and centrifugal. Under special circumstances the main axis of such an extension can also run along a horizontal path. This happens when one walks through a cylinder, for example, through the tubular passages of the London underground.

The architect Steen Eiler Rasmussen writes that the transition from the Gothic to the Renaissance involves a transformation from an architecture of sharp and pointed structures to one of well-shaped cavities, and that just as the Gothic pillar was expanded on all sides into a cluster of shafts, the Renaissance cavity was enlarged by the addition of niches; and he points to Bramante's plan for St. Peter's, which "forms the loveliest ornament of round, domed cavities joined together and expanded on all sides by semicircular niches."

Bramante's plan is indeed a supreme example of negative spaces acquiring figure character by their symmetry and by the concavities in the boundary shapes (Fig. 54). At the same time, however, pillars or columns standing within an interior cannot but counteract the dominant figure character of the hollow space. Whatever their shape, they have a compactness and roundness of their own. As surrounded solids of masonry, they claim a strong positive function and strengthen the same claim on the part of walls, ceiling, and

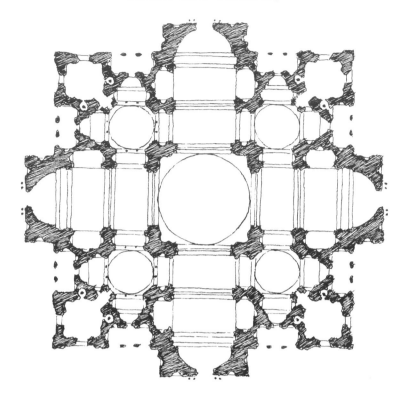

Figure 54

floor. This is particularly evident when, as Rasmussen says, the pillars in Gothic buildings exhibit clusters of convex shafts. In the crypt of the Cathedral of Bourges, for example, the cavities of the pointed vaults, certainly as compelling and well-shaped as those of any Renaissance structure, are in counterpoint to the forceful convexity of the piers (Fig. 55). As the concave surfaces of the arches slide into the convexity of their supports, there results an interplay of hollow and mass and of receding and advancing shapes that is comparable to the complexities of Baroque architecture.

A concave boundary yields to the forces it has itself generated. It provides the expansive hollow space with a maximum of freedom, but at the same time this expansion derives its power from the resistance of the boundary. "The tendency to expand," says Lipps, "depends on the size and narrowness of the delimitation." While yielding to such an expansion, a cupola responds

98

Figure 55

by closing in on the interior space and compressing it from all sides in a gripping pincer movement. The strength of this restraining force reflects the strength of the expansion it contains.

I have observed earlier that the antagonistic play of force and counterforce approaches neutrality when the boundaries are straight lines or planes. A cubic room expands from its center, but it does so less resolutely than a cylindrical one. It is clearly held in balance by the advance toward the center of the walls and the furniture lining them, the bookshelves, the closed doors, etc. In a cubic room, this interplay of centrifugal and centripetal forces tends to take place at a low tension level, but it nonetheless defines the visual dimensions of the room dynamically as a particular ratio of expansion and constriction. The coherence of the cubic shell is strengthened when the corners are defined as mere changes of direction. Frank Lloyd Wright aimed at such continuity when he treated walls and ceilings not as separate planes clashing at the edges and perhaps threatening to cut through one another, but instead as parts of an uninterrupted "folded plane."

99

INTERIORS INTERRELATED

An interior, we noted, is a closed and complete world. Only because the human mind has memory, which enables it to relate a presently perceived sight to the images of things seen before, can a spatial context be established between inside and outside or between different interiors. At best, however, this context remains indirect. In the overview of the architect, interiors appear as either coordinated or nested. We recall here the total perceptual and often functional autonomy of activities on the different floors of a building. The elevator of an office building momentarily pierces the division. As its door opens, one often obtains a glimpse of an alien and self-contained world, unaware of other, similarly autonomous and quite different universes above and below.

Even in the horizontal plane, which allows for easy passage, the autonomy of interiors is compelling. It takes a special mental effort to realize that a wall is a boundary shared with a neighboring space. No contour rivalry arises under such conditions. The contour is peacefully shared because it belongs to each interior separately, and this double function involves no visual contradiction. It is not perceived. The architect is left with the task of giving each room an appropriate degree of autonomy while indicating its place in the whole plan and its connection with adjacent rooms to the desirable extent.

But interiors are also nested, large ones comprehending smaller ones. I quote here a description by the novelist Robert Musil of an Austrian aristocratic official in his palatial office:

He was surrounded by a high-ceilinged room, which was encircled in turn by the large and empty spaces of the anteroom and the library, and these in turn were enveloped, shell over shell, by further rooms, silence, devoutness, solemnity, and the wreath of two swinging stone staircases; at the point where these let out into the driveway, the monumental doorman stood in his heavy, gallooned coat, staff in hand; he looked through the opening of the portal arch into the bright fluidity of the day, and the pedestrians swam past as though in a goldfish bowl. At the boundary of those two worlds rose the playful ornamental vines of a Rococo façade, famous among the art experts not only because of its beauty but also because it height was greater than its width.

In such a synoptic vision the character and meaning of every interior are amplified and sharpened by the surrounding spaces. This is true not only when the entire setting is in harmony, but also when there are disparities, which reveal the often poignant or appalling narrowness of any one of those

100

partial little worlds. I recall older apartment buildings along Riverside Drive in New York City, which preserve some of their past splendor in large entrance halls festooned with gilded columns, huge marble vases, carpets, and even with a doorman of sorts; and upstairs the bleak corridors, the subdivided apartments, some of them with windows opening onto narrow airshafts, through which a meager light trickles. Similar settings abound in hotels, office buildings, and dormitories. Some of their occupants see them in context and are distressed by the pathetic discrepancy; others are taken in by the closedness and exclusive completeness of their particular place and accept it for what it is without making the appropriate invidious comparison.

It has sometimes been argued that an architect's conception need be no more exacting than that of the average inhabitant, and that there is no good reason for providing what will not be noticed. But I shall have occasion to observe that awareness comes at many different levels, not all explicitly conscious, and also that in any profession, as a matter of ethics and self-respect, the most intelligent vision must prevail, irrespective of how fully it will be appreciated by clients, customers, or consumers.

LOOKING FROM BOTH SIDES

Let me return to the particular relation between inside and outside and ask what form it can take and how it is obtained. When one looks at a ceramic bowl thrown on a potter's wheel, one finds that the view from its inside and the view from its outside are not the same. The internal hollow meeting its limits at the concave boundary of the vessel differs in its perceptual character from the convexity of the outside shape, which bulges into unlimited space. Yet there is a physical correspondence or even identity of outer and inner shape, so that if we would repeat the Hagia Sophia experiment and make a plaster cast of the bowl's inside, the result is likely not to be displeasing and, in fact, to nearly duplicate the outer shape. It would be like looking at the metallic core pulled out of one of the old flatirons.

However, not all duplications of an outer shape work well on the inside. I have referred elsewhere to the disconcerting experience of seeing the Statue of Liberty from the inside. Physically the shapes of the outside and the inside of that huge piece of sculpture, which is made of a thin sheet of metal supported by an armature, are identical. Perceptually, however, the inner surface presents a puzzling accumulation of concavities and convexities, without apprehensible meaning and surely without any resemblance to the

101

human body. Here, then, is a case complementing that of the Hagia Sophia cast. In the one instance an outer shape does not work when used as an interior; in the other, an inner shape used on the outside looks wrong.

It would take a careful analysis to establish the cause of the discrepancy. Possibly the shapes of the Statue of Liberty make so little sense from the inside because they are equally chaotic from the outside, with the incoherence camouflaged by the recognizable subject matter. A mold of a human face tends to be a less disconcerting shape from the inside, although it may be as unrecognizable as a photographic negative. But other perceptual factors must also be at play. The internal hollows of the cupolas in Santa Sophia, for example, cannot be directly compared to one another with respect to size, shape, and height, while in the plaster model of the volumes they can.

There are architectural examples, however, in which a close correspondence between outer and inner shape works as beautifully as it does for the ceramic bowl. In some Romanesque buildings, the solid stone construction appears almost like a transparent shell, expressing a reassuring limpidity and simple frankness. The design of the east end of St. Sernin in Toulouse, where, in the words of Henri Focillon, "the volumes build up gradually, from the apsidal chapels to the lantern spire, through the roofs of the chapels, the deambulatory, the choir, and the rectangular mass upon which the belfry rests," holds essentially for the inside as it does for the outside (Fig. 56). At its much higher level of complexity, medieval architecture shares this property with rudimentary huts and cottages, with walls and roofs bounded by parallel planes. As an example from modern architecture, Portoghesi's project for a theater in Cagliari may be cited. The auditorium is outlined by a group of hyperbolic walls whose axes converge towards the stage. The concavities of the outer enclosure are faithfully reflected by the convexities inside, which resemble the opera boxes of traditional Italian theaters and are intended also to aid the acoustics (Fig. 57).

Whether such a correspondence between outside and inside is desirable depends on stylistic preference. The frankly informative appearance of buildings whose inside holds few spatial secrets offers little of the teasing richness and sophisticated complexity found in architectural styles that deviate from such elementary parallelism. Simple parallelism also reflects little of the dramatic struggle by which the architect must plan from the inside and from the outside at the same time—two kinds of planning that typically involve quite different considerations and accordingly different shapes.

Some successful solutions of this problem offer little direct correspondence

102

Figure 56

between the outer and inner facets of a building, but at the same time avoid disconcerting contradiction. It is difficult not to feel uneasy when one discovers, for example, that a palace façade in eighteenth-century English architecture hides a whole row of private houses, or when one looks at a vertical section of the Pantheon in Paris and sees a tall outer dome riding on a much lower inner one as though two buildings had crashed into each other (Fig. 58). A recent example is the Opera House in Sydney, whose tradition-

103

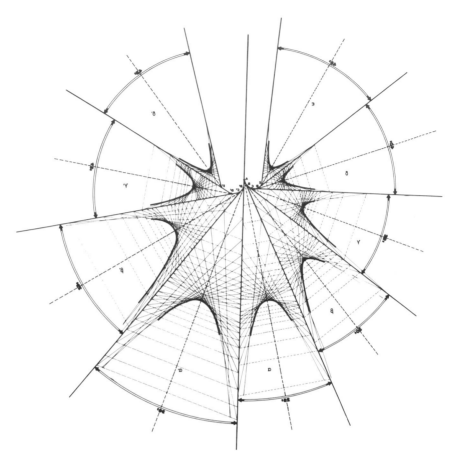

Figure 57. Paolo Portoghesi. Project for a theater in Cagliari.

ally designed performance halls in no way echo the bold sail shapes of Jörn Utzon's outer shells.

What is jarring in these examples is not that the inner shapes differ from the outer ones, but that there is no readable relation between them, or that the same spatial statement is made in two mutually exclusive ways. Two examples, one very simple, the other more complex, will illustrate the principles governing successful solutions. In some early Christian tombs of the Near East, a cross-shaped interior is surrounded by a square exterior in such a way that from the outside the building has the form of a cube (Fig. 59). Although there is no way of guessing that the cube hides a cruciform interior, the two shapes are perfectly relatable to each other in that the outer derives

104

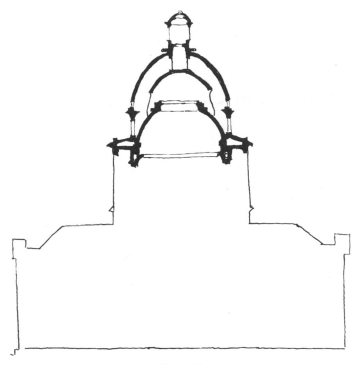

Figure 58

Figure 59. After S. Guyer.

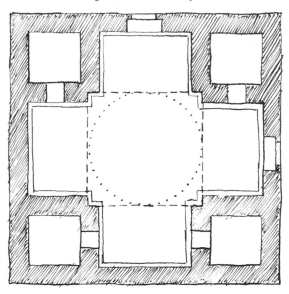

Figure 60. Chapel of Notre-Dame-du-Haut, Ronchamp. *Photo*, John Gay.

from the inner by the addition of four quadratic corner rooms. The internal shape, from which the architectural conception started, is made geometrically simpler by amplification. The different demands made on outside appearance and inside plan are reconciled without contradiction.

A more ambitious example may be found in Le Corbusier's chapel of Notre-Dame du Haut in Ronchamp. Even though this small building is composed of a fairly limited number of shapes, its form is among the most elusive in architecture. To oversimplify somewhat, the basic theme of its design plays on the structural ambiguity of a rectangle that acquires a kind of additional symmetry around one of its diagonals. When one looks at the chapel from the southeast, the sweeping curves of the roof and walls suggest a ship raising its prow on the top of the hill (Fig. 60). The interior, however, is more nearly rectangular, for although the room expands toward the altar wall at the east, this divergence is counteracted by perspective convergence when one views the interior from the west wall (Fig. 61). It is hardly possible to discuss this eminently three-dimensional building only in terms of its plan, but it seems to me that the teasing ambiguity between the relatively stable rectangularity of the interior and the bold dynamics of the external wedge creates a perfectly integrated, though not easily perceived, unity of inside and outside.

Compare also the roof of Le Corbusier's chapel with what I said earlier about the dome of the Pantheon in Paris. The chapel is covered by two thin, curved shells, the one forming the roof, the other the ceiling of the interior.

Figure 61

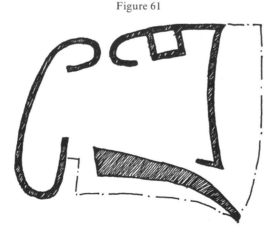

There is a hollow about two meters in diameter between them, but the two surfaces do not result in a contradictory duplication of function, as do the outer and inner dome of Soufflot's Pantheon. They add up to a sculpturally unified "bivalve," as the Abbé Bolle-Reddat has called it.

In a richly documented chapter on inside and outside, unfortunately dedicated to the proposition that contradiction can make for successful relation, Robert Venturi writes:

Designing from the outside in, as well as the inside out, creates necessary tensions, which help make architecture. Since the inside is different from the outside, the wall—the point of change—becomes an architectural event. Architecture occurs at the meeting of interior and exterior forces of use and space. . . . Architecture as the wall between the inside and the outside becomes the spatial record of this resolution and its drama.

This apt description of architectural dynamics suggests two final observations, one psychological, the other aesthetic.

Our examples have shown that a visitor looking at an actual building can never see its outside and inside in the same field of vision. What is possible is to obtain partial glimpses of the direct relation between them by means of vertical and horizontal sections, which can be presented in drawings or models or visualized as mental images. Such sections, however, can only approximate the total relation, and a truly complete conception of inside and outside as an integrated unity is probably beyond any human being's imaginative powers whenever the object is at all complex.

Such a limitation, however, is not at all rare. It operates in the creation and understanding of complex structures everywhere in the arts, in the sciences, in engineering, and so forth. One tries to come as close as possible to a synoptic mastery of the whole by making inroads into the structure from a variety of approaches and by weighing significant relations against one another. Experience shows that such accumulations of partial insights are good enough approximations to make the structure hold together, even though the totality of its aspects transcends the human grasp. An approximate grasp also makes it possible to distinguish with some confidence between structures that are truly integrated and others that are not.

Aesthetically, we conclude that the conception and appreciation of a work of architecture is not limited to what perception can embrace in one field of vision. The next chapter will point out that no three-dimensional object truly

108

satisfies such a rigorous perceptual criterion. And yet, the mind can form a comprehensive visual concept of an object and can submit it to the demands of unity and wholeness. In architecture, only when inside and outside fuse in one integrated vision are we dealing with a work that carries meaning and can be understood as a whole.

IV. AS IT LOOKS AND AS IT IS

N o three-dimensional object can be completely recorded as an optical image by the eye at any one time from one fixed point. This is so because the optical image is a two-dimensional projection, which can portray no more than one point of an object at any one place. When a straight line meets a three-dimensional solid, it does so in at least two places on its outer surface, in the front and in the back. From this limitation of our sense of sight it follows that if the human mind is to grasp a three-dimensional object as a whole, it must transcend the information received from any one angle.

PERCEIVING A SOLID

Fortunately, visual perception and imagination are not limited to the range of the optical images on which they rely. The sense of vision is not a mechanical recording device. It organizes, completes, and synthesizes the structure found in the particular optical images. Figure 62a indicates in section that when the visible part of an object presents enough of a sufficiently compelling structure—for example, the visible part of a sphere or a column—the object will be seen spontaneously as a whole. This perceptual tendency may be misleading when the hidden part of the object does not complete its form in the simplest, most consistent way (Fig. 62b).

In addition, visual experience is not typically limited to one aspect of an object. In the course of moving around in our environment, we see things from different viewpoints. We may change our position deliberately to gain a more comprehensive view. A work of sculpture can only be seen if one walks around it, and the same is true for architecture. From the multiplicity of

110

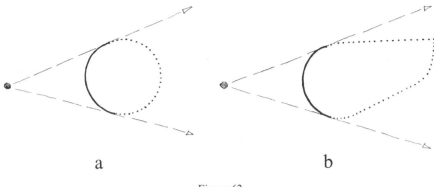

a   b

Figure 62

views the mind synthesizes an image of the sculpture's or building's objective three-dimensional form. Synthesis is aided by the fact that these various views do not come unrelated, as might a series of photographs from which one tries to form an idea of a building. Rather, as the viewer moves around an object, or the object turns in front of his eyes, he receives an orderly sequence of gradually changing projections. The coherence of this sequence greatly facilitates the identification of the object, to which all the particular views refer.

Even so, it is a remarkable achievement of the mind to derive an image of objective shape from discrete views. Many people can picture a cube in its completeness with some precision, and this even though no more than three of the cube's sides can ever be visible at one time. Such a mental image is necessarily derived from partial views, none of which is contained in the "objective" shape of a symmetrical, regular, rightangular cube. Nor is this objective image given in any of the projective views obtainable from the physical object.

A work of architecture, therefore, is an object that never has and never will be seen in its entirety by anybody. It is a mental image synthesized with greater or lesser success from partial views. How easy or difficult it is to obtain that image depends on the shapes used by the architect. Paul Frankl has referred to this difference in distinguishing the architectural style of the period 1420 to 1550 from that of later buildings. In the earlier period, he says, "it suffices for us to view a building from surprisingly few points to gain a complete architectural image." This image is the same, no matter from what angle the building is looked at, and it corresponds to the "actual form."

111

PERSPECTIVE DEFORMATIONS

For a building to be so independent of projective deformation, it must meet two perceptual conditions. Its objective shapes and the relations between them must be sufficiently simple; and the system of distortions imposed upon it by optical projections must be sufficiently detachable from the objective shape. Look at the façade of San Miniato al Monte in Florence from a slight diagonal (Fig. 63). Although the oblique projection distorts all sizes, angles, and proportions of the design as a whole as well as of its parts, we have no trouble seeing undistorted symmetry. This is so because the façade is essentially flat and contains a number of uninterrupted horizontals. The transformation of these objectively parallel edges into a simply family of convergent perspective rays is clearly seen, and it is easily detachable from the actual shapes, which are quite simple in themselves. Detachment of the perspective distortion leaves the rectangles, circles, and arches in their objective simplicity and symmetry. The same is true for the symmetry of the façade as a whole or for the simple order of the five equal arches. The correspondences are so compelling that the homologous elements are seen spontaneously as equal in size and shape. The decisive condition here is not the repetition of similar elements as such, as Norberg-Schulz has suggested,

Figure 63

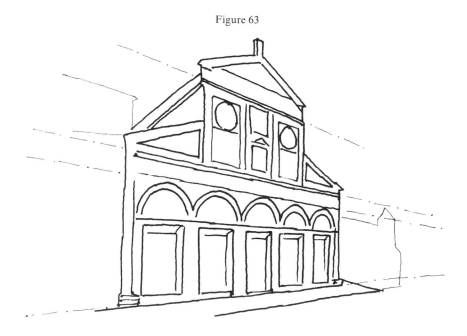

112

but the simplicity and symmetry of the shapes and their overall organization. Repetition of elements in numerical order is not a prerequisite; it merely helps to emphasize correspondences, gradients, and other aspects of visually simple configurations that are overlaid by perspective deformation.

We must not cling, however, to a conceptual dichotomy that has guided the thinking of many art theorists and of some psychologists as well. According to that view, there are two fundamentally different ways of seeing the world. Either it is seen "as it is," that is, with a complete neglect of perspective distortion, of the boundaries of the visual field, and similar conditions of vision; or all these conditions are explicitly acknowledged, as is necessary for example in order to make a perspectively correct painting or drawing. Actually, no such radical either-or exists in perception. On the one hand, the effects of projective vision are never completely excluded; on the other, no draftsman has ever seen a projective image the way he draws it, namely as totally flat, with all distortions, boundaries, etc., fully present. What is actually seen, instead, is an in-between version of partially straightened-out and partially distorted shapes.

A striking example presents itself every time one enters a traditional church through its main portal (Fig. 49). At first glance one sees perhaps an elongated nave, roofed by vaults equidistant from the floor and supported by columns and arches of equal size and height. Paradoxically, however, one may be struck at the same time by the powerful convergence of all orthogonals toward a vanishing point at the altar. The situation is ambiguous and varies somewhat from person to person. For one thing, few people use their eyes to truly look at what they see. Most rely instead on a minimum of information, enough for them to obtain a "norm" image of the situation. Even so, however, and without being aware of it, they may also be impressed and guided by the projective convergence toward the altar.

Some of the persons who perceive this convergence more consciously may nevertheless insist that they see the columns and arches as equal in size and arranged in parallel rows, whereas others cannot free themselves from the impression that the whole interior actually diminishes and converges with increasing distance. The former type of observer sees a building of undistorted shape subjected to what I have called elsewhere the experience of pyramidal space; the other sees the building itself affected by the deformation.

In the case of the church interior, the deformation can be particularly strong because the symmetry of perspective coincides with that of the building and therefore cannot be as easily detached as was possible in the oblique view of San Miniato. It is quite feasible under these conditions for architects or stage designers to strengthen or counteract perspective by deviating from the regular shape of the building. A famous example is Bernini's Scala Regia in the Vatican, a staircase whose colonnades and vault diminish in size and thereby convey the illusion of a much deeper vista.

In a more general sense we can describe these projective effects as instances in which the viewer attributes to the objectively given situation visual qualities that derive from his own position and outlook. A simple example of spatial orientation was sometimes used by Max Wertheimer in his lectures, to illustrate the difference between an egocentric outlook and one that takes the nature of the objective situation into account. A person standing in a rectangular room and facing in the direction indicated by the solid arrow (Fig. 64a) realizes that he is oriented obliquely with regard to the objectively prevailing situation. The discord introduces a tension, which is alleviated if the person changes his position to conform with one of the two structural axes of the rectangular room. But in principle it is also possible for someone to insist on his own orientation as the central axis of the situation and to perceive the walls as standing obliquely and the corners as deviating from the spatial framework. Here, too, tension will create discord, but in this case the way to alleviate the pressure would be for the walls to conform to the occupant's position (Fig. 64b).

In this example of a simple cubic room it would take an almost pathologically egocentric person to feel that the room is out of step with him rather than he with the room. The visual situation is so clear-cut and unambiguous that to overlook its spatial demands is all but impossible. Often, however, the architectural layout leaves room for more than one attitude. S. E. Rasmussen, in his book *Experiencing Architecture*, protests against the art historian Brinckmann's way of looking at the small old town of Nördlingen as though it were a painting or photograph taken from one fixed point. According to Rasmussen, an old town of this kind, clustered around a central church as a web of irregularly spreading streets, prescribes no one view to the visitor, unlike the gardens of Versailles or the Spanish Steps in Rome. In order to see the place properly one needs to interpret every vista as an accidental perspective, not intended in its composition to exclude any other.

THE THREAD OF ARIADNE

Old European towns, which have grown rather than been planned, are much like natural landscapes. To get lost in them is a delight, quite appro-

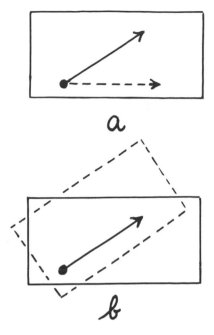

a

b

Figure 64

priate to the situation. One can interpret and enjoy the experience as a sequence of unexpected vistas, stimulating in their variety and not predetermined by a recognizable map of overall order. Such an environment is in the nature of a texture rather than a design; it is held together by its homogeneity, which refuses to assign to any element a particular place determined by the structure of the whole. Instead of trying to discover an objective order in the whole and assigning individual sights their proper location within that order, the mind derives from such circumstances an order of its own. It records the linear sequence of sights, which unfold, more or less unpredictably, as they would in a film. The conditions for such an experience are created deliberately in the so-called stroll gardens of traditional Japan.

In a "grown" setting the objective order is always partial. Villages and towns of this kind come about by sequences of events whose logic is largely historical, just as in a landscape geologically regular structures interact with the accidents caused by particular constellations of natural forces. The liberating and stimulating effects of such surroundings are known to everybody, and an excess of surveyable order has been recognized by city planners as impoverishing urban life.

It makes a difference, however, whether one is roaming through a landscape in quest of pleasant sensations or is trying to find one's way through it to reach a particular place. In the latter case, a mere sequence of disconnected sights offers no guidance. At the very least one has to establish a set of landmarks in the correct temporal order. For more efficient orientation one tries to obtain an overall map, which indicates context and relations, alternatives, distances, and so forth. The same is true for an urban environment. If one wants to live and work in Nördlingen one had better replace the delightful kaleidoscope of first impressions with a precise mental configuration of the pertinent locations and spatial relations. Kevin Lynch has shown that the ease or difficulty of such orientation in a city depends on its physical pattern and a person's ability to grasp structural features. He has also described the forlornness of city dwellers for whom the urban pattern remains inarticulate.

What is true for such environments is imperative for the architecture of individual buildings. Architecture is one of the human occupations and products that, for one reason or another, offer organized form to mind and body. Therefore the historian Paul Frankl must be mistaken in principle when he asserts that from the mid-sixteenth century on, buildings no longer present one coherent image, but a multiplicity of partial images that do not add up to a whole. He says that the first impression received by the visitor is "unstable, momentary, accidental. From a second and third viewpoint the building becomes something we had not expected, and what we have already seen will now seem entirely different." Everybody has had such experiences when he has failed to understand the layout of a building; but when the bewilderment persists one is inclined to suspect that it is the architect who has failed. There is only one type of building designed to transform the architectural experience into an irrational sequence of surprises, and that is the labyrinth. But even the mazes constructed by psychologists for their laboratory rats are meant to be understood eventually, at least to the extent that a path leading from the entrance to the final reward is learned as an orderly sequence.

Occasional attempts have been made to illustrate in a film the architectural experience of walking through a building. An uninterrupted traveling shot can lead through corridors and rooms, along galleries, and all around the walls and across the ceiling of great halls. But since the image on the screen is limited to a small section of the actual space and since the spectator does not experience in his body the sensations of locomotion that would correspond to the camera's path, the film hardly ever conveys a reasonably complete idea of

116

the building's overall form. The result can be of interest in itself, but in no way does it duplicate the interplay between building and visitor that we know as the architectural experience. That interplay takes place between the building's timeless existence in space and the timebound event of its being entered, traversed, and used by the visitor. In the film, the interplay is reduced to the event of the visit, and the only structural invariant holding the sequence together is the visitor's viewpoint. Of the two interacting orders only one is left, namely the suite of impressions characterizing the journey that is portrayed by the camera.

Frankl does not deny that the buildings he describes—essentially those of the Baroque style—have a definite form of their own, but he believes that this form is revealed only as the result of a strenuous inventory taken by a devoted expert, who paces the buildings, investigates every detail, and peers behind every corner. The average visitor is said to know that the variety of his impressions "is caused by something invariable, but this invariable is only of scientific interest. Knowledge of it is gained only for the sake of artistic pedagogy; artistically only the impression of change has value." If this were so, we would be faced with the peculiar state of affairs that the carefully controlled and beautiful order of symmetries, correspondences, and hierarchic groupings conspicuous in every successful Baroque building had no function whatever and was not intended to be seen. What is more, such an order would probably not be the most efficient way of obtaining the kaleidoscopic variety of images they allegedly are intended to produce.

THE READING OF VISTAS

Before offering an alternative description, I would like to illustrate by a further pair of examples the difference between crediting perspective effects to one's own subjective outlook and crediting them to the object itself. Lynch has remarked that since the dome and the campanile of Florence offer a different constellation depending on the direction from which they are seen, one can determine one's own location and orientation by the sight of the two landmarks. Sometimes the clock tower is seen to the right of the dome, sometimes to the left, and sometimes the one is eclipsed by the other (Fig. 65). Using the landmarks for orientation presupposes that the viewer not take their position literally. Rather the sight must be understood as the outcome of the interaction between himself and the architectural constellation, whose objective and invariant nature the viewer has distilled from the experience of walking around the buildings.

117

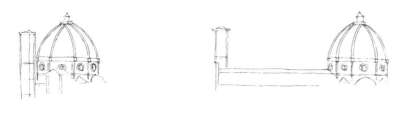

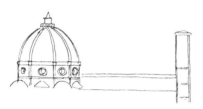

Figure 65

To gain such understanding, one has to liberate oneself from the compelling image of the given particular sight and to see it as accidental, as one among many equally possible and valid ones. This requires mental flexibility, which takes training. The psychologist Jean Piaget has used a small cardboard model of a group of mountains to test children's ability to predict what the constellation will look like when perceived from a position other than their own (Fig. 66). He found that young children distinguish minimally, or not at all between their own viewpoint and that of other observers. At about seven to nine years old, certain relations are understood to vary with changes in the observer's position, but the comprehensive coordination of viewpoints is not achieved until age nine or ten.

The ability to distinguish accident from invariance in evaluating a visual object and to use a particular perspective as a means of determining one's own position is indispensable for practical orientation. Quite different purposes are served by the attitude of painter or photographer who can take such a grouping of objects literally and derive valid symbolic statements from it. This pictorial attitude, or more nearly that of a filmmaker, was adopted in literature by Marcel Proust in the famous episode of the three clock towers

118

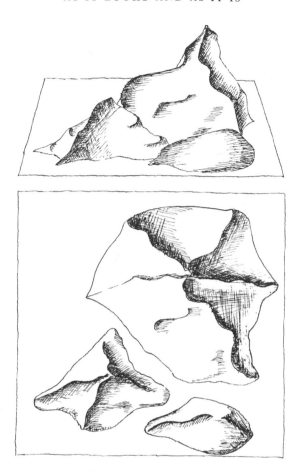

Figure 66. After J. Piaget.

that change their relative position, as the boy, sitting next to the coachman, watches them during an outing. Michel Butor, in an essay on Proust, suggests that we are being presented with a spatial symbol of the liberation from fixed distances in time, which makes it possible for the narrator to play freely with his reminiscences. "The three clock towers are released from their everyday servitude as though they had become birds."

It is not uncommon for an architect to consider his building in the context of the landscape or cityscape in which it will appear and to be aware of the different aspects it will offer in different perspectives. But it seems legitimate to say that in envisioning such sights, the architect does not think of indi-

119

vidual views of his building as pictures that present a unique sight, limited to the one aspect shown. He conceives of them as related to other possible views and to the shape of the building as such. He expects the building to be seen as what it *is*, and he thinks of a given vista only as offering a particular slant on the building's invariant nature. In fact, he will maintain that the particular view makes sense only if it is perceived with an explicit awareness of what the building and its position in the setting objectively are.

It is against the nature of architecture to become subservient to a momentary image or a number of such images, as buildings often do on the stage or in a film. The reason for the difference is that the stage set or film image is made only for the sense of sight and for a particular viewpoint, whereas the creations of the architect are to be used in three-dimensional space and for physical purposes. These physical purposes of orientation, habitation, etc., must be served by the way the building is perceived visually, and even its purely expressive qualities must, as I shall show later, accord with these functions.

For this reason it seems necessary to reinterpret the characteristics of the Baroque and similar styles noted by Frankl. If I am not mistaken, the visual character of those buildings has a much more interesting purpose than offering a dazzling spectacle of everchanging images. It is intended to complicate the viewer's access to the architectural theme and thereby to the fundamental meaning of the building. This tendency is similar to approaches in the other arts at a comparable stylistic stage. Painters such as Pieter Brueghel or Tintoretto often hide the principal theme of a picture by removing it to the background, away from the center of attention; they show it as small and overpowered by the close-up prominence given secondary items. Comparable too, is Shakespeare's roundabout way of introducing his audience to the core of his plot. In all these instances the path leading the visitor to the heart of the matter is beset with obstacles, and the tension created by the discrepancy between the structure of what is to be understood and the appearance of what is being offered to the senses is an essential quality of the work.

Therefore, when an architect chooses to use highly complex shapes that are difficult to survey, he is unlikely to do so for the purpose of making the visitor get lost in a labyrinth. Rather, he organizes his building in such a way that its basic structure is potentially visible but must be extricated from a thicket of elaborations. Figure 67 is meant to illustrate this difference by the profiles of two details, one of them simple and easily surveyable, the other embroidering the basic shape with complications, which, however, neither hide nor distort it.

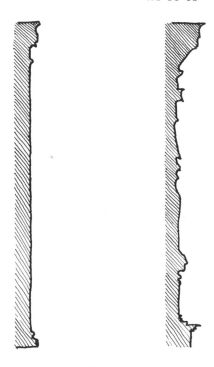

Figure 67

A similar example from music may make the point even more clearly (Fig. 68). Baroque musicians were expected to elaborate the clear melodic line written by the composer. I am reproducing a sample of a sonata by Francesco Geminiani indicating how the soloist, after playing the straight melody of the top stave, repeated it in an ornamented form, an example of which is given on the second stave. One observes the use of trills, which change a steady note into an alternation of adjacent ones and thereby transform a clear-cut statement of pitch level into a vacillation. The exact moment at which a particular tone of the melody is to appear is made unclear by anticipation or delay. The simple downward step of an interval is elaborated into a string of four or more notes involving a small upward movement in addition to the descent, and the same principle enriches the melodic line as a whole. The simple rhythm of the melody is complicated by syncopation, and so forth. The melody is not hidden, since this would defeat the very point of the performance, but transpires in its original simplicity through the teasing intricacies of the ornament.

The idiosyncrasies of Baroque architecture fulfill the same function. The

121

Figure 68

frontal surface of a façade must be visually extracted from curved and oblique elements departing from the plane in all directions. Curves, taking the place of straight corners, make for a gradual change of direction, which is less easily grasped than an abrupt one. Cornices, capitals, swellings, and spiral twists complicate the verticality of supports. Sometimes two different shapes are combined to serve the same function, for example, when a doorway is topped by a triangular pediment, inscribed with an arch. Convexity at one level of the building is contradicted and supplemented contrapuntally by concavity at another. Instead of stating a consistent height, a row of elements creates a visual trill by alternating between somewhat lower and somewhat higher units. Interrupted shapes call for completion, and perspective overlays violate each other's integrity.

MODELS AND SIZES

I have described the Baroque principle at some length because it illustrates dramatically the general problem I am discussing here, namely that of the relation between objective architectural form and its particular appearance. Earlier I pointed out that a building, like any other three-dimensional object, can never be seen in its entirety but only in projectively deformed aspects. This is true not only for the completed structure but also for its conception in the architect's mind, and since he cannot conceive his design without an integrated overview, he resorts to working with small models.

No doubt, the architect must imagine with some degree of precision what the actual building will look like when approached from the street or seen from the inside. But much of the actual shaping must be done on thought models of the whole building, mental images that are supported sooner or later by small-scale models built at the office (Fig. 69). Such models, being easily comprehended in the visual field, are much more surveyable than the

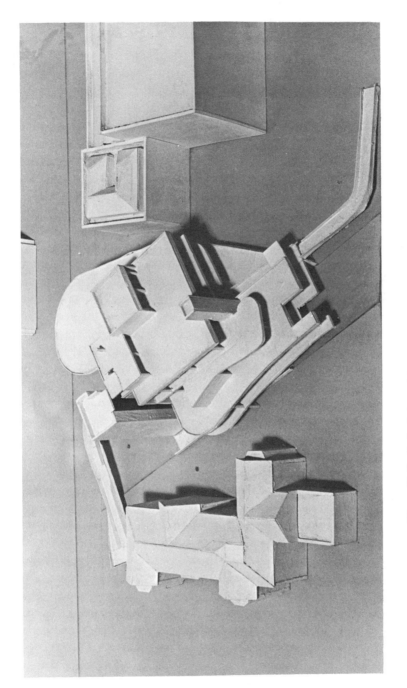

Figure 69. Le Corbusier's model of the Carpenter Center for the Visual Arts. *Photo*, Todd Stuart.

executed structures. Claude Lévi-Strauss, talking about the artist's habit of making pictures and sculpture smaller than the subjects they represent, says that reduction seems to reverse the cognitive process: the viewer, instead of beginning with the parts in the usual way, is invited first to comprehend the whole. Whereas a viewer normally tries to overcome the resistance of a large object by dividing it into parts, scale reduction reverses the situation:

The smaller the totality of the object, the less redoubtable it appears; by being quantitatively diminished it seems qualitatively simplified. More precisely, this quantitative transposition increases and diversifies our power over an analogue of the thing, by means of which the thing itself can be taken hold of, weighed in the hand, comprehended with a single glance.

Lévi-Strauss's speculations are borne out by recent experimental studies of the ability to handle mental images. It has been shown not only that spatial relations, such as comparisons of size, can be "read off" from three-dimensional thought models but that the average person is also quite capable of rotating such models either in the frontal plane or in depth if a task requires it. What can be seen in imagination tends, of course, to be less detailed and more generalized, but nevertheless the handling of a mental image bears a striking resemblance to the manipulation of an actual model with one's hands.

The advantages of using models are evident. To avoid being misled, however, the architect must keep in mind that the final product of his labors is a huge structure to be seen and used by small creatures. The difference between a small model and an actual building may lead to psychological discrepancies that are worth elucidating here. For this purpose I shall draw upon analogies to what the physical and natural sciences tell us about allometry, that is, about the dependence of shape on size and the ensuing effect of size on function. "Absolute size decrees that the lion will never fly nor the robin soar," writes Peter Stevens, on whose handy presentation of the subject I shall rely in what follows.

Allometry derives from the fact that geometrically a large object has more volume in relation to its surface than a small object; more precisely, surface increases by the second power of the linear dimension whereas volume increases by the third. In the weightless space of mathematics such a transposition makes no difference, but when it occurs in the physical world under the influence of a constant gravitational pull, the difference matters a great deal. To the extent that an increase in volume means an increase in weight, the relation between weight and shape is altered when size changes.

In the psychological world of perceptual awareness, the constant factor

124

that makes for a similar difference is the disproportion in size between man and his dwelling place. The human animal is relatively small and confined to the ground, and since his locomotion is accordingly slow, he builds for himself environments in which the local distances are small. The shorter the distance from an object, the greater the visual angle, which determines the size of an image received by the eyes. In a constricted environment, therefore, a relatively small part of a building or space between buildings fills a large area of the visual field and may be surveyable only if the eyes and the head rove back and forth in scanning motions.

The resulting visual experiences are qualitatively different from those received when one looks at a small model. Thus, for example, the spaces between windows in the model may be easily bridged by the eye. The rhythmical alternation between windows and spaces is effective because the horizontal row is surveyed as a whole (Fig. 70). When the actual building is seen from nearby, however, the distance between two windows may look so great that the alternation of the visual units cannot be perceived. Similarly, intended correspondences between the lower and upper parts of a building may be evident in a small model but unobservable from the street. The front view of Le Corbusier's Carpenter Center for the Visual Arts shows a drum

Figure 70

containing a studio and next to it an upright cube containing the staircase, the two being separated from each other by an opening, which closes on the top floors. When students who saw the building every day were asked to draw it from memory, quite a few showed two disconnected units, a drum and a cube with empty space between them. A similar but more extreme phenomenon obtains for high rise buildings as seen by pedestrians. One walks past the Empire State Building without an inkling of the gigantic presence towering over neighboring roofs that the more distant sees.

Allometrically a small cube is relatively free from the pull of gravity. It can be moved by the flick of a finger like a matchbox. Perceptually also, a small model looks light, perhaps insufficiently anchored to the ground. The architect may feel tempted to strengthen the connection. The visual weight of the actual building, however, may be such that one sees it press down unmistakably. Relevant here is Stevens's observation that a spherical building, such as the United States Pavilion designed by Buckminster Fuller for the Montreal World's Fair in 1967, is much more subject to gravity than a small ball lying on the floor. This is also true visually. The contradiction between the symmetry of the shape and the asymmetry of the spatial field is all the more evident when the sphere is very large.

In relation to human size, an actual building is, of course, imposingly large. But the larger its dimensions, the greater the visual discrepancy between the volume of the interiors and the partitions creating them. With increasing size, the architectural shell looks flimsier, even though its dimensions have been enlarged proportionately. The walls of a larger room seem to look thinner, they fulfill their function of shielding the room against the outside less convincingly, because their specific visual density decreases with size. Stevens points out that the surface tension in a drop of water can hold together only so much liquid. "If the volume of water is too great, the little skin will burst. The volume must remain commensurate with the strength of the surface." Visually, too, the texture of a wall needs to be given more substance with increasing area, lest it seem to burst under the impact of the large hollow space.

The same is true for the ceiling. Stevens gives the example of a beam resting on two posts. Physically it will break under its own weight if it is made much longer. In the same way the center of a large ceiling, quite distant from the supporting walls, looks commensurately less firm, regardless of the actual statics.

Columns or pilotis supporting a bulky architectural volume look thinner than they do in a small model even though their girth has been increased proportionately. The legs of an insect look gracefully thin and those of an elephant quite clumsy when one compares pictures that make the two animals the same size. In nature the difference looks much less pronounced.

Although the walls surrounding a large interior may look flimsy, they also seem more constrictive because volume grows more rapidly than surface. The walls of the Pantheon in Rome surround us more tightly than a smaller version of it would. This seems paradoxical since the smaller interior restricts our locomotion so much more severely. But as I shall try to show in the next chapter, visual space and motor space do not always produce similar perceptual effects. Just as all biological cells come essentially in the same size, regardless of the size of the animal, so there is an optimal size for the living space of man: if it is too large, the boundaries may look too flimsy and too confining, even though the person may feel forlorn in the excessive interior expanse; if it is too small, the boundaries become unsurveyable, but the room for action is constricted. Needless to say, these purely perceptual factors interact with the conditions derived from the function and meaning of the room. Is the small interior a study or a prison cell? Is the large one a ceremonial hall or a pretentious private dining room?

THE RANGE OF IMAGES

Let me return to the disproportion in size between man and his buildings. In a purely visual sense this creates obstacles when a building is to be surveyed as a whole and in its parts from different distances. Furthermore, because the building is not only an object to be contemplated but also a part of the human environment in which man and building are to interact, man must be able to integrate himself and the building in a perceptual continuum. How can this be done given the discrepancy in size between the two?

When may we call an object surveyable? In a purely optical sense that condition is met when the object in its entirety can be accommodated within the visual field. Since we are dealing with a projective image, its size will depend on the physical area occupied by the visible part of the object in its relation to viewing distance. The field available to human vision is approximately a half circle in the horizontal direction at any one moment. In the human head both eyes look straight ahead and each one compensates for the obstruction on the nasal side of the other eye's field. As Figure 71 shows, each eye covers an approximate angle of 145°, which creates a central overlap of about 110°, available for binocular vision. In the vertical direction, of course,

127

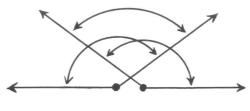

Figure 71

the two fields do not complete one another. The vertical range comes to about 110°, with roughly 45° above eye level and 65° below.

The extent of the field has considerable bearing on visual experience, as one can easily verify by shielding its outer reaches with cupped hands. When the context in which the centrally located portions appear is restricted, space no longer surrounds the viewer but looks like a picture in front of him. It is as though one were looking at a photograph or the framed image on the cinema screen. However, we must immediately add that sharp vision is limited to a small angle of about one degree, so that all but the tiniest images must be scanned by eye movements in order to be properly perceived. This limits truly comprehensive vision to an area that can be comfortably covered by the human eyes unassisted by head movements.

Paintings require such comprehensive vision since each part of the image should be seen in relation to the whole. H. Maertens has established that from a distance twice the length of a painting's longer dimension, the whole will be seen comfortably at an angle subtending about 27°. At such a distance and size, the range of the visual field includes the boundaries of the picture, so that any part fixated by the eyes is seen as located at its place in the whole. To a lesser degree other aspects, such as direction, shape, size, and color, will also be seen in the context of the total composition. It seems safe to assert that unless the total visual pattern is comprehended within this range, it cannot be seen and judged as an integrated whole.

What is essential for the surveyable unity of the visual image is not only the defined range of the object within the field, but also the fact that as long as the head stays still and only the eyes move, the perceived image also is seen as standing still. Compensating for the displacements of the projective image on the retinas of the eye is the feedback that carries information from the motor impulses controlling the eye muscles to the brain centers controlling vision. As soon as the viewer's head moves, however, the visual field is seen as

128

moving in the opposite direction, perhaps because under these circumstances the eyes are carried along as passive passengers by the vehicle of the head.

In addition, as long as the eyes move in their sockets but retain the same position in space, objects at different distances from the observer maintain a constant relation to one another. But when the head moves, the eyes are displaced, which changes perspective relations; for example, one sees the landscape outside move in relation to the window frame. Similarly, the boundaries of the visual field are seen as being displaced in relation to the objects contained within the field. The same thing happens when one views a film, and this is one reason why the effect of head movement resembles the locomotion observed on the cinema screen when the camera has been rotated or tilted. However, the effect does not equal the nauseating experience of vertigo, where the world actually seems to spin around the afflicted person.

The displacement of the image caused by head movement seems to be sufficient to interfere with the persistent identity of the image perceived in simultaneity. As I move my head what I see is different from what I saw a moment ago, and the two sights do not integrate as parts of the same thing as convincingly as when only my eyes move. Head movement typically prevails when one looks at buildings, as opposed to small architectural models or photographs. Much of the time the viewer is not far enough to profit from the 27° angle optimal for detached contemplation. The usual vertical angle more closely approximates 45° above eye level, which is the case when the viewer's distance from the building is equal to its height.

Under such conditions the eye roving across the building experiences a sequence rather than a unified image. This is bound to prevent the viewer from seeing the architectural design truly as a whole—a condition that would be fatal for the perception of most paintings but is not for most buildings. The visual structure of any part of a building tends to be simpler than that of most paintings. It is content with a few basic shapes, and the formal units, such as windows or columns, are often lined up in rows, which not only makes sequential viewing more acceptable but almost invites it. A building, moreover, being a three-dimensional solid, is not made to be stared at from a fixed point, but to unfold as one walks around it—a sequential experience, which seems to go well with an equally sequential survey of any one of its aspects, as distinguished from the restful simultaneity of a picture.

When we employ head movements to survey a building, we make it move and thereby give it the quality of an event rather than see it merely as a static

129

object. And since moving the head is more of a physical activity than the mere roving of the eyeballs in the immobile head, scanning by head movement is not simply an extension of static contemplation but makes the viewing of architecture a part of our body's daily activity. That is, this mobile mode of viewing makes architecture not something we stop to see, but something we become aware of as we go about our business.

There are other reasons that make the sequential viewing of buildings not unwelcome. When a person has to raise his head in order to survey a large object, he confirms in his motor behavior the visual experience of facing majestic height. This works to the advantage of monumental buildings, when the viewer's eyes climb, as it were, from their own level upward in a sort of pilgrimage to the crowning shapes of roof and towers. "I will lift up mine eyes unto the hills, from whence cometh my help."

When the range to be covered by sight becomes still larger, head movements no longer suffice, and the viewer's whole body must turn or change place. This is true for the viewing of any interior space. Here it becomes even harder to integrate the image of one total shape from successive impressions. Therefore, the design of interiors intended to be seen as timeless spatial wholes tends to be simple: a cube, a cylinder. Otherwise the experience becomes distinctly sequential—for example, when the viewer winds his way along a corridor or passes from room to room.

THE PARTS OF THE WHOLE

It will by now be evident that in dealing with architecture we must constantly shuttle back and forth between the building as an object seen as a whole in space by a contemplating mind, and the building as an event in time experienced by man in action. Having pointed to the meaning of the building as a sequential experience, I now return to the importance of the unified image comprehended as a synoptic whole. Although the viewer's image of the building adds up to a unified whole when he scans it from bottom to top, he will see an incomplete and therefore meaningless thing at any one moment unless the designer takes the necessary precautions. In fact, it has been good architectural practice through the ages to compose the total image of a building, which can be fitted into the visual field only from considerable distance, out of smaller subwholes whose completeness can be encompassed even from short distances.

The composition of a whole from relatively self-contained parts is not the exclusive privilege of architecture. Most paintings are composed of subwholes, a method with several advantages. Perceptually, it enables the viewer to grasp manageable units, easily surveyed by the eye, and to attain an image of the whole by finding the relations between components. This approach "from below" complements very helpfully the approach "from above," that is, the breaking down of the whole into its parts. It also enables the painter to present his statement as an interplay between relatively complete entities. This makes the work correspondingly richer, just as a dialogue can be richer than a monologue.

The parts of a whole can either be coordinated, as with windows that form a row, or subordinated in a hierarchy, as in the relation of the single window to the whole row and, in turn, the relation of the rows to the façade as a whole. Hierarchic subordination aids the viewer in gauging the size of a large object. It is true that in most instances the physical dimensions of such an object are understood by comparison with the size of surrounding objects. But as we know from many a commercial skyscraper, a building may be seen as covering much space and yet not look large. Conversely, a small structure like Bramante's Tempietto may be organized in such a way that it looks monumental. The perception of size turns out to be a highly dynamic process. A building attains its size by presenting a hierarchy of subdivisions, which lead from small units to progressively larger ones. One might say that we see the building not simply as *having* size but as *acquiring* it while our eyes climb from the small units to larger and larger ones, until the size of the whole can be measured perceptually by the scale of sizes that has been traversed. To a considerable extent, size is a matter of internal relations.

There is an essential difference between the way a viewer interrelates parts in a picture and the way he does so in a building. The parts of a painting are all directed toward the viewer in the same way: they are about the same distance from him, they all appear together in the context of the whole composition, they are available for inspection in any sequence, and while one of them is looked at, the others are present, though out of focus, in the visual field. The same is true for architecture only when one surveys, e.g., the façade of the cathedral of Amiens from some distance, that is, as a picture. The eyes are free to roam across its surface, pick out the rose window, see it surrounded by a frame of rectangular units, compare the vertical extensions with the horizontal ones, and so forth (Fig. 72a).

As one approaches the building, however, the diminishing distance restricts the view concentrically. The sequence of sights is no longer entirely at the pleasure of the viewer but is constrained by the narrowing range of the image. More exactly, the image shows things larger, but at the same time the image itself becomes narrower, like a film scene taken with a zoom lens. And

a

b

Figure 72

since the visitor approaches on the ground level, the entrance of the building is the center toward which the sight converges. This shift of focus is the appropriate visual equivalent of the functional relation being established between the visitor and the building. Instead of contemplating it as a detached viewer, he is preparing to use it by entering it.

There is visual logic to giving the meeting between visitor and entrance a completeness of its own. At Amiens, for example, the portals of the west façade are really three small gothic buildings of their own (Fig. 72b), each closed off from the rest of the façade by a protruding gable and each enriched by a world of sculptural figures, more than enough to monopolize the viewer's attention. The same is true for well-designed interiors. Otto Schubert, who describes the use of subdivision as additive seeing ("additives Sehen"), observes, for example, that if St. Peter's Cathedral had been executed according to Michelangelo's design, the visitor, upon entering the church, would have been close enough to the crossing to see included in a visual range of 27° the inscription "Tu es Petrus . . . " at the foot of the drum within the hollow of the cupola. In the same building, Bernini's baldachin, erected on the crossing, absorbs our attention with a complete shape and meaning of its own.

If human beings are to interact with a building functionally, they must be united with it by visual continuity. Huge though a building may be as a whole, it can make contact with the visitor by providing a range of sizes, some small enough to be directly relatable to the human body. These human-sized architectural elements serve as connecting links between the organic inhabitant and the inorganic habitation. The most explicit use of this principle is offered in Le Corbusier's *Modulor*, a scale of sizes growing according to the rule of the Fibonacci series. In this series, each interval is equal to the sum of the preceding two—for example, in one of the two sequences picked by Le Corbusier, 33, 53, 86, 140, 226, 336 cm., extended in both directions. With respect to the human body, these values are supposed to be derived from the proportions of the limbs, the torso, etc., and therefore the system amounts to conceiving of the building as an extension of man. Elsewhere I have described it as follows:

To Le Corbusier, man and the world he builds are an indivisible unity. Just as man is an outgrowth of nature, so the building, the furniture, the machine, the painting or statue, are outgrowths of man. The builder and his work are interdependent like the snail and its shell. Man enlarges his scope by his works, and the works receive their meaning from man's use of them. It follows from this Romantic view that man and his creation must be conceived as one integrated organism.

133

The golden section, regarded by Renaissance architects as a symbolic formula of cosmic perfection, is used by Le Corbusier in the closely related form of the Fibonacci series, controlling progressions in plant growth and shape. Thus man appears as grown from nature according to its inherent rules, and as applying these rules in turn to his own extensions of nature in his works. In the language of the old philosophers, man is presented as *natura naturata* and as *natura naturans*.

THE BUILDING MADE VISIBLE

In evaluating the visual properties of a building, one is inclined to distinguish between those that belong to the building itself and others by which the building seems explicitly to acknowledge and accommodate the beholder. This is not a tidy distinction, since all visible properties of a building are conceived in response to its sighted masters, and conversely, all considerations of projective and perspective appearance produce shapes that are at the same time objective elements of the building. But the distinction helps to point again to the dual nature of the building, which is the theme of the present chapter.

When the building takes into account man's ability to see, it does so in order to display and explain not only its practical functions but also the three-dimensional nature of its shapes and their expressive qualities. In practice, all these functions are closely related. As Paul Frankl has pointed out, in buildings designed to give a clear overview, the architectural elements face the viewer orthogonally, that is, frontally. This is true for walls and ceilings but also for cylindrical concavities, for example, an apse, in which "everything is turned toward its center point." By assuming a frontal position a building or any of its parts adopts the stance of a good servant paying full attention to his master's wishes. Frontality establishes a kind of eye contact. But eye contact is a two-way matter; not only is the building receptive to the master's orders, it also looks him straight in the face with an almost aggressive initiative. A frontally faced building is always a little like the locomotive frightening the audience of Louis Lumière's first films with its head-on approach. There is truly a confrontation.

Frontality, then, displays a principal aspect of the building fully, indeed, allows this one aspect to monopolize the scene. When one faces a cube head-on, one gets to see nothing but the frontal plane. One can, however, combine, the best of both worlds by using isometric perspective (Fig. 73). Here the front face appears in its full, undistorted extent, but at the same time

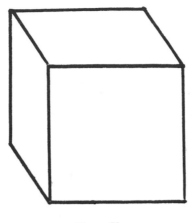

Figure 73

two of the orthogonal faces, for example, the top and one side face, are visible. Such an image is accepted in the two-dimensional plane as a representation of a regular cube. But a three-dimensional solid would yield this projection only if it were crooked, oblique, and divergent—not a likely candidate for architecture.

There are ways, however, by which the architect can display the three-dimensionality of shape and preserve frontality at the same time; one example is the bay window, whose side faces diverge and are therefore visible despite the foreshortening (Fig. 74). Hexagonal or octagonal buildings, such as baptisteries, also display their volume for the viewer, and the same is true for buildings at the intersection of two streets. Figure 75 shows one of the octagonal turrets of San Antonio in Padua. Artists, too, take advantage of this device when they are not bound by the rules of central perspective.

The problem of losing the visual sense of the depth dimension is less acute in the reverse case of the cubic hollow, e.g., in U-shaped buildings like the Casino Borghese in Rome. If the viewer is not too far away, he will see the foreshortened side wings. From a greater distance, however, he will not see them unless the wings diverge toward the front (Fig. 76).

The side faces of a cube become visible as one abandons the orthogonal position and walks around it. A flat roof, however, hides the top face of a building from anybody who is looking up to it, and therefore the stark roof line of such a building tends to make it look flat, like a sheet of paper. A pitched or hipped roof, apart from its practical functions, continues the shape of the building beyond the frontal plane; it makes it enter the depth dimen-

135

Figure 74

sion and thereby helps to define it for the eyes as a solid. Setbacks do something similar for taller buildings.

I spoke of the effect of frontality; but actually, of course, a building faces the viewer orthogonally only from a great distance. Viewed from close by, the walls lean backward, and the tall structure seems to address itself to concerns of its own size without regard to the small creatures at its feet. This is

136

Figure 75. S. Antonio, Padua. *Photo*, John Gay.

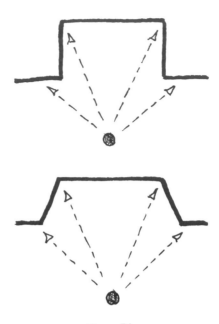

Figure 76

particularly true for buildings locked in by their neighbors, and we have already noted that relatively closed and complete subwholes, such as the porch of a traditional church, tend to act as representatives of the whole and mostly invisible building for the benefit of the approaching visitor. The building can also take notice of the visitor by bending down toward him. The overhanging houses of old towns often make this friendly gesture, and Marcel Breuer's Whitney Museum in New York leans protectively over the pedestrian and thereby exposes itself to him more directly. Such inclination is even more effective as a countermeasure when the building stands on a hill and is therefore approached by visitors at a particularly oblique angle. The hyperactive Goddard Library at Clark University has windows on stalks like crayfish eyes, peering down at what is going on outside (Fig. 77).

OBLIQUENESS AND DEPTH

The projective effects received by the viewer have been treated here as genuine properties of architecture. A few further remarks on this subject will complete the present chapter. I said earlier that if an observer stands at an oblique horizontal angle to an architectural setting, only a very egocentric

138

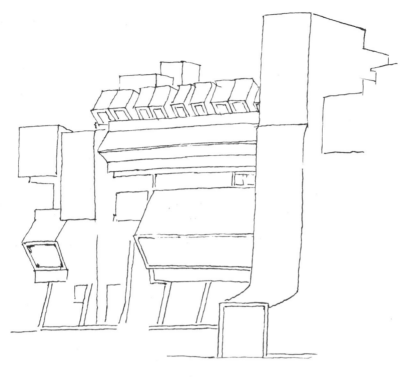

Figure 77

person would view the resulting visual effect as a property of the objective situation. As a rule, an obliquely placed person sees himself as being out of step with the spatial framework of the place, not the place as facing him obliquely.

It would be a mistake, however, to overlook the effects of relative position. Much depends on whether or not the architectural setting lays out its own spatial framework, which asks the visitor to conform. No such framework is imposed on us, for example, by the Acropolis in Athens. As one enters through the Propylaea, the axis of that building provides the only determinant of spatial orientation. This axis seems to be departed from, or even ignored by, the temples, which stand—at least in the present condition of the site—on essentially unstructured ground. No direct visual connection makes the building look forward to the arriving visitor either as his servant or as his master. The strict framework of the Parthenon does not determine the

139

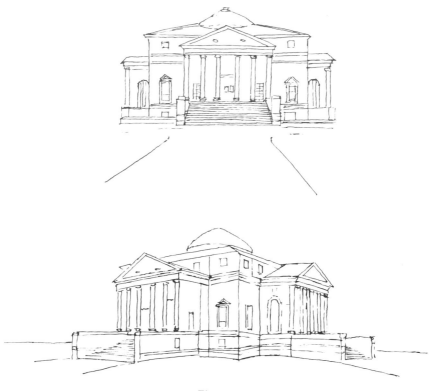

Figure 78

visual shape of its environment. The temple has to be approached from nowhere and without explicit invitation. The visitor must conform to the uncompromising demands of the building.

An oblique orientation does not fail to convey its particular expression to the viewer. This is true especially for architectural renderings on paper because a picture freezes the viewer's station point and bestows significance upon the slant. If the draftsman shows the building at an angle in order to avoid the uninformative flatness of the head-on view, he also characterizes it as turned away, dwelling in a world of its own, minding its own business. The oblique position of the building suggests that if anybody wants to approach it, he must provide his own bridge, look for the entrance, and seek out the rules of the place in order to comply with them. Conversely, a pictorial rendering that places the viewer in an orthogonal position to the entrance of the building may not tell him much about the building as a three-dimen-

140

Figure 79

sional whole; but it rolls out the carpet of invitation by providing visual conformity between the framework of the architecture and that of the viewer. (Fig. 78 shows two views of Palladio's Villa Rotonda near Vicenza.)

Looked at obliquely, a building is delivered of its flatness and visibly embedded in the framework of spatial dimensions. Except for the outer contours, every one of its edges is a crossing of planes running in different directions and thereby defining one of the corners of the building's volume. It

141

matters in principle, however, whether such an angular image is obtained from the ground or in a bird's-eye view. Above eye level the angles at the edges point upward and hide the roof plane of any cube. That we are seeing a closed solid must be accepted on faith. But since it towers over the viewer it looks gigantic.

When a building is seen from above, it presents itself more nearly as a whole. In this case the cube's three planes represent all three spatial dimensions. But the building looks small, remote, and inaccessible because no walkable plane connects it to the viewer. Like a small model, it appears as a work of man, and by revealing itself in its overall shape, which is hidden to all terrestrials, it endows the viewer with superhumanly complete sight. Only from above can we truly grasp the basic theme of, say, the cathedral of Bamberg—the elegant slimness of its Gothic body, and the correspondence between its two pairs of clock towers, one of them freely exposed, the other tightly held by the angles between the crossing and the western apse. Only from above do we see the slim nave hugged on one side by the cloister and opened on the other to the large square (Fig. 79).

And only from such a high vantage point can one see a courtyard surrounded by walls on all four sides or a castle embedded in its gardens. A conspicuous work of architecture is perceived within the cityscape in relation to other landmarks, the river, the bridges, the countryside. Bird's-eye views approach the orthogonality of geographical maps without suffering from their flatness. The maps of the seventeenth century, which accomplish the feat of presenting a city from an airplane perspective no human eye had ever enjoyed, come closest to giving us the image of an architectural setting, not as an inhabited environment but seen from afar as a creation of the human mind.

I return once more to ground level and the effect of perspective. Architectural perspective, I suggested earlier, forms so simple and compelling a system of converging edges that it detaches itself easily from the building and thereby enables the viewer to see the building in its objective shape. This is true, but it has also become clear that the deformations wrought by perspective are never entirely absent from the building's appearance and that their effect is felt even though they are not commonly acknowledged as objective properties of the building itself.

Perspective removes the building from the stable repose of the frontal plane and conveys it into the dimension of depth. Because depth is the realm of coming and going, when a building's shapes conform to perspective, the

Figure 80

building partakes in a movement (Fig. 80). This visual movement can be read in two directions, either as a departure toward the horizon or as an arrival from it. In many cases there are two or even three vanishing points, each the focus of a system of rays that recklessly traverses the building and subjugates its edges. By allowing itself to be thus deformed in deference to an encompassing spatial order, the building defines itself as a part of a larger event.

V. MOBILITY

NATURE quite in general and man in particular expend much effort on the interfaces that connect and separate creatures in their environment and relate them to it. What is needed is a protective shield, as well as something to house the end organs of observation and communication. The interface takes many forms, from skin, fur, harness, all the way to the walls of modern buildings with their windows, doors, and air conditioners. For our present purpose, the essential distinction is not so much that between natural and man-made envelopes, but the difference between containers that move with the creature and independent enclosures that serve as temporary dwellings. Skin and fur are made and shaped by the inhabitant's body; they are a part of the organism, more or less permanently attached, and they reflect its shape with varying degrees of fidelity. Whatever mobility they have is imparted to them by their carriers. This is true also for human clothing, for harnesses, and even for the more self-sustaining suits of divers and astronauts.

THE AUTONOMY OF CONTAINERS

The bird's egg is the prototype of an independent dwelling. It is not made by its inhabitant, and rather than being a manifestation of the inhabitant's size and shape, it merely accommodates its own shape and size to those of the inhabitant as far as necessary. Essentially the shape of such a container derives from requirements of its own—stability, simplicity, etc. This is true for all containers, including human housing. Therefore, although made for a mobile creature, the shape of the container depends on how little or how much mobility it requires for its own functioning. The egg must lend itself to easy movement within the hen's body, and therefore it is smooth, round,

144

well-enclosed. But most buildings will live out their lives on the spot where they are built; they need to be firmly rooted in the ground and to show that they are. Being made for a particular location, they often reflect the particular conditions to which they respond.

If, as Vincent Scully has speculated, the mobile home is the germ of tomorrow's architecture, which will not only prefabricate fully equipped houses in the factory but also make possible a more mobile lifestyle, this changed function will fundamentally affect the appearance of buildings. The automobile, although more a vehicle than a home, displays what will be the new architecture's basic characteristics. It is detached from the ground, and therefore the bottom surface needs to be well protected. Ideally, the sidefaces should not be designed just for their relation to the road, but should continue across the bottom edge. The mobile building must be a fully enclosed container—a development anticipated by our architecture on stilts, which presents boxes of potential mobility. The mobile box discourages open form, balconies and bridges—that is, the sort of continuity with the surroundings cherished by Frank Lloyd Wright. It is a capsule, whose skin is pierced for access only at some risk. Getting in and out, opening the wall to look out or to let air in must be basically retractable acts. The difference between the protruding portal of a church and an airplane door, which reduces itself to a seam in the capsule, illustrates the point. The symbolic message carried by such a shape is that of isolation and detachment.

This isolation involves self-sufficiency and independence of location. Instead of adapting its size, shape, and color to the lay of the land, to the avenues of access and vistas, to light and weather conditions, the mobile building, like the automobile, must be designed to serve adequately in all situations and with distinctive appropriateness in none. Its individual appearance derives from its own character, not from that of a particular location it is intended to fit. Like all kinds of mobility, it contravenes the wealth of local variation. Just as the Volkswagen runs on the city street, the country road, and the alpine pass, the standard mobile home replaces the urban apartment, the rural farm house, and the mountain cottage. During the Renaissance, sculpture and painting broke loose from their moorings and became adaptable to the requirements of any customer who happened to buy them, and therefore had to be geared to the average needs of a fairly broad clientele. Architecture, largely standardized and internationalized even now, may be moving in the same direction.

The traditional house, rooted in the ground, has always served the pro-

145

ductive role of counterpoint to human mobility. In opposing the one-sidedness of a nomadic lifestyle, the stable home establishes a richer pattern of being and dwelling pitted against moving, acting, and changing. When everything changes constantly, change loses much of its creative power. Architecture, therefore, has always acted as a tangible symbol of what is given, what can be relied upon, but also what must be reckoned with as a constant condition.

This productive opposition of Being versus Becoming is particularly valuable for life in a man-made environment. There is something threateningly incestuous about man living in the company of nothing but his own tools and facilities, things created entirely for his own convenience. Coping with counterforces is a prerequisite to maturity, and nature has always been the great provider of antagonists against which man had to maintain himself. With nature largely excluded from the urban precinct, it is all the more important that man's environment should compel him to set the various aspects of his being against one another. The counterpoint of mobility versus dwelling place is one of those indispensable antinomies.

DIGNIFIED IMMOBILITY

The building profits from the dignity of things that transcend change. Images of divine powers are made of durable materials, and the heavy stone walls of temples, fortresses, and palaces have always served as a suitable metaphor for temporal and spiritual power. There is a particular poignancy to architectural ruins. Although they concern us less personally than a human corpse, the destruction of a building displays the mortality of monuments that stood for duration.

Change of place, though less drastically than destruction, also affects the permanence of an object. When an object changes context, it changes character. This is a subtle notion but also a very basic one, as can be seen in the anxious resistance of so-called primitives and of children to having things removed from their accustomed place. Alberti, in his book on architecture, discusses

the very whimsical though very old persuasion which is firmly rooted in the minds of the vulgar that a picture of God or of some saint in one place shall hear the prayer of votaries, when in another place the statue of the very same God or saint shall be utterly deaf to them. Nay, and what is still more nonsensical, if you do but remove the very same statue, for which the people used to have the highest veneration, to some other station, they seem to look upon it as a bankrupt and will neither trust it with their prayers nor take the least notice of it. Such statues should therefore have seats that are fixed, eminent, and peculiar to themselves.

146

Even for someone who does not count himself among the vulgar, there is something disturbingly undignified, indeed threatening, about seeing a piece of sculpture taken from its place and moved around for purposes of shipping, cleaning, or repairing. It is equally disconcerting to see a good house being moved or reconstructed elsewhere. This sensation has two different psychological aspects. One of them, already mentioned, derives from the fact that by changing context an object changes character and thereby loses some of its constant identity. The other is that by handling the object at will, one deprives it of some of its autonomy. The object is forced to surrender its own initiative. It was somewhat risky to set the venerated statue of the Virgin at the Ronchamp chapel on a rotating pedestal, as Le Corbusier did, so that the image could be switched from indoor to outdoor service by a simple turn of 180°. Since the image is defined by its surroundings as much as by its own nature, it displays a somewhat inappropriate variability, which is likely to be manifest also in its changing of appearance when it is lit by electricity and candles in the narrow and dark chapel or exposed to bright daylight in endless natural space.

Furthermore, the handling of the statue, its defenseless acquiescence to anybody's will, breaches its autonomy. Compare here the effect obtained when a religious image is borne in procession. Physical evidence notwithstanding, the image does not appear to be carried around willfully. The saintly figure is merely supported in her or his journey by subservient followers. The figure is undertaking a visit on its own initiative. Thus it is not motion as such that endangers the integrity of the object, but its being reduced to a passive tool. A moving automobile looks distinctly different depending on whether one conceives of it as powerfully carrying its passengers or as responding mechanically to the commands of the person in the driver's seat. In the latter case the driver is visually defined as what Freud called the "Prothesengott," the prosthetic god, endowed with superhuman powers by his technological appendages.

When mobility is perceived as derived from the object's own initiative, it may increase rather than diminish the object's power. This is true for kinetic sculpture, which gives the impression of generating its own action and therefore of being animated by a more elemental dynamics than an immobile piece. The same could be true for architecture. There is compelling power in the slow advance of a large ship, and rotating penthouse platforms on tall buildings enhance the imposing structure's vitality. Such considerations are remote from most architects' minds today; but as mobility becomes more feasible, such notions may look less strange in the future.

For the time being, architecture as we know it is the stable counterpart to man's mobility. This relation between the two goes much beyond the mutually enlivening contrast characteristic of our dealings with sculpture. Sculpture reposes in its self-contained completeness; it takes notice of the customer only by exposing itself, that is, it complies with the need for readability by deploying its shape. But most sculpture admits of no penetration other than that by the viewer's eyes. It dwells in a closed precinct and serves as a tool only to the extent of making itself visible and touchable. It provides for no other physical handling. The viewer's locomotions are structurally alien to the sculptural form. He may walk around it in any direction he pleases, and he may let his eyes scan the object in any sequence. The course of his exploration in no way affects the timeless nature of the sculptural object.

Architecture also complements the coming and going of people by its own timeless permanence, but it interacts with them in a much more tangible physical sense. By offering facilities to be entered, walked through, lived in, it acknowledges in its form the human presence, just as a bridge is incomplete without the image of cars and pedestrians moving across it, or as a pair of scissors looks empty without fingers through its loops. The relationship between the architectural object and its users is one of intense interaction. In all interaction, each partner must work out a suitable ratio between adapting himself to the other's character and requiring the partner to adapt to him. On the one extreme the inhabitant derives his needs from the idiosyncrasies of the building; on the other, the building's character is effaced in the selfless service of the user.

SHELTER AND BURROW

With respect to mobility, the architectural task admits of two basic solutions, which I shall call the shelter and the burrow. A shelter is a container, which, as I mentioned in reference to the egg, derives its form from its own function and acknowledges its users's presence only secondarily. The logical shape of a container is one of simple centric symmetry, especially roundness. A recent architectural example is the stark cylinder of the Hirshhorn Museum in Washington (Fig. 81). When this sort of container building is taken to its theoretical extreme, we are faced with a structure that tolerates entrances and exits only as interruptions of its integrity and as concessions to an imposed function. Access may be obtained surreptitiously through openings left by the building for its own purposes, for example, through the arches

148

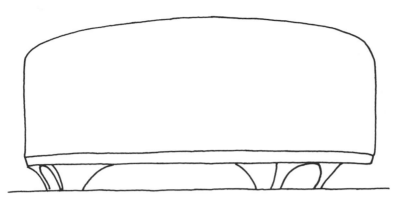

Figure 81

between supports. Such a building is populated without actually playing the host, and it is not really incomplete when deserted. Its open spaces admit access but provide no active accommodation for the visitor. Certain tracks conform to the building's design, for example, in a centralized hall the movement toward the center and away from it; but these paths do not serve the user's needs unless he is an architectural devotee who moves around for the purpose of exploring the building's design. Otherwise, the visitor's pattern of movements is as unrelated to the structure as that of someone walking around a sculpture in order to see it.

The opposite kind of building is the burrow, which, taken again as a pure abstract type, is simply the result of the inhabitant's physical penetration. The track left by digging serves as the channel for future use. It therefore prescribes the user's itinerary as inescapably as a railroad track; and when it offers a larger area, it does so because the user wants more freedom of direction or needs more space, not because the structure requires it as an element of its shape (Fig. 82). Taken as a whole, the burrow can be as three-dimensional as the shelter, but its three-dimensionality is formed by a system of linear channels, not by inherently three-dimensional shapes. If Wright's Guggenheim Museum consisted of nothing but the spiraling corridor that constitutes its principal exhibition space, it would add up to a cylinder, but without employing cylindrical shape.

Frankl has said of such a building that it is conceived as a network of pathways, quite disembodied at first, that is, at an early stage of conception, because it is not yet clothed in material shapes. The shapes are derived secondarily from the direction and arrangement of the channels. In fact, it is

149

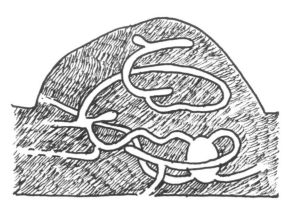

Figure 82. Section through a mole's hill. After von Frisch.

quite common for the programming of buildings to begin at the even more abstract level of functional relations. For example, if there is to be an area of central activity from which a number of more specialized functions are to derive, the arrows describing these functions are at first not even embodied in the image of physically moving persons but simply indicate the directions to be taken in the course of business (Fig. 83a). At a somewhat more concrete level of conception, these vectors become the images of people who come and go, and only at a third level do the channels begin to suggest material shape.

The conception of such a "burrow," if it comes about by plan, is as purely dynamic and as devoid of tangible matter as a piece of music written for no instruments in particular. A building of the shelter type, by contrast, is conceived as a timeless form, whose functions are foreseen essentially by the grouping of areas, differing in size and shape and relating to one another as required by the necessary connections (Fig. 83b). It, too, may derive from an abstract plan, that results only secondarily in the invention of shapes, but such a plan of the building's functions is more like a tree or a skeleton than an arterial network. It is an arrangement of specified containers, held together by a functional order. The relations between these containers are connections rather than directional channels, and the design is further concretized not as a network of pathways but as an agglomeration of spaces.

What I am describing here are fictitious extremes. In practice, any architectural project combines features of both approaches in some ratio; but in order to describe the ratio, one must first define the poles of the scale. It also is evident that these two conceptions are not simply two methods of designing a building, but spring from deep-seated ways of viewing human existence

150

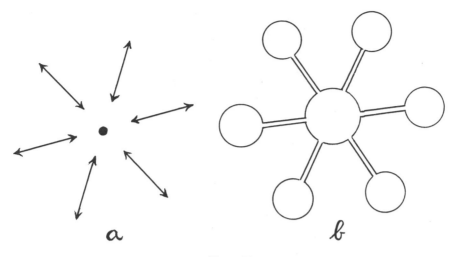

a   *b*

Figure 83

and hence from two different architectural styles. One can express this difference by saying that the conceiver of shelters is essentially a builder, whereas the conceiver of burrows is a digger; or in sculptural terms, that the one is a modeler, the other a carver. To the builder or modeler, paths are interstices between volumes; to the digger or carver they are the primary ducts, around which the supporting matter accumulates. And although the architect, who conceives of the building in his head and on his drawing board, does not do any of the modeling and carving himself, it seems sensible to suggest that mental refinements of these physical activities steer his imagination as he invents his shapes.

MOTOR BEHAVIOR

The shelter type of architecture is dominated by visually conceived forms; the burrow type derives from motor behavior. This difference of control favors different shapes. The study of handwriting shows that letters conceived for visual effect tend to prefer symmetry and right angles. For the purpose of neat distinction they leave space between units. When motor behavior dominates writing, it tends to favor an uninterrupted flow and to smooth abrupt changes of direction into gradual curves (Fig. 84). The same tendencies are observed wherever motor behavior has its way, e.g., when a rolling marble leaves its track on a sandy slope or when students tramp shortcut paths across carefully kept lawns on a campus. Highways designed

151

Figure 84

for the convenience of speedy cars avoid sharp turns and renounce angles between straight lines. By the same token, a building laid out as a system of arteries will run to smooth, flowing, uninterrupted curves, and will avoid angular breaks. This is true also in the vertical dimension, when ramps replace zigzagging steps. If steps are indispensable, the mobility-conscious architect will design them keeping in mind not just their visual effect of patterned obliqueness, but also the particular kinesthetic rhythm produced by the alternation of riser and tread, i.e., the ratio of laborious lifting versus victorious advancing.

In a fragmentary note on architecture, Goethe goes so far as to remark:

One would think that architecture as a fine art works solely for the eyes. Instead, it should work primarily for the sense of mechanical motion in the human body— something to which scant attention is paid. When in dance we move according to definite rules, we experience a pleasant sensation. A similar sensation should be aroused in someone who is led blindfolded through a well-built house. This involves the difficult and complicated doctrine of proportions, which gives the building and its various parts their character.

Mobility is linear and forward-directed. The greater the velocity, the stronger the impulse, and the more effort it takes to deflect it from its course. Rasmussen tells us that in ancient China the main entrance to a dwelling was placed somewhat to one side of the north-south axis leading toward the place. This was done to prevent evil spirits from rushing straight into the house. One supposes that if the spirits arrived at a leisurely pace, the device would not have deterred them. Quite in general, however, any deviation from the course is an impediment. Movement tends to straighten the course and eliminate deviations.

152

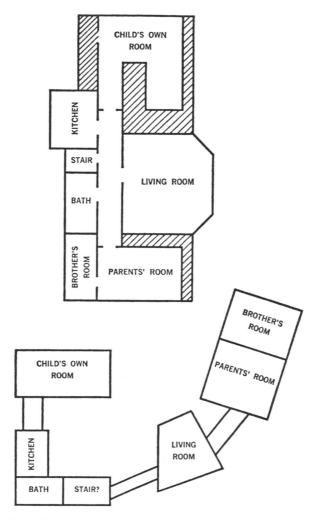

Figure 85. From J. Church, *Language and the Discovery of Reality*.

This is true also for the mental images of spatial connections based on motor experiences. In recalling city layouts one tends to overlook bends that complicate the overall direction of a street or route. The same happens to orientation in a building. Any deviation from an overall direction is hard to conceive and invites spatial confusion. Figure 85 is a schematic version of a map drawn by a five-year-old girl when she was asked to depict her parents' apartment. At the top is the actual plan of the apartment. In presenting the

153

map, the child psychologist Joseph Church comments: "We must insist on the difference between space given as a field of locomotion and space given visually or as a container for objects other than oneself." The two-dimensional layout of the apartment has been reduced by the girl to a linear sequence. The mind can grasp a linear sequence more easily than the multiple simultaneous connections in a two-dimensional manifold. This simplification also corresponds to the child's motor experience of coming and going, through which she acquired her image of the apartment. Spatial simultaneity is experienced as temporal sequence.

The example shows, furthermore, that reduction to a linear sequence does considerable violence to the actual topological relations. The motor approach generates misinformation. This is particularly important if we keep in mind that one rarely acquires the image of a spatial configuration, be it of a house or a city, by looking at a plan or map or just by looking around. Rather, one's knowledge derives primarily from what one observes in the course of purposeful locomotion. This favors a very particular kind of conception. In a study of the perceptual image young married couples form of their apartments, Glenn Lym found that by no means all of them harbor an image of the overall plan. Their living quarters consist for them of functional connections between particular units, e.g., the living room and the bedroom; and although these partial motor links cross one another, they do not necessarily add up to a unified pattern. The fact that the apartment "really has an L-shape" may come as a surprise; it may come only when the inhabitants are invited to look at their place as a whole. Therefore, when an architect wishes to design an environment that conveys to its users an overall image of its spatial form and arrangement, he must consider conditions much more complex than the visual simplicity of the total pattern.

The difference between the overall contemplation of a spatial pattern, obtainable only through the eyes, and its exploration through linear motor forays may also account for the well-known experience of returning to an old apartment or house only to be surprised at how much smaller it is in fact than it was in memory. What the returning visitor receives on seeing his old study after an absence is a visual overview, something quite different from the pattern of functional relations the place represented when he traveled as an active user back and forth between desk and bookshelves, windows and filing cabinet. Such local action creates a much more pronounced sense of space than the same distances convey when looked at as parts of a purely visual whole—as it were, from the outside.

In these last examples I have, almost inevitably, shifted the discussion from the purely physical conditions of mobility to the visual experiences accompanying locomotion in space. Vision is the principal steering instrument of motor behavior. The eyes look ahead to the space that can be traversed; they discover openings and directions and gauge the ease or difficulty of progress. During physical movement the mind sees the world ahead as a map of potential paths. The same visual distance conveys different images depending on whether it permits motor access or not. The moon looks different when it is seen as the target of space travel rather than as a heavenly body way off in the sky. Looking up to a cupola, one receives a sight affected by unreachability, as distinguished from a target attainable on the ground at the same distance. When one drives through Boston on an elevated highway, a nearby building may appear unreachably far away because no path connects it with the road on which one is traveling. Any railing, fence, or balustrade enhances the visual subdivision of space by the potential motor information that the place is inaccessible and therefore "farther away."

THE DYNAMICS OF THE CHANNEL

In the preceding chapter I commented on the difference between an object seen from a particular viewpoint and its objective visual shape. The same is true for the perspective distortion of channels. A regularly shaped road or corridor is seen as converging in the distance ahead. This renders the path more dynamic visually because any wedge shape looks more dynamic than a pair of parallel edges. At the same time, however, a convergence offers the prospect of a gradual narrowing and ultimate blocking of the road, which inhibits forward progress. Yet, paradoxically, that convergence remains at the same distance. It never comes closer, but offers instead an unchanging image, a visual standstill, which contradicts the walker's or driver's sensation of moving forward. All this adds up to a subtly frustrating experience, which counteracts the exhilarating freedom of the open road. The effect is the opposite of what we feel when there opens ahead of us a crescendo, a gradually expanding vista.

The visual experience of locomotion is always a relative matter. It is conveyed by displacement with regard to the environment that serves as the frame of reference. Paradoxically again, as we move, our own body or vehicle remains visually immobile. It is only the displacement in the things around us that confirms for the eyes the kinesthetic information of locomotion. When

155

flying through fog or dense clouds, one sees no progress, and the same is true amidst the deadening monotony of corridors in office buildings or hotels. The street grid of Manhattan, spelled out by rows of anonymous buildings, tires the pedestrian because he must supplement his muscular exertion with the psychological effort of convincing himself that he is making headway. Since the impulse is not supported from the outside, it must be generated within.

Defeatist boredom is relieved when, for example, a street or a pedestrian underpass is lined with store windows, or a highway with trees, farms, and bridges. Such enrichment helps not only because it gives the traveler an enlivening variety of things to look at. Landmarks, big and small, subdivide the endless road and provide short-term goals: one sees the tall willow tree approaching and one reaches it. A stretch of the journey has been completed.

In addition, passing targets change appearance as one comes closer. A store window, contracted and almost invisible from a distance, gradually broadens and unfolds its full display as one passes by it. This perspective unfolding is an essential part of the experience that transforms the simultaneity of space into a sequence in time. As we walk or drive, the environment becomes a happening, in which things follow one another and change shape while they change position. A building in which nothing is designed for sequence is a depressing experience. The staircases of Baroque palaces offer a grandiose overture when one enters the building and when, as it were, the curtain rises. Pevsner describes the winding staircase in the Bruchsal episcopal palace as it existed before it was damaged during the war.

On the ground floor it is a somber room, painted with rocks in the rustic manner of Italian grotto imitations. The staircase itself then unfolded between two curved walls, the outside wall solid, that on the inside opened in arcades through which one looked down into the semi-darkness of the oval grotto. The height of the arcade openings, of course, diminished as the staircase ascended. And while you walked up, it grew lighter and lighter around you, until you reached the main floor and a platform the size of the oval room beneath.

Such a description reminds us that the visitor experiences not only a sequence of sights but the constant gradual transformation created by perspective and lighting in every wall or constellation of elements. The architect has helped to translate the visitor's purely physical movement into a corresponding visual event. Kevin Lynch speaks appropriately of the "melodic" path that leads, for example, from Oakland across the Bay to San Francisco: the approaching towers of the bridge, the rhythmically swinging garlands of the steel cables, the island of Alcatraz sliding by on the water in the distance, the approach of Yerba Buena Island, the entrance into the tunnel, the revelation of the city skyline as one emerges from the darkness.

By their very nature, buildings must combine passages and dwelling places. Physically, of course, all spaces persist in rigid immobility; but visually the occupant must not be smothered by the stagnancy of an assemblage of containers, tied together by corridors that convey no progression. I spoke earlier of the exhilarating crescendo of a vista that diverges before an approaching walker. But a temporary narrowing of the path can also act dynamically, by generating the tension of constriction, resolved into new expansion. There is furthermore the stimulating effect of the sudden surprise: the opening up of an unforeseen space, of which the most spectacular example remains the approach to Bernini's square in front of St. Peter's. This impressive *coup de théâtre* has survived even Mussolini's misguided attempt to create monumental access by removing the "spina" between the two narrow streets that led from the Tiber to the Vatican. On a more modest scale, any passage from a corridor to the sudden expanse of a room quickens the visitor's experience with a small visual shock.

Strict control by a narrow channel is not the only means of guiding locomotion. Propelled by a sufficiently directive impulse, the walker may find himself traversing a room whose main axis he crosses at a right angle (Fig. 86). Suddenly without support, he enjoys the freedom tinged with anxiety of being on his own, a sense of power and adventure. Architecture

Figure 86

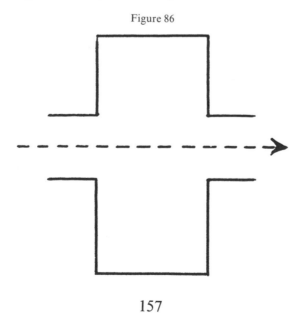

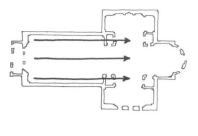

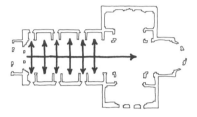

Figure 87

often guides not by channels but by the magnetism of a target. Arches and niches beckon. Here again we are served by an example of Pevsner's. In Sant' Andrea in Mantua, Alberti "replaces the traditional nave and aisles arrangement by a series of side chapels taking the place of the aisles and connected with the nave alternately by tall and wide and low and narrow openings. The aisles thus cease to be part of the eastward movement and become a series of minor centers accompanying the spacious tunnel-vaulted nave" (Fig. 87). Whereas the visitor is guided by the aisles as strictly as a ball rolling in a groove, in Alberti's church he retains the initiative of deciding whether or not to accede to the invitation of the lateral chapels and deflect, by a side step or two, his course toward the main altar. In some cases a simple strong color on the end wall of a corridor suffices to transform the static passage into a goal-directed track. The statue in the far corner of Mies van der Rohe's Barcelona pavilion (Fig. 11) is a more explicit example.

Temporary retardation is known in the arts as a strong incentive toward forward movement. It is also a standard device of traditional drama, and is constantly used in music to dam the melodic flow before a new surge of power. Suspense derives from the temporary suspension of action. The overcoming of obstacles similarly intensifies a walker's or runner's striving toward his goal. An elemenary antagonism occurs in almost every experience of locomotion by virtue of the fact that as a person advances, the

158

setting seems to move toward him in the opposite direction. The effect of a traveling shot on the cinema screen reveals that a visual experience of motion occurs when we see the world fly apart from the vanishing point in front of us and pass by us to the left, to the right, and up above.

James J. Gibson has described this perspective effect as a means of orientation for airplane pilots during landing. The higher the speed, the more noticeable the countermovement of the environment. In our time we may have grown unaware of these visual phenomena even from a fast-moving car; but during the nineteenth century, the dynamic experience of transportation was very impressive. Testimony from French writers of the period has been collected by Claude Pichois, who quotes from Théophile Gautier and Victor Hugo and, in particular, cites a poem written by Gérard de Nerval in 1832. The poet describes how, on awakening in a moving coach, he sees the trees on the road in disorderly flight like a routed army, and the church towers shepherding their villages like flocks through the plains; the mountains are staggering drunks, and the river leaps toward them from the valley like a boa constrictor seeking to capture them in its squeeze.

Such high-pitched examples remind us that even under the calmer conditions of architectural experience, the environment marches toward the visitor as he enters a building and walks through a lobby or crosses a hall. Accordingly, architectural shapes are designed not only as features of statically reposing spaces, but as members of a kind of reception committee, assembled to greet the arriving visitor. Depending on their appearance, they will either facilitate the entrance or restrain it. A gate, be it a triumphal arch or a Japanese torii, offers an opening, but at the same time stands in the way as a temporary impediment. A door is a wall's reluctant contribution to passage.

A conspicuous example of the teasing Baroque play with the attraction and retardation of movement is the Spanish Steps in Rome. After climbing the first groups of steps, one runs into a balustrade, which splits the flow of traffic toward the left and the right; and hardly has the flow reunited when it is stopped again by another bulwark, surmounted by an obelisk. All this leads to the crowning church of Trinità de' Monti, which is the goal and ultimate stop (Fig. 88).

Less dramatic but more applicable to the skillful handling of architectural dynamics in interiors is an example cited by Robert Venturi. Access to the church of St.-Madeleine in Vézelay is blocked, as so often happens, by a column in the center of the portal, and again, more conspicuously, by an

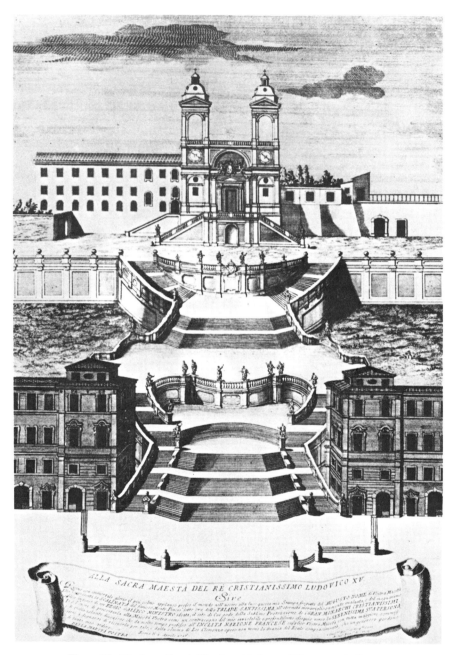

Figure 88. Girolamo Rossi, *The Spanish Steps of Francesco de Sanctis.*

Figure 89

ornamented post subdividing the inner door, which leads from the narthex to the nave (Fig. 89). This traffic-stopping post directly supports a stone relief on which the large frontal figure of Christ towers over the disciples—an arresting image that gives emphasis and meaning to the imposed physical pause. The visitor, briefly retained by the impressive Biblical scene, is released with a new momentum into the main hall of the sanctuary. The theme of the great interplay between the mobility of man and the stony persistence of his dwellings is performed in miniature by an architectural element and the response it evokes.

161

VI. ORDER AND DISORDER

T HE MEANING of the term order has been distorted by a controversy that identifies order in general with a very particular kind of order, praised by one generation of designers, artists, and architects, and rejected as irksomely restrictive by another. Order has come to mean a reduction to simple geometrical shape and the standardization of everything for everybody, the favoring of basic physical function over expression and of rationality at the expense of spontaneous invention.

Controversies over stylistic preferences come and go. They constitute the dialectic of art in history and supply a needed impetus for change. But they must not be permitted to deprive us of concepts that are indispensable to an understanding of fundamental facts. Nothing but confusion can result when order is considered a quality that can equally well be accepted or abandoned, one man's meat and the other man's poison, something that can be forgone and replaced by something else. Order must be understood as indispensable to the functioning of any organized system, whether its function be physical or mental. Just as neither an engine nor an orchestra nor a sports team can perform without the integrated cooperation of all its parts, so a work of art or architecture cannot fulfill its function and transmit its message unless it presents an ordered pattern. Order is possible at any level of complexity: in statues as simple as those on Easter Island or as intricate as those by Bernini, in a farmhouse and in a Borromini church. But if there is no order, there is no way of telling what the work is trying to say.

CONTRADICTION IS A FLAW

This basic fact has been effectively beclouded in a book by Robert Venturi. As buttressing for his aversion to the ascetic sobriety of the Bauhaus and the International Style in architecture—an aversion to which he is certainly

162

entitled—he offers a well-documented review of tendencies toward complexity and intricacy throughout the history of architecture. This demonstration would be useful indeed were it offered as a reminder of how compatible a rich variety of formal invention is with architectural order. Instead, Venturi maintains that his examples display and thereby justify inherent contradiction. If this assertion amounted simply to the incorrect use of a term of logic, it would merit little attention. But the choice of the term is deliberate. It is invoked to defend disorder, confusion, the vulgar agglomeration of incompatibles, and other symptoms of the modern pathology for which, in theory at least, Venturi professes a liking.

Self-contradiction, which is what Venturi has in mind, is an offense against order. It is a mistake committed out of ignorance or oversight or for a misguided purpose. When it occurs in a statement, it consists in attributing to some object or fact a particular predicate while at the same time denying it that predicate. It is a violation of the rule of the excluded third, which holds that any predicate must be either attributed or denied to any thing. One is in error if one asserts that something exists and does not exist at the same time.

Nor is it possible for one thing to possess two mutually exclusive properties in the same place at the same time. It is quite feasible for an object to be partly red and partly blue, or to look blue in the morning and red in the evening, or to look blue to one person and red to another. But the same parts cannot be both red and blue under the same conditions, although the object can be any mixture of the two. It can fulfill several functions, provided those functions are compatible. It can also be ambiguous, in the sense of an alternation between two versions. All these are possible and acceptable kinds of order. But if you say about a thing that it is this and also that and the two are mutually exclusive, and similarly if a thing reports to you that it is this and at the same time also that and the two are mutually exclusive, then what is said is nonsense, what is being created is confusion, and order becomes disorder. Such a turbulent state of affairs may be to your or my liking; but it prevents the thing from exercising its function, at least to the extent that these functions rely on an orderly statement.

For our present purpose I shall assume that the form of any object or mechanism should be such as to serve the object's or mechanism's purpose. An incorrectly built engine can blow up a factory, which might benefit society but does not serve the purpose for which the engine was made; and if an orchestra's bassoon player decided to play his part sometimes but not always, instead playing the violin part off and on, the result might be fascinating but the intended musical statement would be sabotaged. Can we agree that, as one of the basic prerequisites for the functioning of our world, each object or event should project an intelligible statement of its nature and purpose? If so, we must require that these statements be orderly. A building unable to tell whether it is straight or crooked, in one piece or in several pieces, symmetrical or asymmetrical, simple or complex, exalting or depressing, will fulfill its purpose only if that purpose is to puzzle—not much of a goal in most cases.

THE CONSTRAINTS OF ORDER

Order is so fundamental a tendency in inorganic and organic nature that we can make the following assertion: Order comes about unless special circumstances prevent it. Or: In any situation as much order will obtain as circumstances permit. If a situation is a closed system of forces, these forces will arrange themselves so that the tension in the system is at a minimum. At that level of lowest tension all action ceases and the system holds itself in equilibrium unless new forces are introduced from outside to change conditions. The ordering process stops at the level determined by the constraints inherent in the system. If there are no constraints at all, the process continues until a state of complete homogeneity is attained—a state exemplified by a perfectly shuffled deck of cards, a well-shaken mix, or the distribution of molecules in boiling water. In this latter case, order consists in nothing but the prevalence of the same situation everywhere in the field. Any parts could exchange places without any modification of the system. Homogeneity is the lowest possible level and the least fruitful one, but a state of order it is—even though the physicists, for purposes of their own, prefer to describe it as a state of disorder.

Architecture approaches this lowest level of order in the identical housing units of a so-called subdivision, where all homes are interchangeable and the visitor finds himself in the same place wherever he goes. This distressing condition is avoided in most other instances because the tendency toward order is constrained by a countertendency, which we may call the *theme* of a system. The theme is what is being ordered. In a piece of music, the composer's "idea" and the given structure of the musical system are constraining features, to which the best possible order is applied. In architecture, the program of a building, its transformation into a design idea, the requirements deriving from the needs the building is to meet, as well as the symbols it is to express—all these factors keep the ordering process from proceeding toward further simplicity, symmetry, regularity, etc. At the same time, the factors constituting the theme are subjected to the ordering process to ensure their

164

optimal realization. Ordering serves to organize the parts in the whole and thereby to avoid redundancy, conflict, self-contradiction—all those deficiencies that would prevent the work from being truly itself and fulfilling its various psychological and physical functions.

The admirable structures found in nature—crystals, atomic systems, flowers —reveal configurations of forces that are arrested at some level by the constraints of their theme and left sufficiently alone to realize their form perfectly. They are governed by such rules as: Similarity of function makes for similarity of form; and whatever has no reason to look different will look the same. The petals of a daisy are alike in color and shape and have the same relation to the center because they all play the same role in the system. That sameness of role expresses itself in sameness of appearance.

THREE MODIFICATIONS OF ORDER

The foregoing is the rationale of order in its purest manifestation. Pure perfection, however, is modified by a number of principles, of which I shall mention three.

1. Symmetry or other kinds of regularity are highly ordered themes, but being themes they apply only where they suit the program. Symmetry is contraindicated by dissimilarity of function. A tree or a tower can afford to be centrically symmetrical when there is no reason for it to respond differently to different directions. In most animals special treatment must be accorded to the principal direction of their mobility, and therefore their symmetry cannot be centric. The human face is a necessarily one-sided modification of the spherical container housing the brain. The façade of a building visibly acknowledges the importance of approach, entrance, and exit.

Regularity is not acceptable when the mind for which the object is made thirsts for irregularity. A box can be a simple cube when all it is meant to fulfill and express is the physical function of a container. Depending on its size, it can suitably house a file of index cards, an electronic computer, or five thousand heads of office personnel. A simple cube can serve as a symbol of something monolithic, such as power or permanence, but it cannot reflect the complexity of the human mind. Complex structure can be housed but not expressed by simple shape.

2. Every thing has some independence and completeness of its own, but at the same time is a part of larger contexts. It may acknowledge very little of this dependence, but it can never be wholly self-contained. There is much closure in an apple's symmetry, yet its shape recognizes its dependence upon

165

the stem from which it grew. A building may be designed without regard to its neighbors, but almost always it at least shows its subservience to the force of gravity, and it commonly provides entrances and exits and adapts its shape to the intake of air and light. Such modification of the object's intrinsic order by its interaction with the environment is not only indispensable to its functioning, but also desirable for its form and appearance. An object that behaves as though it were independent while being in fact dependent, harbors a discrepancy that may be experienced as self-contradiction and therefore as disturbing. Untruth interferes with functioning.

It makes a difference whether an object's dependence upon a context manifests itself as interference with its shape or as a modulation of it. A tree impeded by its neighbors may be stunted on one side. In a natural setting, this partial setback makes sense as a response to prevailing conditions, and to that extent it fits the ecological order of its surroundings. Even so, looked at by itself, the tree may be ugly. This is so not because its inherent structure has been interfered with, but because the interference has rent, not modified, the structure. If in comparison one looks at the windswept pines of the California coast, there, too, one notices incompleteness unless one perceives the wind as a part of the order. In the latter case, the trees' deflection from their inherent symmetry does not play havoc with structure. It rather overlays it with a new vector, which has been incorporated in a restructuring of the whole. The order of the object has been shifted to a higher level of complexity.

The architect faces this sort of problem, for example, when he has to adapt his design to a sloping or otherwise irregular site. Whether or not his solution works can hardly be decided by objective measurement. What we can and must do, however, is to formulate the principles relevant to the evaluation of the particular case. Let me cite a rather extreme example. What are we to say of the Hôtel de Matignon, erected in Paris in the late eighteenth century, a building cited with approval by both Venturi and Pevsner (Fig. 90)? The problem that "the front towards the *cour d'honneur* and the back towards the garden should both be symmetrical in themselves and even when they did not lie on the same axis" is solved by the building shifting its axis, as it were, in midstream. Two symmetrical structures are entwined in such a way that a wing of the one becomes the central axis of the other. The solution is unquestionably ingenious, but one cannot let the example pass without asking whether the resulting design is a successful unification of two structures or a monster, in the precise biological meaning of that term.

166

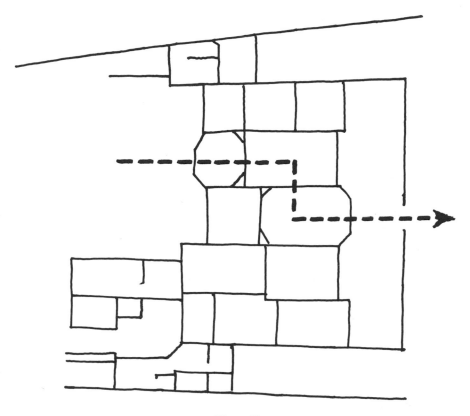

Figure 90

The device used by the architect cannot but remind us of what musicians call an enharmonic modulation, that is, the almost imperceptible shift from one key to another, in the course of which certain tones act as bridges by fulfilling different functions in the two keys and thereby display a double allegiance. The transitional moment generates a slight sensation of seasickness, unwelcome or exhilarating depending on the listener's disposition, because the frame of reference is temporarily lost.

(As a simple example of what I am discussing, Figure 91 reproduces a passage from a violin sonata by Jean-Marie Leclair [1697–1764]. Two notes refer to the same tone, but they are written differently because the *b*-flat is experienced dynamically as the outcome of a steep ascent in the key of D, which has, as it were, overshot the mark by a half tone and is straining

167

Figure 91

downward toward the dominant, *a*. The same tone written as an *a*-sharp presses upward as the leading tone in the new key of B, thereby assuming a new function in a different structural context.)

In music, most characteristically perhaps in the work of Richard Wagner, this device is considered not only a workable one but an important stylistic means of expressing a liberation from absolute standards, characteristic of a particular philosophical attitude. It is not possible, however, simply to equate the architectural modulation with the musical one. To be sure, as the visitor walks through the Paris Hôtel, he will be moved gradually from the initial framework to the one that displaces it—an experience rather analogous to that of listening to the music just discussed, including the transitional phase of disorientation. But music is a sequential event by its very nature, and therefore the shifting from one frame of reference to another is a change of scene for the work as a whole, as though in a play the story had moved from a boat to an island. An architectural experience that is purely sequential, however, can never do full justice to a building, because a building is a spatial entity that persists as a whole.

In the case of the building, the two symmetry systems coexist in the total spatial image that must be obtained if the building is to be understood, even though in direct perception no such simultaneity is ever accessible. Therefore it is necessary to transcend the sequential perception of the visitor and look at the building's total design. To be sure, since the Hôtel de Matignon is intended to serve a dual role with regard to its environment, its design must be considered in that context. But a building of that kind is so much a structure of its own that while fulfilling its assignment as a connecting link in the surrounding context, it must also present a form that holds together within itself. Although the verdict on the building's success or failure rests

168

with the critics, the principles on which they should base their judgment can be established with precision.

The reference to Richard Wagner, that is, to a musical style of a roughly comparable period, makes it evident that the French architect's plan cannot be treated simply as a clever solution to a practical problem. The nature of the device employed and the fact that it is considered acceptable and perhaps even desirable must be seen as a stylistic symptom; and since all architectural experience is by its nature symbolic, we must take note of the architect's willingness to create a spatial metaphor of a relativistic worldview.

3. There is a third principle modifying the perfect embodiment of pure order. It has to do with the difference between intended or inherent pattern and practical execution. An ornamental pattern representing the corolla of a daisy can please us by exhibiting the symmetrical star shape to perfection. This perfection, however, can also be considered cold and lifeless. We may find it suitable for decor intended to surround us with undisturbed harmony, but it is hardly appropriate as an image of life in a fuller sense. Life appears to us for the most part as an interaction between intended patterns and the impediments, variations, imperfections, imposed upon them because our world is not a machine shop run by infallible powers. The petals of an actual daisy are often not exactly alike and do not array themselves in perfect order. We may welcome this imperfection as an image of our own way of behaving by a variety of individual impulses, which we cherish because they document our freedom from mechanical replication.

HOW TO MAKE NOISE

It is well to remember, however, that this romantic affection for the "noise" qualities of natural behavior is a particular stylistic preference, not a universal principle. Architecture in particular has almost always aimed at geometrical perfection and symmetry. The builder endeavors to make parallel elements exactly alike, and slight deviations, such as the "refinements" of the Greek temples, are introduced for a particular purpose. When we cherish the erosions by which the marble of the ancient columns reveals its affinity with the mountains of its origin, we indulge in a sentimentality not shared by the men who carved it. Similarly, the imperfections of "anonymous" architecture are not mainly due to a taste for the rustic.

Architecture has ways of expressing tension, interference, distortion, and similar modifications of undisturbed harmony, but the "noise" of organic

169

and inorganic imperfection is not generally one of them. Recently, however, resentment against the tidiness of simple order has stimulated attempts to include such effects among the architect's legitimate devices. By what principles can we evaluate such attempts? Take the following example. Some of the old sidewalks in Cambridge, Massachusetts, are still paved with bricks. Loosely fitted in the sand, the bricks are heaved by the frost in winter, pushed around by tree roots, and displaced by pedestrians' feet. This irregularity makes walking laborious and hazardous, but also has the charm of pre-industrial handicrafts and the rough paths of the pioneers. Obviously, to imitate such an effect deliberately would be ludicrous. It is valued precisely because it shows the forces of physical circumstance at work against the mechanizing efforts of man. Portoghesi has made this point in a reference to "anonymous" architecture:

Modern architecture has discovered the fascination of spontaneous composition, or architecture without architects, and of the unrepeatable harmony that comes about when similar units produced by different hands at different times are placed next to one another. Once this type of beauty, created by time and by the sediment left from generation to generation, had been discovered and celebrated in the literature, one tried naively to capture it and to replicate it in the laboratory by vaguely imitating its form, without understanding that a form born from a process cannot be retrieved without the process sustaining it.

Imitating the effect in the absence of the cause would be mischievous trickery. (The saving grace of wax flowers is that they present plants with a sort of Platonic perfection. When they go further and imitate the imperfections of individual specimens and the deterioration that comes with wilting, they become truly contemptible.) A designer inspired by the unruly bricks would probably propose to enliven the flat road bed by some rhythmical variation or a controlled random distribution of ups and downs—that is, some kind of order invented and imposed by him. An alternative would be that of letting the forces of chance do their work, in search of the sort of effect used in aleatory music or in the recent unappetizing example of a life-sized human figure, made from foodstuff and left in the street to be worn away by the assaults of animals and climate. The mechanical copying of chance effects, however, is rejected in practice by most artists as an embarrassing trick, although it may be advocated in theory.

The same considerations hold with regard to the fascinating irrationalities of an old town, in which partial planning is offset by contrary efforts, one generation contradicts the next, gaps are filled by designs of different intent, lack of funds and changes of mind interfere with the original ideas, and the forces of nature modify what the builders wrought. It takes extraordinary tolerance to derive a similar pleasure from the shrill dissonances of our own agglomerations of filling stations, ice cream parlors, motels, bars, and used car lots. The vulgarity of the ingredients distinguishes these modern examples of disorder from their older counterparts, as much as the fact that the "noise" of the disorganized inputs is raised to a strident clamor. Furthermore, the traditional examples typically show an unimpaired sense of visual and functional organization, which acts with much sensitivity on the irrational patterns thrown together by the vicissitudes of time; whereas our own commercial pollution of traffic arteries suffers from a brutal neglect of context in the interest of immediate personal profit.

What matters most for my present argument, however, is that all these instances, attractive and repulsive ones alike, have come about logically through complex constellations of impulses and motives. There is an authentic causality behind each of their many elements If a designer, attracted by this unruly complexity, were to use it as an inspiration, he could interpret it by a design of his own invention and control, but he could not simply copy or adopt it. The forces of society and history and those of nature may manifest themselves disturbingly, but they are powers of awesome grandeur and inevitability, different in principle from the naughty irresponsibilities of immature individuals.

DISORDER, ITS CAUSES AND EFFECTS

What is meant by disorder? Not simply the maximum absence of order. I mentioned earlier that as structural articulation is reduced, components become interchangeable and the prevailing texture homogeneous. I also said that, contrary to the terminology of physicists, such homogeneity needs to be considered a state of order, even though at a very simple level. Disorder is something else. It is brought about by discord between partial orders, by the lack of orderly relations between them. The relations existing in a disorderly situation could equally well be some other way; they are purely accidental. An orderly arrangement is governed by an overall principle; a disorderly one is not.

However, the components of a disorderly arrangement must be orderly within themselves, or the lack of controlled relations between them would disrupt nothing, frustrate nobody. You cannot sabotage a melody unless there is one, and one melody cannot be incompatible with another unless each of them possesses a structure of its own. I therefore define disorder as "a clash of uncoordinated orders."

171

Figure 92. *Photo*, John Gay.

Before analyzing more ambitious examples in some detail I invite the reader to cast an eye on Figure 92, taken from the façade of an apartment building, which will remain unidentified. Each element is clearly defined and ordered: the outlines of the vertical bays, the windows, the colored rectangles, the spaces between them. Yet the total design is unreadable, because

Figure 93. Certosa, Pavia. *Photo*, McAllister.

each relation one tries to follow is destroyed by unrelatable counteraction. Each element is pushed back and forth, up and down, depending on the connection one tries to establish. The result is confusion.

An example worthy of closer attention may be found in the façade of the Certosa in Pavia (Fig. 93). The exterior of this monastery shows the transition from Gothic to Renaissance style. Fletcher in his *History of Architecture* reports that the west façade of the church was constructed in marble between 1473 and 1540. In this work the sculptor and architect Giovanni Amadeo

contributed both as a sculptor and in the design, having been given charge of the work in 1491, at which time certain of the prepared marbles were ready for assembly in position. Several other sculptors took part. The upper half is simpler, owing to a halt

173

in the progress of the work. The framework of the façade, with its canopied and pinnacled buttresses, still is partly Gothic, but filled in with Renaissance features, such as profusely ornamented windows, arcaded galleries and statues in niches, which, together with carved ornament and medallions, make it one of the most elaborate combinations of architecture and sculpture in Western history.

Add to this that the façade is not complete. On top, the "coronamento," as the Guida d'Italia calls it, is missing.

Works of architecture are often built under unfavorable conditions, and in this particular case the resulting visual disorder is apparent. In approaching the building from the west we see a complexly structured surface, not clearly subdivided by any prominent features except the arched central door and the rose window with its pediment. The openings placed in the central bay mark the façade's axis of symmetry, and this center is flanked by a pair of bays of similar width and height on each side. The whole is framed by two narrower turrets, each crowned with a finial. This basic theme, however, can be extracted from the design of the whole façade only with some effort and against counterevidence. The central bay does not really dominate the visual structure because the strongly articulated lateral bays do not acquiesce in the role of subservient wings. They suggest five coordinated vertical units of roughly equal strength and thereby contradict the hierarchy of the symmetrical design. One cannot tell what is intended because the two structural versions fight each other. The homogenizing of the surface is furthered by the low arcaded gallery, which cuts like a girdle across all five bays, and by the lack of differentiation in the roofline among the three central bays. Moreover, the gallery suggests a division between the upper and lower parts of the façade that is not borne out by an appropriate self-sufficiency of the horizontal expanses at either the higher or the lower level.

Everywhere the viewer is disoriented by the struggle between contradictory relations. The four windows on the ground floor are too similar to justify the difference between the open and closed ones and too dissimilar to sustain the similarity. Above the arcade we see an array of structures standing alongside one another like the tops of unrelated buildings, in number either five or seven depending on whether one counts the three central bays as three separate units or as one—a decision not facilitated by anything the design itself tells us. The pointed endings of the four lateral units are not reflected in the roofline of the three central bays, which therefore look cut short, deprived of their tops, as in fact they are. The resulting disorder among unresolved relations prevents the viewer from comprehending what the building is trying to tell him.

174

Disorderly results stem from the action of uncoordinated forces. In a disorderly mind, team, or society, forces pushing in different directions are unable to come to a working agreement. A disorderly piece of writing or work of art is one whose creator has left various ideas or themes in a state of raw agglomeration. Because of the unresolved clash, disorderly systems exhibit high tension, directed toward a resolution, by which tension will be reduced. When the forces in a field situation can interact freely they reorganize in the direction of the best obtainable order. Such freedom is not available, of course, once the constellation is frozen. When a building or a complex of buildings has been erected, the constraint is final, and there can be no remedy except radical surgery or total destruction. In looking at such frozen constellations of disorder, however, one senses in the incoherent elements a tendency to separate or to shift to a better arrangement, and this blocked striving in the mishandled shapes creates the discomfort characteristic of an encounter with ugliness.

The forces responsible for disorderly results may operate at a fairly superficial level. Under special cultural conditions the sure sense of good form, unimpaired in the artwork of any healthy child, ceases to operate. Intellectually acquired standards and measurements, mindless imitation, piecemeal production, replace the intuitive sense of what goes well together; and when cheap mass manufacture relieves the common man and woman from the need to invent and shape things with their own hands, the inherent sense of order shrivels from neglect. This may deprive the young architect of the one indispensable resource the teacher cannot give him but at best awaken and restore in him.

Destructive though such interference with the spontaneous sense of form may be to the appearance of our world, it does not necessarily manifest deeper discords in personal or social structure. The disturbance can be superficial. It seems fairly evident, however, that in the present condition of the Western world, the painful ugliness of so many of the things we put together reflects an atomized mind, in which diverse ways of thinking and behaving accumulate without coordination and no basic directives have strength enough to control the endless stream of possibilities. Similarly atomized is our social life, which induces us to view the human community as a collection of individuals, ignoring and neglecting one another as much as possible and competing rather than cooperating in their affairs. The lack of relation among buildings we put up is an outcome of this anomie, as sociologists have called it.

Disorderly situations can be spotted intuitively by the discomfort their

175

Figure 94

overall appearance causes. One can try to explain them by analyzing discrepancies between parts. But by definition there is no structure to the whole. Faced with unrelatable units, one can respond to them only by picking particular items out of context and dealing with them without regard to the others. An atomized environment therefore encourages focusing on disconnected items, vision handicapped by blinders, which cannot but interfere with intelligent behavior.

We close our eyes to protect them from harmfully strong light. A similar biologically elementary response makes us turn off our spontaneous effort to organize the world around us when we confront overwhelming disorder. Instead we concentrate on the isolated targets of our immediate purposes. For the same reason we may find it exhausting to respond to an undisturbed urban setting in an old Italian or Dutch town. Every building addresses us with a discourse so compellingly understandable that we cannot ignore it, and the coherence of a whole street or square prevents us from limiting our attention comfortably to one item at a time. The protective blindness pro-

176

voked by a chaotic home environment cannot operate when a perceivable order demands comprehension. We find ourselves raised to a painful level of intelligent alertness.

In one of the focal squares of West Berlin, the ruin of a neo-Romanesque church built in 1893 and all but destroyed during the Second World War has been preserved as a historical reminder of the dark years. At the same time, however, the ruin has been supplemented by a modern church designed in a different style and consisting of a simple octagon and an equally geometrical clock tower (Fig. 94). There is no way of integrating the two buildings in one image, and therefore, in spite of their contiguity, the mind cannot apprehend them both at the same time. When one accepts the reality of the black, burned-out Romanesque ruin, the modern building evaporates into a ghostly apparition; conversely, the ruin disappears when the neatly complete solids of the new church impose themselves on us. This happens because one way of coping with two incompatible elements is to eliminate one of them and leave the other uncontested.

Compare this effect with that of the temple of Antoninus and Faustina in the Forum Romanum in Rome (Fig. 95). To the Roman temple erected there in the second century A. D., a Renaissance façade was added in 1602. The portico is classically severe, but the Corinthian capitals prepare us for the addition of a more flexible superstructure. The attic conforms to the Roman structure's rectangularity; at the same time it enriches it, in accordance with a new taste, by a play of outward-swinging scrolls and convergent wings at the top. The harmonious development from a simpler base toward a more elaborate crowning introduces an element of order.

One might object to my description of the viewer's reaction to the two incompatible churches in Berlin. To avoid seeing them together may be criticized as a refusal to receive the very message of the architectural statement, namely the contrast between the imperial ruin destroyed in response to dictatorial madness and the sanity of a new era. Such a confrontation, however, cannot be obtained by the disorderly yoking of unrelatable buildings. Contrast or conflict are relations and therefore can be brought about only by an order comprehending both parties. The components of a disorderly arrangement cannot come to grips with each other, either for harmony or discord, because they bypass each other. They cannot meet. Paradoxically, disorder can be represented only by order. Only a controlled description, be it in a historical report or a painting or a musical composition, can define the nature, location, and orientation of the contending forces and thereby show their lack of interrelation.

Figure 95

Such a demonstration, however, is hardly the function of architectural design. A building may be intended to house the conflicts between politicians, judges and lawyers, or boxers, but it cannot take part in their squabbles. It may provide an arena for the contending forces, and accordingly it may choose to depict them, as the west pediment of the Parthenon showed Athena and Poseidon brandishing their weapons in their fight for the possession of Attica; but it can present them only as elements of an integrated whole. A building cannot afford to be disorderly. A disorderly object can act as a symptom of disorder but not as a symbol or intepretation of it. If a building is disorderly in itself, it makes no statement about the existing disorder, but merely compounds it.

LEVELS OF COMPLEXITY

Order is found at all levels of complexity. The more complex the structure, the greater the need for order and the more admirable its achievement, because it is harder to obtain. Venturi shows many excellent examples of complexity. But he misleads in asserting that these complexities involve

178

contradiction and therefore are disorderly, which in fact most of them are not. The misuse of the term contradiction must not be permitted to justify the existence of chaotic willfulness, caused in our time by the atomization of society and the breakdown of the sense of form.

I will try to illustrate the difference by a look at the notion of contrast. In any two-dimensional pattern, for example, the vertical and horizontal dimensions contrast. But rather than making contradictory statements, they together complete the framework of the surface. They hold each other in balance. The same is true for every kind of symmetry. It always balances contrasting directions. Earlier I mentioned the perceptual experience of an architectural setting's seeming to move toward the visitor as he approaches and traverses it. There again is contrast, but by no means intrinsic contradiction. The opposing movements pertain to different components of the situation. If the same object were seen as coming forward and receding at the same time, then the result would be contradictory and confusing.

Here, I must again mention ambiguity and specify that there are two kinds of ambiguity. Orderly ambiguity can make one and the same building look tall when it is perceived in one context and small when perceived in another. There is no contradiction here, only enriching complexity. However, ambiguity becomes disturbing when the same thing under the same conditions vacillates when, for example, it looks curved one moment and straight another, thereby upsetting its particular visual function in the design as a whole.

In a complex musical rhythm a pianist may play triplets with his right hand and straight sixteenths with the left. This produces no contradiction. Nor is there any when in the Wieskirche "the colonnade, which runs closely parallel to the walls makes changing rhythmic juxtapositions against the pilasters and window openings of the walls" (Venturi). To be sure, it takes an effort to integrate the discrepant parallel sequences in such a building, but discerning the order in their relation is a rewarding experience.

One could argue that there is contradiction in a horizontal slab that serves as the floor of the space above it and the ceiling of the space below; and in fact, in the drawing of an elevation, the section of the slab appearing as a mere line between the two floors might give the viewer a case of "contour rivalry." No such rivalry, however, exists for the building's occupants. The floor of the upper story and the ceiling of the story below appear in different universes of perceptual discourse, and only if an inquisitive explorer tried to visualize the double allegiance of the slab in a single image might a sensation of seasickness result.

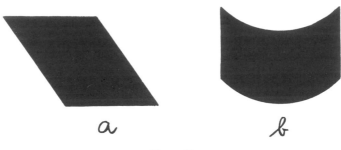

Figure 96

One of the most common sources of orderly complexity is deviation from a norm. When Figure 96*a* is seen as a leaning rectangle, it is not a shape in its own right but a deformation of a simpler shape, which serves as the norm. The norm is a genuine aspect of the percept itself, although not tangibly present. Any perceived deviation from a virtually present norm endows the object with strong dynamic tension, directed either toward the norm or away from it. Dynamics is created by this means in all the arts, especially music, where, for example, deviation from the diatonic base provides expressive tension in the pitch dimension of the melody, and syncopation gives tension to the rhythmical sequence. The angles and curves by which Baroque façades deviate from a flat front supply strong visual dynamics. They give the impression of an originally straight front that has been contracted by squeezing and bending. A simpler example from the sixteenth century is the convex façade of the Palazzo Massimi in Rome, which suggests to the passerby a bulging deformation like Figure 96*b*. This shape adapted the building to the original curvature of the street and therefore represents an example of what I described earlier as deviations from simple order in response to a spatial context.

The enemy of complexity is incompatibility, i.e., disorder. A complex pattern unites elements of different sizes and shapes, different directions, colors, and textures in the same structure, and often builds the whole from a multitude of more or less dependent parts. So divergent a setup can easily fall apart. It would therefore be most useful if a thorough study were made to determine the conditions that make a complex structure succeed or fail. I can offer here only the sketchiest observations.

A strong basic structure can tolerate a certain amount of deviation without being endangered by it. This is particularly true when the deviations are random, so that they are perceived as mere "noise" rather than as shapes in their own right. Paul Zucker has described as the "nuclear square" a loose

180

arrangement held together by a strong central accent, such as a monument, a fountain, or an obelisk, which ties "the heterogenous elements of the periphery into one visual unit. This spatial oneness is not endangered by an irregularity of the general layout or by the haphazard position, size, or shape of the adjacent buildings." A strong structure will impose itself, even if realized only approximately. It can handle a certain amount of impurity. This can be observed in fragmentation and erosion, or when a building has remained incomplete or has been altered by rebuilding.

Order is endangered when the deviations are strong enough to upset the pattern of the whole. A problem of this kind was created in Boston when the huge office building of the John Hancock Tower drove a visual wedge obliquely into an area governed by an attractive rectangular square (Fig. 6). The new giant structure betrays its guilty conscience in its reflective glass sheath. Let me suggest in passing that the perceptual effect of total reflection deserves more attention than it has been given. Reflection injects a portion of a visually unrelated world, for example, a piece of street and sky. But a design can absorb only a limited amount of alien matter without losing its identity. A building entirely covered with reflective glass creates a painful contradiction by offering a visual denial of the fact that physically it is indeed present. Is there any merit to introducing the mystery of the Invisible Man into architecture?

Figure 97a schematically depicts an example in which an intruder, too strong for absorption into the governing structure, is nonetheless too weak to act as a balancing counterforce. This balance is achieved in Figure 97b, in which both units are assumed to be strong enough to form together a super-ordinate structure of the whole. It will be seen that the relationship between the subwholes can rely either on coordination or on subordination. In a setup such as that of Figure 97c, the necessary balance is obtained either when the diagonal unit is equal in visual weight to the surrounding framework or when either of the contending parties clearly subordinates the other to its own framework. If such a balance is not achieved, the constellation wavers indecisively. It looks as though it had been stopped on its way to a stable solution, and therefore it fails to offer a readable statement of its character and meaning. An instructive example of spatial disorientation, due to a historic accident, is offered by the cathedral of Siena. After the original church had been built in the thirteenth and fourteenth centuries, it was decided to add a large new nave at a right angle in such a way that the original church would become the transept of a much larger one. The project was not completed, but enough of the added nave is standing to suggest the contradiction that

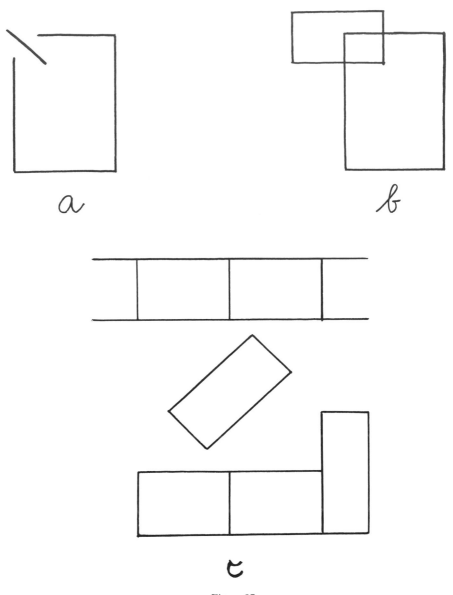

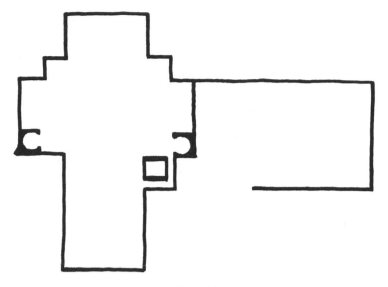

Figure 98

would probably have been created between two mutually exclusive versions of the church (Fig. 98). The original building, when considered in this larger context, looks large but also small, dominant but also subordinate, complete but also incomplete—all at the same time.

As I mentioned before, there is no way of proving objectively that a certain constellation of shapes is orderly and therefore successful, or disorderly and therefore unsuitable for the architectural purpose. Such judgments, although based on objective perceptual features, are intuitive because they derive from a weighing of the various visual forces in their interrelation. What seems in balance to one viewer may not to another. In the presence of the object, however, one can point out the various dynamic components, their function and relative strength, and thereby persuade someone, who saw the constellation differently. It is also possible to establish objectively the criteria for order that the intuitive evaluation follows. I have therefore chosen a classic example that has aroused divergent opinions, in an attempt to show how complexity works.

THE PORTA PIA

Speaking of Michelangelo's design for the Porta Pia in Rome, an experienced observer, S. E. Rasmussen, asserts that "the spectator who tries to take in every detail of this gateway will feel no sense of harmony or balance.

183

Figure 99. Porta Pia, Rome. *Photo*, Alinari.

It is impossible to choose any one form and attempt to get a lucid picture of it without having its antithesis force its way into the picture demanding to be noticed" (Fig. 99). Rasmussen's description continues in some detail and concludes that Michelangelo achieves a deliberately restless design by drawing together "an unbelievable number of Baroque details . . . from the large flat wall to the center, where they clash in mighty conflict." A more balanced and perceptive judgment comes from Jakob Burckhardt, who, in the *Cicerone*, calls the Porta Pia

an ill-famed building, seemingly a mere caprice; but an intrinsic law, which the master creates for himself, lives in the proportions and in the local effect of the particular shapes, totally arbitrary though they are in themselves. Those windows, that pediment with its strong shadows, etc., together with the main lines, form a whole that even at first glance one will attribute to none other than a great, though misguided artist. The arbitrariness is governed by a determination that appears almost as a necessity.

As far as the criticism refers to the portal itself in its relation to the attic, there can be little disagreement. The attic continues the vertical dimension of the portal beyond the crenelated roofline and roughly repeats the portal in size and shape. This relation creates a typical instance of disorder. The two units are neither truly alike nor truly different. If they were sufficiently similar, their relation could be read as a duplication, that is, as a definite order in a purely formal sense. But even in that case the similarity of form would conflict with the difference in both practical and visual functions of gate and tower. Nor can these two units be seen as continuing each other, because the gate does not present itself as a base for the attic nor does the attic develop a pattern taken from the gate. So there is indeed disorder here; but this particular relation is hardly a suitable subject for a discussion of architectural intent, because not only is Michelangelo unlikely to have been directly involved in the design of the attic, but its present shape is a nineteenth-century restoration of the original, which seems to have been somewhat lower. I shall therefore limit this discussion to the portal itself, on which Michelangelo in fact concentrated his own interest.

The portal presents itself as an upright structure, about twice as high as it is broad, fitted in a wall but quite independent and complete in itself. Its verticality is continued beyond the roof by the attic and serves as counterpoint to the horizontality of the Aurelian wall, of which it was an integral part. The portal is a visual indicator of the opening in the wall, embellished

185

with the emblems and associations befitting a principal gateway to and from the papal city. The portal's design is echoed by the two satellite windows to the right and left; they compensate for the isolating self-sufficiency of the door by connecting it to the wall through their similarity of shape while at the same time making the doorway loom larger by virtue of their own relative smallness. Taken by itself, the portal has the form of an arrow, which probes the resistance of the roofline without unduly disrupting it. We witness the dynamic interplay between the solid mass of the wall and the upright challenger of the wall's forbidding integrity.

The balancing of contending forces continues within the design of the portal itself. The verticality of the overall arrow shape is underscored by the fluted pilasters of the frame. The whole structure would fly upward if this vertical were not countered by the horizontals above and below the architrave and at street level. The architrave acts as a strongly horizontal counter. The upward movement is further opposed by the overhanging pediment and cornices, which burden the relief of the portal with downward-straining loads.

In its overall outline the arrow shape has its focus in the tip of the pediment. But to stay in place the structure must compensate for the drive of this outward-directed peak with an internal center around which its masses arrange themselves. This center lies within the opening, roughly halfway up the whole portal, and is pointed out by concentric grooves in the door frame. If this internal center ruled uncontested, however, the equal distribution of weights upward and downward would sabotage the soaring effect of the whole. An additional center is therefore supplied in the mask of the architrave. This mask accentuates the architrave as the centerpiece of a tripartite division in the vertical: the horizontal block of the architrave lies between the opening below and the pediment above. Being placed rather high up, however, it raises the center of gravity to the upper half of the structure—another enhancement of the upward movement.

The upward movement is also introduced from below, where the actual opening is magnified into the visual monument of the arrow-shaped portal. This progression takes place in three principal stages. A crescendo begins with the arch of the opening, which is stopped and flattened into a horizontal lintel. At the next level, the arch is permitted to run its semi-circular course, and at the third level a final increase of intensity transforms the arch into the pointed gable. Within the gable, which is the area of strongest uplift, counters are once more provided: the garland presses downward with considerable

186

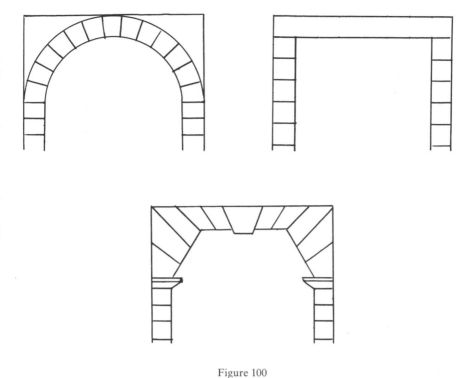

Figure 100

weight, and the rectangular tablet seconds the retardative effect of the horizontal architrave.

A description of this sort can at best enumerate various vectors and indicate their directions and approximate strengths as well as the principal interrelations between them. What the description cannot do is prove the underlying assertion that all these dynamic agents balance one another in a beautiful order. And yet the fact of this order is essential. Without it, the dynamic theme of Michelangelo's gateway could not make the statement it is trying to make.

The design of the Porta Pia comprises mainly simple geometrical shapes: rectangles, triangles, circles, segments. But there are also more complex shapes, for example in the frame of the opening, which is a hybrid between an arch and a rectangular combination of post and lintel (Fig. 100). Much tension is created between the parent shapes: the arch tries to eliminate the angular breaks and to press the flat horizontal into a curve; lintel and post try to complete their rectangular pattern by freeing the corners of their trunca-

187

tion. These antagonistic forces hold each other in an orderly balance. Further tension is introduced by the voussoirs, which have lost the symmetry they each would possess in an undisturbed arch. They appear as deformations of the norm shape displayed in the keystone.

Other deviations from norm shapes occur in the horizontal borders of the architrave. They are broken into three parts in order to continue the framing function of the jambs. Again there is a delicate balance between antagonistic forces, the vertical and the horizontal, each interrupted in deference to the other, but sufficiently continuous to sustain its own complete extension. All in all, we notice in Michelangelo's design a characteristic difference between a summation of simple shapes, each complete in itself, and the mutual impingement of shapes that complete one another within a larger whole. By combining the simpler with the more complex organization of shapes, the Porta Pia exemplifies the transition between an earlier and a later architectural style, representing two levels of order.

INTERACTION OF SHAPES

An order in which wholes are composed of simply shaped, self-sufficient parts is easy on the human mind. Each part, being a whole within itself, can be dealt with alone. It can be understood and judged in terms of its own organization, and the interrelation between components is relatively loose. Early forms of visual conception favor such compositions. They are found, for example, in children's drawings, composed of simply controlled geometric units, and in other types of primitive art. The mode is also a characteristic of visual control, as distinguished from the more dynamic shapes favored by motor control (cf. p. 151). The most elementary form of such additive conception in architecture consists in deriving the whole building from modular units. This procedure is exemplified technically by combining bricks to form a wall, or by the traditional Japanese method of deriving the measurements of a house from the size and the two-to-one proportions of the standardized tatami floormat.

Wherever builders put together stones or sticks or wooden boards, they proceed analytically. The corresponding psychological method of composing a whole from simple, autonomous parts is a kind of fundamentalism, to which the architect, like his colleagues in other media, returns when imagination has become so exuberant that perceptual organization has reached the limits of the complexity it can handle. As a dialectic countermove to the rich orchestration of the Gothic style, architects of the early Renaissance such

188

Figure 101. House Van den Doel, Ilpendam. *Photo*, Cornelis Nettinga.

as Brunelleschi and Alberti returned to the geometrically simple units from which the design of Romanesque buildings, for example, San Miniato in Florence, was derived. Symbolically, a style that leaves much autonomy and independence to the parts may be considered congenial to a society in which every citizen, town, or state rules its own little kingdom and tries to protect its individual integrity.

In spite of the relative independence of the elements, such patterns can be held together by a tightly organized order. A symmetrical façade is composed of identical units left and right. A series of arches or windows adds up to a unified horizontal row. An asymmetrical structure, such as Gerrit Rietveld's House van den Doel, built in Ilpendam, Holland, in 1958–59, leaves the units more independence (Fig. 101). Nevertheless, the rectangular elements continue and counterbalance one another in a highly integrated whole. Notice also that the visual dynamics of such a pattern is much more complex than is suggested by the shapes that strike the observer's eyes. For instance, as the cubic units add up to a kind of pyramid, peaking in the chimney, each of them incorporates a diagonal pull, in conformity to the profile of the whole building. Two more specific examples may illustrate this phenomenon of perceptual interaction.

Each of the two rectangles of Figure 102 is symmetrical within itself.

189

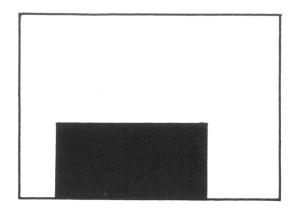

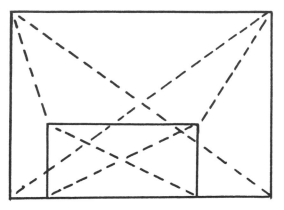

Figure 102

However, the difference in their proportions as well as their oblique relation to each other, creates a complex dynamics. Lying off center, the black shape squeezes the space on the left and pulls wide the space on the right as though it were a rubber sheet. The oblique arrangement introduces an emphasis on diagonals; and consequently several oblique but not quite parallel lines try to get along with one another: the diagonals of the rectangles and the connections between their upper corners. Thus a simple combination of simple shapes creates considerable tension.

Or look at the spandrels of the arcade of Brunelleschi's Foundling Hospital in Florence (Figure 103). They are decorated with della Robbia's well-known medallions, which are circular—the simplest, least disturbable shape. And yet, squeezed in a narrow space, they are pressed by their neighbors, namely

190

Figure 103

the horizontal cornice above and the expansive arches on both sides. If these neighbors had their way, the discs of the medallions would be deformed into a somewhat triangular shape. The medallions, in turn, exert counterpressure, pushing upward against the cornice and threatening to dent the perfection of the arches. Although these various pressures produce no physical effect, they have a strong influence on the perceptual dynamics, which enlivens the simple geometry of the shapes and generates a complex interaction between them. The various elements seem tied together by their reciprocal influence; the result is a more intimate cohesion of the total design.

If perceptual tensions had the power actually to deform the architectural elements, they would offer examples of what Venturi, adopting a term proposed by Trystan Edwards, calls inflected parts. I suggest that inflected shapes must be expected to meet the following perceptual conditions. They must be seen as deformations of simpler norm shapes; and the deformations must be seen as caused by the pulls and pushes of the surrounding constellation. Also the disequilibrium resulting from the deformation must be compensated for within the balanced pattern of the whole. The distorted voussoirs in the door frame of the Porta Pia are an example (Fig. 100).

Inflection will be recognized as the sort of interference with potentially simple order I discussed on page 166: the Monterey pines are inflected by the wind. The term inflected is well chosen because it is used by grammarians to describe a similar process in verbal language, namely the deformation of a noun within its own body in order to express the noun's function in the sentence, its dependence on another noun, its serving as a target or tool, etc. Such inflection occurs in Latin, as distinguished, for example, from English

191

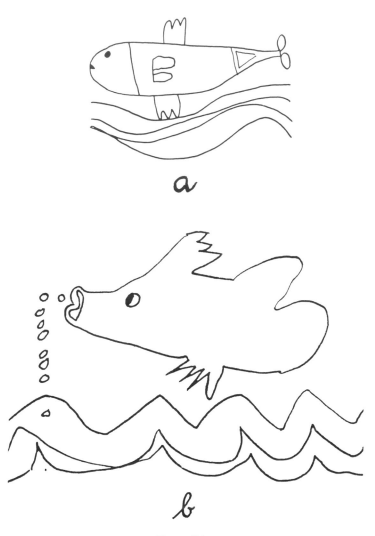

Figure 104

nouns, which remain untouched and express relations by the addition of prepositions.

I have pointed to this parallel between visual and linguistic form in an analysis of children's drawings, where inflection comes about by the fusion of elements into more complex wholes. Figure 104a shows the drawing of a fish fitted together from relatively simple units; Figure 104b, drawn by the same child somewhat later, fuses the components in a unitary but much more

192

complex whole. A parallel example from architecture is the fusion of post and lintel in Gothic shafts that unfold into the ribs of the vault, for example, in the "palm trees" of the Church of the Jacobins in Toulouse, or the "lily pad columns" of Wright's Johnson Wax building. As long as the vertical and horizontal dimensions are assigned to different elements, the shapes remain simple, tension low, and the coherence of the whole loose. But when a single visual unit performs the inflection by bending from the vertical of the support into the horizontal of the roof, the shapes become complex, curves create tension, and the continuous unity of the whole is superimposed on the subdivisions (Fig. 105).

An additional source of dynamic tension derives from the reliance of spatial orientation on the framework of vertical and horizontal. As long as this framework is explicitly represented by discrete elements, orientation is easy. But when the two dimensions are integrated in continuous shapes, the mind must extricate them from their disguise. The disparity between observed unity and underlying separation creates tension, an increase in dynamics, which may be welcomed or rejected.

A designer composing a pattern from simple shapes uses a procedure comparable to that of a builder who constructs a wall from elements, such as stones. On the other hand, the fusion of basic functions and directions in complex wholes is analogous to organic growth, which builds by seamless continuity and treats even the joints as links rather than distinct parts. Poured concrete is most congenial to such biomorphic imagery, while there is always something awkward and almost dishonest in constructing indivisible shapes from separate components.

Order based on "inflected" components stresses the lines of force in the building's structural skeleton. Like a painting by Rubens or a fugue by Bach, it does not allow the isolation of any of its parts for separate consideration. It therefore calls for a more sophisticated mental effort than the combination of elementary units. The observer must consider the design almost entirely "from above," that is, proceeding from the whole to the parts, and does not get very far following the opposite principle, which traces the relations between parts "from below."

BALANCING ELEMENTS

The distinction between organization from above and organization from below suggests still another way of describing different kinds of order. One more look at Rietveld's house (Fig. 101) will illustrate the point. Its design

Figure 105

certainly gives the impression of a well-organized whole. Definite rules of conduct apply to all constituents. All shapes meet at right angles, in conformity to a basic three-dimensional framework. Taken as a whole, the house has a roughly rectangular plan and builds from a broad base in several steps toward the upright peak of the chimney. At the same time the house looks as though its design did not start with the conception of a master shape, as is the case with a Greek temple, a medieval church, or a Florentine palazzo. Rather it looks as though a number of fundamental cubes and slabs had been fitted

194

together, adapted to one another in their sizes and proportions, and moved back and forth until the relations looked just right and created a satisfying whole, not susceptible to further change.

This procedure of arriving at a design by the fitting together of building blocks seems to have few precedents in the history of architecture, although it is familiar to children and is used wherever some sort of shelter or monument is put together from given materials. But there certainly can be no objection to such a procedure, and in fact it may be particularly congenial to a modern way of approaching aesthetic and social organization. The principal difference between the two methods of designing is that traditionally the overall pattern of plan and elevation, once decided upon, governs the formation of components. In the Greek temple, gable and architrave, columns and base, had their pre-established place and character, and even though the individual builder was on his own when it came to the exact number, proportions, and interstices between elements, the organization took place essentially "from above." A dominant schema determined the place and function of every individual component.

In the approach exemplified in the Rietveld house, by contrast, the relation between elements is primary. Each element derives from its character certain capacities and requirements: it can serve some purposes, is unsuitable for others, needs certain conditions in order to function, etc. On the basis of these characteristics of the units, the whole arranges itself. The weight and importance of each element derives from a sort of power play, with the aspirations of every individual unit confronting those of its neighbors. A solution is obtained when the demands of all participants are balanced against one another.

It is a system of free enterprise, in which the components' independent initiative, by the pushes and pulls of individual adaptation, leads to a *modus vivendi*. There is an essential difference, however, between free enterprise as we see it in action around us and the interplay of components in good architecture. In the economics or politics of an individualistic society, each participant is permitted, indeed encouraged, to base his plans exclusively on his own selfish interests and to get away with as much as the others allow him. The result is the chaos familiar to us—a situation in which the government, as one party among others, uses its powers to pursue its own particular aims. The architectural manifestation of this disorder is the ugly incompatibility of the shapes that constitute so many of our streets and cities. Such disorder is tolerated only as long as no common purpose imposes itself, and it can hardly prevail in a single mind except under pathological conditions. What we see at

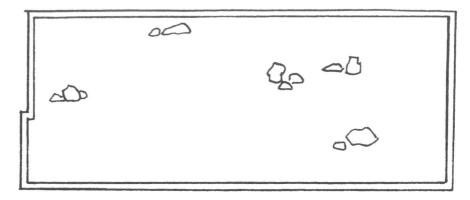

Figure 106

work in a successful piece of architecture of the kind exemplified by the Rietveld house is the search for a sensible whole achieved by balancing individual relations. Such an arrangement resembles the attempt of a group of musicians to improvise a piece of music: each player contributes the character of his instrument, proceeds according to that character, and puts forward some melodic invention of his own, responding and being responded to, trying to serve the emerging piece of music to the best of his ability. Together the musicians search for the theme of the whole. It is a spirit of collective cooperation, not of atomistic competition.

The particular quality of the visual patterns deriving from this procedure may be illustrated by the simple example of the five heaps of stones in the famous gravel garden of Ryoanji in Kyoto, a Zen temple of the fifteenth century (Fig. 106). Viewed from the temple's wooden platform the five small heaps of two, three, or five stones seem to be distributed over the rectangular surface of the garden in a perfectly balanced order. The objective configuration can be seen when one looks at the plan. In practice, the order does not reveal itself from any one vantage point and is therefore impossible to photograph; it emerges from the entirety of the infinite number of perspective arrangements that glide into one another as one walks back and forth along the platform. What strikes the visitor about this ancient order is its perfection and its elusiveness. The constellation of the five units is not definable; they form neither a circle nor a pentagon nor a quincunx. Their locations avoid any hierarchical patterning, but are determined solely by a delicate weighing of their interrelation. It is as though five magnets of un-

196

equal power, attracting and repelling one another, were floating on water, free to find the position in which their fields of forces are in perfect equilibrium. It looks like a good way for five individuals to get along with one another, practicing mutual respect unassisted by any government coercion.

The forces at work in such balanced distributions can also be compared with the biological and physical processes involved in the branching of blood capillaries, the venation of leaves, or electrostatic discharges. To be sure, in all these examples systematic diffusion from a center provides an overall pattern, but this superordinate organization does not account for the delicate distribution of space between branches—an admirable illustration of the achievement of order by unpredictable relations. The biologist Paul Weiss writes:

> Descriptively, the regularity is reflected in the near-constancy of distances between the branches; dynamically, it reflects a growth pattern elaborated by interactions of the component branches, both among one another and with the cellulated matrix they pervade. In oversimplified terms, the interactions involved are a kind of competition. This, then, is interaction no longer in contiguity, but at a distance. Each branch may be viewed as surrounded by a shell of influences of graded strengths— domains, which keep each other at a respectful standard distance.

In these examples from nature the forces controlling the spatial distribution are physical. The same may be the case when the human mind intuitively balances the components of a perceptual design. The mind is governed by the sensation of pushes and pulls that are perceived as located in the perceived items and that suggest changes by which equilibrium can be attained. These perceptual pushes and pulls are the sensed effects of physiological processes that must be assumed to be occurring in the corresponding brainfields—processes attempting to cope with the perceptual inputs from the sense organs and to reestablish the equilibrium upset by the intruder. Intuitive ordering can be considered a reflection of physical field processes that take place in the nervous system and are related to natural branching systems by a link more direct than mere analogy.

Organization "from below" makes for loose ties between parts that are relatively complete in themselves. In some modern architecture, this has led to the dissolution of compact mass—a development paralleled in sculpture. The traditional piece of sculpture is typically a single body, modified by limbs and draperies on the periphery. In the twentieth century there occurs, for example, a thinning and multiplying of the units in the work of Lehmbruck or Giacometti; a puncturing of volumes and planes in Moore or David

197

Smith; the connection of parts by mobile joints in Calder; and finally, the creation of constellations from groups of independently made and loosely welded groups of elements in the recent work of Anthony Caro. In architecture, similar developments have been constrained by the inescapable need for any shelter to be a sufficiently closed container. Even so, a steel skeleton sheathed in glass shows a distinct thinning of the limbs and is a skeleton composed of separate units rather than a mass. To be sure, the cubes of highrise buildings are conceived very much from above, as unitary volumes. But at the same time, architects have begun to favor screens and free-standing panels, cantilevered canopies, open galleries, and multiple interruptions of the walls—a gradual dismantling of the dominant volume. In extreme cases, for example, in certain California houses influenced by Japanese design, the building looks like an assembly of sticks and slabs, called together to agree on an overall shape, with plenty of air circulating between them and large windows contributing additional openings. Such an order relies on a delicate balancing of weights and distances and on the rhythmic alternation of closed and open spaces.

Perhaps one of the properties that fascinate some architects in the honky-tonk landscapes around our towns and cities is the extreme looseness of coverage, the lack of closed volume and solidity, resulting from the flimsiness of the investment and the momentary stimulation and ephemeral contacts these establishments are intended to serve. They are certainly symbolic of the mobility of modern life and therefore can spur the imagination of the architect who is seeking a form congenial to our time. But it is one thing to gather suggestions for expressive characteristics wherever they can be found and translate them into new versions of order, and quite another to swallow the vulgarity and disorder of a blighted commercialism and pretend that noise is vitality and chaos complexity, and that the raw materials of titillation can transfer their power to environments conceived by the human mind for its own well being.

THE RANGE OF ORDERS

Of necessity, order is coercion. Order prescribes the place and function of everybody and everything participating in it. The principles and purposes from which the order of a system derives are unlikely simply to duplicate those governing the components. Consider examples from social life. The rules of conduct a teacher prescribes cannot possibly meet the needs of every student, and even if they did, the student should not wholly surrender his

198

initiative. The same holds for the workers in a factory. It is not true, however, for the components of an engine. An engine does not contain centers of initiative independent of those given it by the planner. Even its degrees of freedom, its ranges of adaptation, its ways of responding to circumstances must be prearranged, however sophisticated the sensors and computers it employs. The same is true for any organism: it contains a number of highly complete systems, e.g., of blood circulation or endocrine balance, but all these particular orders must be governed from above by a central administration if the organism is to function properly.

Different in principle is the kind of order that rules ecological or social systems. There, overall functioning depends on the coordination of initiatives from independent centers. If the arrangement is left to chance, a persistent struggle may lead to an unproductive solution. On the other hand, if it is controlled entirely from above, the solution may be equally unproductive because dictatorial impositions on subsystems can prevent them from fulfilling their potential. In architecture the problem calls for constantly renewed solutions in two areas: the relations between the planners and the builders, and those between the builders and the clients.

A collective enterprise in which all individual inputs are subject to the final judgment of a commanding authority may produce friction but involves no theoretical problems of organization. Serious questions can arise, however, when components of a principal architect's work are left to the independent initiative of others. This may lead to disappointing results—for example, when the head architect designs only the outer shell of a building and leaves the distribution of inside spaces to assistants. Such an arrangement may work when the theme of the external shape has in fact nothing to contribute to the internal structure; but it will falter when the design of the outside has implications for the inside, or vice versa, and these requirements are not met by an integrated design. This leads to a structural break, the sort of alienation between outside and inside I referred to in an earlier chapter.

The same is true for an unsuccessful compromise, which comes about, for example, when the demands of the client and the ideas of the architect cannot be accommodated in an integrated order. The visual result is unreadability, the kind of ambiguity that prevents the design from making its character manifest without self-contradiction. I recall an instance of an automobile manufacturer consulting a market research agency because one of their new models was dogged by a persistent popular rumor, to the effect that the car was not solidly built, but was liable to break apart in the middle. No such

199

structural flaw existed. The cause of the rumor turned out to be a visual inconsistency in the car's shape. The designers had been asked to combine the smart, speedy look of a sports car with the roomy comfort of a family wagon. The resulting compromise did not add up to a unified visual order; like the proverbial camel, the car was "an animal designed by a committee."

There are examples of later additions by other hands that successfully amplify a building's original form. They change it but do not conflict with it. The "ass's ears" Bernini added to the façade of the Roman Pantheon have not stood the test of time because, in violation of the original character, they were meant to adapt the old building to Baroque taste; whereas a spire added to the crossing of a church may provide a structurally suitable accent. Sculptural ornamentation in architecture is a perennial case in point. A building may call for or at least be able to accommodate statues, gargoyles, or reliefs; these additions, too, may supply indispensable accents—as did Kolbe's figure in the Barcelona pavilion—or offer secondary elaborations of the main architectural theme.

The principle governing all such attempts, happy and unhappy, derives from the basic characteristics of structure. Different parts of a structural context are not equally sensitive to change. Certain features are structurally so central that one cannot touch them without changing the whole. Make a Greek cross into a Latin cross by lengthening one of the arms, and you change the centric symmetry of the whole plan into a bilateral one. None of the relations between parts remains untouched by this change. But in a church it might be possible to substitute a classical colonnade for the arches that separate the nave from the aisles without fundamentally disturbing the building's overall scheme. The function of the columns in the total design is not basically different from that of the arches. Again, the exact nature of a piece of sculpture may not matter as long as its size and location are right. One can place an obelisk on the back of an elephant and thereby fit it to a larger structure, but one can hardly change the shape of the obelisk itself without making it unrecognizable. Quantitatively large changes matter relatively little when they leave the structural skeleton unimpaired; small changes applied to a sensitive spot can overthrow the whole system.

It is on the whole less risky for an architectural design to be changed or completed by another hand than a painting or sculpture. Many works of the fine arts tend to be so personal in the smallest detail of form, color, and texture that, whereas the artist himself might be able to alter the composition, no one else could do so with impunity. Architecture operates with a more generic vocabulary. It is safer to top a bank of windows by Antonio da

Sangallo with one by Michelangelo than to add a figure to one of Michelangelo's Pietàs.

DIFFERENT FUNCTIONS, DIFFERENT ORDERS

So far I have discussed tolerance in an order intended to govern a structure as a whole. But there is an obvious difference between the relatively tight order controlling all architectural features that contribute to the design of a church, and the relation of that church to adjoining facilities, such as the sacristy, a monastery or cloister, a crypt, etc. The stage of a theater or concert hall is more directly integrated with the auditorium than are the public spaces with those backstage: dressing rooms, scenery storage rooms, etc. The same is true for the public halls of a law court as against the chambers of the judges. Within the overall order that integrates the various functions of a building or complex of buildings, components devoted to different functions require more autonomy than can be permitted in a space or group of spaces serving a single function.

Here we come to the principle that the appropriate degree of unity among various components of an architectural whole is directly related to the functional relations between them. By no means is maximum unity an absolute desideratum irrespective of what is being unified. The formal yoking of distinctly different functions may only mislead and confuse the building's users.

On the other hand, it would be naïvely dogmatic to insist that all functions should automatically be differentiated in appearance. In discussing the relationship between inside and outside we caught an inkling of the problem's actual complexity. The various functions of a building, like the parts of any other whole, are related to one another by a more or less intricate pattern of connections and separations, to which the architect may do justice by providing different ratios of unity and diversity at different levels of the design.

Take the extreme case of a building that combines a church and a bank in a unitary design—a combination that might have definite practical advantages. If the services of both institutions were separated and meant to be independent, a unitary design would indeed be misleading. But if the purpose were to show that the cultivation both of the citizen's soul and of his purse is offered as an integrated social service and meant to be understood as such, the architect would contribute to the success of the undertaking by a strongly unified design. He would still face the task of making sure that a client entering the building to see his investment counselor would not end up in the confessional.

Unity at the level of overall design may indicate a common role and function superordinate to differences at a lower level. For example, under certain cultural conditions there is little objection to the sheltering of different lifestyles in the same apartment building. The uniformity of the building corresponds to what is accepted as uniform in the various families' needs. Different though they may be otherwise, they all ask for a similar kind and amount of space offering similar facilities at the same location. The overall formal order reaches precisely as far as the functional order, and the discontinuation of this order behind the front door of each apartment is acceptable because in fact a separate way of life quite legitimately reigns in each family's living quarters. It may be that the monotonous equality of one-family homes in so-called subdivisions is the more objectionable because in theory the independent single-family house provides for an individuality that in the subdivision either remains hidden or does not exist. While the uniformity of the apartment building symbolizes a shared purpose, the architectural conception of the subdivision suggests a standardization of minds.

What we are advocating here is a hierarchic structure, in which an overarching order reaches only as far and as deeply as the functional unity between components. At one extreme distinct orders may border upon one another with no pretense to a unity governing them all. Quite legitimately, there may be no relations between them other than the connecting links required for minimal interaction. At the other extreme are settlements in which a common purpose obliterates all distinction—for example, military camps or medieval fortress towns. Such settlements are laid out according to a simple geometrical schema. The same is true for founded cities, dreamed-up utopias, and the unrestrained fancies of city planning (Fig. 107). In each case a system for which a comprehensive order is a perfect match prescribes uniform functioning for everyone and everything. This order may be one of additive coordination, such as the gridiron system, which has no center and is susceptible to endless expansion; or it may be centrically symmetrical like the utopian towns of a Filarete or a Scamozzi. Those of the latter indicate a governing focus and are laid out in a concentric hierarchy, in which the importance of each circular layer is defined by its distance from the center. These highly ordered plans, resembling not by accident the regular shapes of mandalas, brooches, crystals, and radiolaria, are the visual expression of totally unified fields of force, conceived as ideals of harmony, peace, and devotion to a common theme.

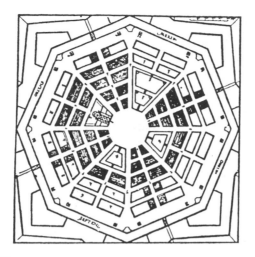

Figure 107. Daniel Speckle. Plan for an ideal city. 1598.

But I have already pointed out that undisturbed perfection is deadly when it is offered as a reflection of life and coercive when meant to inform all human activity. Under more natural conditions we find that each order has a limited range. A country is made up of settlements, which grow independently, each as an order of its own, until an increasing need for more contact creates a network of roads, railways, and airplane routes. These connections impose a comprehensive order, no simpler in shape than functionally required, and having no more influence on the character of each center than necessary. We also note that separate orders bordering upon each other without connection do not necessarily create disorder because disorder presupposes a clash, and no clash results from mere coexistence. Ethnic neighborhoods of totally different character, for example, may border upon each other, as different countries do, with no more pretense of orderly continuity than is required by essential communication between them.

Psychologists operate with the concept of "life space," introduced by Kurt Lewin. For our purpose this notion must be applied in two different ways. Perceptually, a person's life space reaches only to the limits of the environment as he conceives of it. For those attending a court trial, their present life space may be limited by the courtroom walls. The judge, the lawyers, etc., arrive as it were from nowhere. But when the jury is absent and deliberating, the jury room, although not perceivable, becomes a part of the life space for everybody in the courtroom.

Different from the psychological life space is the technically functional

203

one. Thus, although for the hospital patient the physicians and nurses, as well as the food trays and the laboratory cart, may arrive from nowhere, the facilities off-stage are directly linked to the work on the wards. The architect must facilitate these connections by an integrated order relating the wards to the other work areas. But at the same time he must help the patient to surround himself with a world of his own, where he can find shelter from the sights and sounds of avoidable disturbance and anxiety. The life spaces of the patients and those of the medical personnel, and the needs to be satisfied within them, are different, and the architect must try to serve them all.

A person has as many particular life spaces as he has environments: his home, his place of work, the streets of his neighborhood, etc. Each of these spaces requires an order of its own. In relation to one another they are either coordinated or subordinated. A person may walk out of the world of his apartment into a totally unconnected setting, that of the public neighborhood, and this minimal coordination of two separate orders may appropriately reflect the absence of relation between the individual and his community. On the other hand, someone's house may flow into the landscape, be open to it and entered by it, in which case the orders of the life inside and of the environment may be parts of an overarching order integrating them both. Between these extremes there exist all degrees and kinds of connection, tying things together and keeping them apart, relating them in some ways and separating them in others. Appropriate orders can be worked out for any one of them.

I want to emphasize once more that a lack of relation between adjoining orders does not necessarily create a disorderly clash. Clash presupposes relation, and disorder comes about when relation is suggested but not provided. We find disorder in the visual appearance of a city street, not because no relation is discoverable between the various components, but because such a relation is called for by the street's coherent parallelism. The best possible way of ordering the elements of an atomized society might be one involving no discernible relations, a world in which each individual unit were visibly on its own, like the walking figures of Giacometti or the stone heaps of Ryoanji, balanced against one another only by the attractions and repulsions that derive from the properties of each. Such atomization may not be the desirable way for individuals, families, populations, and peoples to live together. But that is preeminently a social problem.

204

VII. SYMBOLS THROUGH DYNAMICS

B UILDINGS are visible to the human eye. But being visible does not necessarily mean that appearance is purposively shaped and colored to
convey a visual message. Rocks, water, and clouds tell us a great deal by
the way they look, but unintentionally, as it were; and even plants and
animals have developed their shapes and colors only secondarily as visual
means of protection, attraction, or deterrence. Man, however, rarely makes
an implement with total disregard for the image it presents to the eyes.

Buildings are expected to show how they can be used. For most purposes it
is desirable that the design of the exterior tell the approaching visitor where
the entrance is. There is something wrong with a lobby in which people
looking for the elevator constantly end up in the boiler room. When two
staircases have the same function and lead to the same place, it is helpful for
them to be shaped symmetrically, that is, interchangeably.

The simple principle to which all this comes down is that in a well-designed
building there is a structural correspondence between visual properties and
functional characteristics. Similar function should be reflected in similar
shape; different functions in different shapes. Visual accents should occur in
places of importance. The image of the building should lead, not mislead, in
its overall arrangement as well as in detail. This principle of correspondence
between function and appearance has a purely practical aspect, to which
architects have given much thought and on which I need not dwell here; it
also relates to visual expression, on which more will be said in the last
chapter.

205

VISUAL LABELS

The varying shapes of buildings in a cityscape add up to a kind of visual language, which provides a different "word" for each kind of structure. To some extent one can tell simply by looking what kind of building one is facing. This distinctiveness of appearance derives in part from differences in practical function. A motel or a hospital cannot look like a fire station or a public library and should not try to. As a useful contribution to the semantics of architecture one could investigate the range of variation among particular types of buildings. What are the invariables that cannot be neglected with impunity? How is a hotel or a bank recognized as such, and what features might mislead the user? When the standard image is jettisoned, how does the design try to redefine the image? Such a study would also have to consider changes that types of buildings undergo over time. For example, a motion picture theater or a department store built forty years ago looks different from one built today, for reasons that deserve exploration.

These semantic aspects are particularly relevant for buildings that are essentially bearers of an ideology. In some modern church architecture one can observe an almost desperate attempt to disclaim any allegiance to the tradition expressed in a neo-gothic or neo-romanesque style and to proclaim that religion has kept up with the times. In religious architecture, caprice has been offered almost unlimited liberty, and eagerness to attract a dwindling clientele at almost any cost is expressed externally in ostentatious shape and color. Inevitably churches have taken their cues from their leading competitors, the entertainment and catering industries and their barbarous imagery. Such willingness to sacrifice the end to highly dubious means is possible only because the very nature of religion and its tasks are now so open to question that their external expression is no longer governed by reliable standards. These tendencies make all the more rewarding those examples of church architecture that succeed in translating dignity and spiritual devotion into twentieth-century idioms.

However, the semantics of architecture is another topic on which I shall not dwell here. I shall only add that the prevailing individualism of our civilization has led to an emphasis on "proper names," that is, to a stress on the uniqueness of particular buildings and their distinctiveness among their neighbors. In integrated cultures, individual differences are held within the framework of a common style and thereby enrich rather than disrupt the image of the community as a whole. In our own case, individualism often takes the form of commercial competition, which in turn has distorted the

206

notion of originality to mean something divergent from its neighbors. Some commercial enterprises try to make their buildings stand out at all cost. Thus the remains of the San Francisco skyline have been punctured by a unique but unsightly pyramid. Similarly, some architects draw attention to their work by making it spectacularly different from their competitors.

SYMBOLISM

We come closer to what principally concerns me here when we inquire into the nature of symbolism, a concept that has been grossly misused in our century. To be sure, as long as a term is not standardized, anybody is free to use it as he pleases. But it is also true that we badly need the word *symbol* to designate a basic function of visual expression. This function has been neglected in discussions of visual communication, and accordingly the meaning of the word *symbol* has been flattened out to refer to mere signs, that is, to conventional indicators or images. Thus, letters, words, and numbers are often referred to as symbols, although they are only conventional signs. Signs displaying the names of gasoline brands, motels, or hospitals are not symbols, but mere inscriptions. They add to the meaning conveyed by a building, but to equate them with architectural expression only sows confusion.

Architectural symbolism begins to come into play when a building's design uses shapes that carry a conventional meaning. The medieval mind, in particular, was inclined to see such a message in every shape. Pevsner makes this point in discussing the Gothic cathedral. For example, "to Guilielmus Durandus the cruciform church represented the Cross, and the weathercock on the spire the preacher who rouses the sleeping from the night of sin. The mortar, he says, consists of lime, i.e. love, sand, i.e. earthly toil which love has taken upon itself, and water, uniting heavenly love and our earthly world." Similarly, Otto von Simson suggests that the Abbot Suger may have selected twelve columns each for the ambulatory and the choir of St. Denis because of the Biblical metaphor of building spiritually upon the foundation of Apostles and Prophets, Jesus Christ being the keystone that joins one wall to the other. In our time, the thirty-six columns of the Lincoln Memorial in Washington refer to the number of states constituting the country at the time of the president's death.

Alfred Lorenzer observes that "intentional and consciously applied symbolism is always superficial. When Ledoux and Vaudoyer in the eighteenth century designed a sawmill owner's house in the shape of a sawblade or the

207

house of a cosmopolite in the shape of a terrestrial globe, the symbolic correspondence remained at a relatively shallow level." Successful architecture, therefore, rarely limits symbolism to arbitrary convention, but rather seeks to ally it with features of more basic, spontaneous expression. When Etienne-Louis Boullée proposes fashioning the outer walls of a law court as the tablets of constitutional law, he is not going beyond superficial labeling; but when he suggests placing the prison entrance underneath that same building, he is relying on a direct visual symbolism, plausible to the mind: "By presenting that august edifice as elevated above the dark cave of crime, it seemed to me that I could not only emphasize the nobility of the architecture, by the resulting contrast, but also offer metaphorically an imposing picture of vices crushed under the load of justice." Similarly in the example from St. Denis the symbol of the keystone is not chosen at random. Placed in the highest position and holding the vault together, it offers the physical equivalent of the ideas being expressed.

All genuine metaphors derive from expressive shapes and actions in the physical world. We speak of "high" hopes and "deep" thoughts, and it is only by analogy to such elementary qualities of the perceivable world that we can understand and describe non-physical properties. A work of architecture, as a whole and in its parts, acts as a symbolic statement, which conveys, through our senses, humanly relevant qualities and situations.

The more firmly a traditional symbol attaches itself to an appropriate physical image, the more convincingly it survives changes in philosophy and doctrine. The morning light falling through the choir windows onto the altar carries with strong immediacy a sense of enlightenment and blessing. Instead of transmitting the specific message of, say, Neoplatonist metaphysics, it conveys a broader, more generic experience, of which that doctrine is but one application. Sensory symbolism reveals the general in the particular and thereby raises the latter to a higher level of relevance. These heightened expressive qualities may survive in a building and continue to create a powerful experience when the specific nuance of the builders' message can be retrieved only by historical research. The cupola of a dome may no longer specifically signify a religious image of heaven; but as an overarching and surrounding hollow it forever preserves a spontaneous affinity with the natural sky and shares some of its principal expressive connotations.

The conventional symbols just mentioned are best described as a special case of what I will call open symbols. The spontaneously perceivable analogy between the visual character and behavior of an object and a corresponding

208

mental or spiritual character and behavior relies on very generic attributes, such as height or depth, openness or enclosure, outgoingness or withdrawal. In a conventional symbol, the generic nature of the signifier is applied to a specific thing signified, and the symbol is thereby officially withheld from the many other meanings it could convey. Without such limitation, the highly abstract qualities of the signifier remain open to an infinite number of potential applications. For example, when a Christian church is given a cruciform shape, all other connotations of the cross are limited at most to unofficial overtones. But the cross form as such can symbolize the conjunction of opposites, the action of centrifugal or centripetal forces, the spreading of life or fire, crossroads, the relation of vertical striving to horizontal stability, and so on. In discussing symbolism it is most important to realize that conventional symbols, with their relatively limited meaning, are not the prototype but only a limited application. The artist, the architect, is concerned first of all with the broad metaphoric quality of perceptual expression.

Symbols could not rely on the expressive qualities of sensory experience if that experience were not endowed with metaphoric overtones in daily practice. Sunlight streaming through the windows when the shades are raised in the morning is not perceived as a mere change in brightness level. Only because it is received as a gift of life, exposing the world to us and us to the world, can illumination serve us as a broadly valid symbol. The most powerful symbols derive from the most elementary perceptual sensations because they refer to the basic human experiences on which all others depend. A person watering his plants would have a frighteningly flattened mental life if he sensed in this activity no connotation of offering refreshment to the thirsty. The effort invested, the affection felt, the help given, the flow of the cool and sparkling liquid, the silent acceptance by the recipients—all these sensory qualities give this simple daily chore a halo of spontaneous nobility. The symbolic overtones of practical life have been beautifully described by Jean Giono in a passage of his novel *Que ma joie demeure*:

One gets the impression that basically people do not know very well what they are doing. They build with stones, but they do not see that every one of the gestures they make in setting a stone in mortar is accompanied by the shadow of a gesture that sets the shadow of a stone in the shadow of the mortar. And the shadow building is what counts.

The symbolism of the arts, of which architecture is the most important, could not be so effective, could not move us so profoundly and prevail over changes in cultural convention, were it not rooted in the strongest, most universal human experiences. Dagobert Frey says that the steplike ascent of Indian Sikhara spires conform to the stages of the *via purgativa* by which the yogi ascends toward full redemption in Nirvana. This symbolic endowment of architectural shape is compelling only because the humble daily experience of climbing stairs reverberates with the connotations of overcoming the weight of gravity and rising victoriously toward the heights.

It is true that the spontaneous symbolism of practical experience has paled in our own civilization, not only because the traditional foundation of philosophical and religious ideas has all but vanished, but also because physical activity and contact with nature have been so largely replaced by the handling of rarefied concepts, especially in buying and selling. The strongest resources of spontaneous symbolism have thus been sadly depleted. Works of art, such as buildings, must now serve somewhat artificially to revive our weakened experience.

The most important cognitive virtue of a civilization probably consists in the working interrelation between practical physical activity and so-called abstract thought. The mental life of a civilization is broken asunder when, on the one hand, the meaning of walking, eating, cleaning, sleeping, exploring, and making things is reduced to the material and physical gain accruing from these activities, and when, on the other hand, the principles by which we understand the nature of things and govern our conduct are reduced to intellectually defined concepts, which no longer benefit from their perceptual sources. For the architect this means that to the extent he succeeds in reinforcing the deep-seated spiritual connotations inherent in all the simple aspects of domesticity, he is contributing to the healing of a split in our civilization. He can do this by cultivating the expressive qualities in the shapes he invents.

INHERENT EXPRESSION

Spontaneous symbolism derives from the expression inherent in perceived objects. To be seen as expressive, the shape of an object must be seen as dynamic. There is nothing expressive, and therefore nothing symbolic, in a set of stairs or a staircase as long as it is seen as a mere geometrical configuration. Only when one perceives the gradual rising of the steps from the ground as a dynamic crescendo does the configuration exhibit an expressive quality, which carries a self-evident symbolism. Once this is understood, it will also be apparent why spontaneous symbolism is found in all shapes, including architecture, even when they are not equipped with conventional

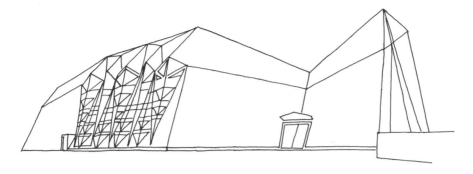

Figure 108

symbols, such as the escutcheon of the Medicis or a metallic eagle spreading its wings over an embassy roof.

On the contrary, the use of identifiable subject matter as a component of architectural shape may interfere with a building's spontaneous symbolism because of the concessions its dynamics must make to the shape of that subject matter. One could argue that the expressive qualities of an entirely un-"symbolical" Mies van der Rohe building come across more clearly than those of Eero Saarinen's TWA air terminal, which might soar more purely if it looked less like a bird. Or that the Presbyterian church built in Stamford, Connecticut, by Harrison and Abramovitz might express a more religious attitude if it did not try to be symbolical by resembling a fish (Fig. 108). It is true, of course, that connotations other than spontaneous expression can strongly determine the meaning of a building. Cylindrical towers of roughly similar shape may impress us quite differently depending on whether we are looking at the clock tower of Sant' Apollinare in Classe or at the grain silo of a midwestern farm. But these are indirect effects, based on intellectual information, and therefore are architecturally less compelling than the direct messages of perceived form.

At this point I must refer at least briefly to the psychological basis of perceptual expression—a subject I have discussed more extensively in other writings. Of the several theories that propose to account for expression, I shall mention here only the most influential one, namely the doctrine of empathy. This term, a translation of the German *Einfühlung*, is associated with Theodor Lipps, who dealt with the concept most systematically. For our present purpose it might be appropriate to cite the version of this theory set forth in Heinrich Wölfflin's 1886 doctoral dissertation for the University of

211

Munich, "Prolegomena to a Psychology of Architecture." Although Wölfflin's reasoning on empathy closely resembles that of Lipps, Lipps is not among the sources Wölfflin cites, and I cannot attempt here to investigate to what extent the two men knew of each other's work or drew on common sources.

Wölfflin bases his theory of perceptual expression on the assertion that "the organization of our own bodies is the form that determines our apprehension of all physical bodies." And he proposes to show that the fundamental elements of architecture, namely, matter and form, gravitational weight and force, depend on experiences we have had within ourselves. Like Lipps he uses the example of the column: "We have carried heavy loads and have known pressure and counterpressure. We have collapsed on the ground when we no longer had the energy to oppose the downward pull of our own body's weight. That is why we are able to appreciate the proud happiness of a column and to understand the tendency of all matter to spread shapelessly on the ground." Every oblique line, he says, is perceived as rising, and every asymmetrical triangle impresses us as a violation of equilibrium. He emphasizes muscular responses, especially in respiration: "Powerful columns produce energetic innervations in us, and the wideness or narrowness of spatial proportions controls respiration. We innervate our muscles as though we were those load-bearing columns, and we breathe as deeply and fully as though our chest had the width of those halls."

Wölfflin and Lipps were obviously aware of the expressive qualities inherent in architectural shapes, but in keeping with the psychological theory current in their day they interpreted them as projections of the observer's own muscular sensations. As I have shown elsewhere, the primary effect of visual expression is more convincingly derived from, and controlled by, formal properties of the visual shapes themselves, and muscular responses can best be understood as secondary reactions to the primary visual dynamics.

It would be misleading, however, to derive these perceptual sensations from the physical forces that control the statics of the building. Those forces may be inferred intellectually from what is seen and known, but obviously the observer receives no direct effect from the strains and stresses in the building materials. What he receives is the visual image of the surface shapes, which acquire their dynamic character as the image is processed by the observer's nervous system. I have argued that the physiological forces which organize sensory raw materials into the shapes we perceive are the same ones

212

we experience as the dynamic components of visual images. There is no need to resort to another sensory modality, such as kinesthetic awareness, to explain this primary effect.

The dynamic quality of perceptual experiences accounts also for the difference between mere intellectual information received indirectly through the eyes and the direct reverberation within us of the forces we experience in the objects we see. An engineer who gathers information on the quantity and type of materials in a building may draw inferences about the physical forces operative in it. But viewing a work of architecture lets the observer sense within himself perceptual forces of load and resistance, of pull and push, and so forth. This immediate resonance of the forces observed in visual objects accompanies all perception, but it is particularly decisive for aesthetic experience, which is based on expression.

The dynamics of perceptual experience is the fundamental component of visual images. However, it is so largely suppressed in the daily use of our eyes for information-gathering that some persons find conscious awareness of the phenomenon difficult to achieve. They may be helped by the following curious passage from Moholy-Nagy's book on architecture, even though it relies once again on kinesthesis:

As long as there is any relation between two entities, there exists the possibility of tension, be it biological, psychological, spatial, etc. For example, when one holds a finger tip of the left hand and one of the right hand against each other and then pulls them apart very slowly, farther and farther until, with the arms extended, they point outward, one perhaps gets an inkling of the degree to which relations can be controlled, subjectively and objectively.

THE ARTIFACT IN NATURE

The basic fact of architectural expression is that of the building as a man-made object placed in a natural setting. There are other such objects, but architecture is distinguished from them by the particular way it supplements nature's resources and facilities, while at the same time insisting on a particularly human function, different in principle from those fulfilled by nature. A cultivated field, a ladder leaning against a fruit tree, a wooden board bridging a stream, are distinctly human in many of their formal qualities, such as their regularity of shape, but they typically are experienced as enhancements of nature, added by man for his own benefit. One might include in this category even agricultural machinery, river boats, and indeed the unpretentious architecture of the farmhouse and the barn.

213

This was the view of the architect Adolf Loos, who said of farmhouses and village churches that they looked as though they had been built not by human hand but by God. He also admitted to this unspoiled company the creations of engineers, boats and railways, but complained that architecture, in the narrower sense of the term, desecrated the landscape, even when the buildings were designed by a "good" architect. Clearly, Loos thought architecture should serve merely as an extension of nature, namely as objects whose visual features seemed derived entirely from the physical functions they performed, just like the form of a tree or an animal's body. He objected wherever architecture went clearly beyond that limit and proclaimed the specifically human privilege of making a symbolic statement.

Such a symbolic statement can assume one of two basic attitudes toward nature. Although not attempting literally to imitate nature or to pretend that his buildings are products of nature, the architect can conceive of man as an outgrowth of nature. From this point of view, architectural creations, although unashamedly human in origin, should conform to nature and be shaped in the manner of nature. Buildings should grow out of the landscape, "in the image of the tree," as Frank Lloyd Wright said, and perhaps incline toward biomorphic shapes rather than geometrical ones. Such "organic" architecture may favor curving deviations from the straight line or plane, and merge in the continuous flow of a landscape that eschews the clear definition of elements, so characteristic of human reasoning. Nature, of course, can be conceived of in different ways. The identification of nature with biological growth is a romantic interpretation conveyed by the type of architecture I am referring to here.

On the other hand, man can use the forms of architecture to declare himself a rational creature generating rational shapes. As such he feels antagonistic to nature's appearance and perhaps superior to it. He may even undertake to make nature itself conform to this ideal of rationality. This was done in the French gardens of the seventeenth century, with their symmetrical layout and geometrical trees and flowerbeds, in direct continuation of the equally formalized palace architecture. In comparison with the mathematical concepts embodied in stone by man, untreated nature thus becomes an inferior wilderness.

While in the gardens of his own making man imposes his order on the irrationality of nature, he can also point up an order underlying nature's disorderly appearance. If all natural things consist ultimately of the five regular stereometric solids, as Plato maintained in the *Timaeus*, or if the multifarious variety of natural appearance is derived from the complex application of simple laws, then this inherent lawfulness can perhaps be evoked in nature by the presence of the pure geometrical shapes that only man can conceive and build. Thus a tower on a hill creates an accent around which nature may organize itself in a comprehensible order. This idea is made poetically tangible in Wallace Stevens's *Anecdote of the Jar*:

> I placed a jar in Tennessee,
> And round it was, upon a hill.
> It made the slovenly wilderness
> Surround that hill.
>
> The wilderness rose up to it,
> And sprawled around, no longer wild.
> The jar was round upon the ground
> And tall and of a port in air.
>
> It took dominion everywhere.
> The jar was gray and bare.
> It did not give of bird or bush,
> Like nothing else in Tennessee.

Whatever the style of architecture, buildings always have a curiously ambiguous relationship to their human setting. A comparison with sculpture will make the point. Primitively, sculpture serves to create icons, especially of divine figures, which are not so much portraits of superhuman powers dwelling elsewhere as embodiments of the powers themselves. The wooden or stone idol is endowed with the potency of the god or demon it represents, and is addressed accordingly as the bodily presence of that power. Such an icon takes its place in the human environment as a bona fide inhabitant. The great Buddha of Kamakura has his address in the park where he stands. You can go see him and he receives you, although in a strangely unresponsive and remote manner.

Elsewhere I have called this early conception of a sculpture or picture a "self-image" because "it visibly expresses its own properties," as distinguished from a "likeness," which is an image or representation of some individual person, kind of person, animal, etc. In this new role, gradually assumed, a sculpture's place and function in the human environment is as an object of detached cognition. Its location becomes arbitrary because a "likeness" may be kept any place, just as other pieces of information may be. The figure has become a signifier of something that is elsewhere, anywhere, or everywhere. It does not altogether lose the power of a "self-image," and therefore its ontological status is peculiarly ambiguous. As an embodiment of its own particular powers it has its defined place and function, like a mirror or washbowl; as a "likeness" or representation it dwells in the world to which it refers but has no claim to a fixed address in it. The world is complete without it, just as a concept is a statement about the world and not a part of it.

A building, too, is a "self-image" as well as a likeness. The primordial hut, the shack or cabin, is essentially an implement, shaped to suit its function. By its appearance it simply defines itself and its own kind. But the overtone of symbolism is present even then. The general notion of protective shelter is embodied in the particular shelter serving a particular person or living group, and the position of man in his world is reflected in the inhabitant's moving about within his four walls, adapting himself to this framework, receiving from it and acting upon it. In this way even the simplest dwelling, intentionally or not, acts as a "likeness," which transcends the here and now.

The further culture develops beyond elementary necessity, the more explicitly its architecture serves the need for a symbolism that makes buildings the bearers of a broad visual statement. A successful church or temple, a palace, an imaginatively designed private home, are statements of man's spiritual aspirations, definitions of worldly power, a person's conception of his own existence in his surroundings. As we walk in a town or city, we see ways of life reflected in each building, some clear and powerful, some confused and dull, some pretentious or humble, old-fashioned or bold, bare or exuberant.

A similar display of character is found, of course, in works of the visual arts, and yet there is a significant difference between the likenesses offered by buildings and those embodied in paintings and sculpture, as we know and make them nowadays. The works of the fine arts have become so thoroughly independent of their context that we expect each of them, in its own way, to present a valid image of human existence as a whole, though viewing it in a particular perspective. The abstract sculpture of a Jean Arp, in which swelling, curved shapes, vaguely evocative of human bodies or plants, move in harmonious and complex action, are surely limited in their presentation of our world, but rich enough to be accepted as a world view. The same is true for a cubist painting, in which a whole—*the* whole!—is shown as consisting of loosely interacting units.

A work of architecture need not aspire to such comprehensive symbolism

216

because it is limited in its expression by its particular function as a dwelling. A building is conceived, for the most part, as a stable refuge amidst the hubbub of human activity. Therefore, its meaning must be seen in the context of that setting, not as a self-sufficient statement. Being a shelter, its expression can be limited to ways of being a shelter and container, a gathering place for particular human activities.

Quite properly, for example, architecture is often symmetrical, whereas symmetry is rare in the fine arts. For the purpose of most paintings and much sculpture, the stable, simple order of symmetry would imply too limited a view of human experience. Significantly, however, monumental images of gods and rulers often show symmetry. They resemble architecture in proclaiming by their appearance that they are not susceptible to change, interaction, or interference. A rose window with its centric symmetry, beautiful as a symbol of undisturbed concentration in the façade of a church, would look irritatingly "ornamental" if presented as a painting. It would offer more harmony than can be reconciled with the turmoil of the world.

Although a building is complete in itself as a formal design, it is an implement of physical utility and therefore reveals its full meaning only by embracing the presence of man. André Malraux, in his *Antimémoires*, recalls the story of an Indian prince who spent many years building the most beautiful tomb in the world for his wife, whom he had loved. After the work was completed, her coffin was moved in, but it disturbed the harmony of the funeral chamber. "Take this away!" said the prince. The building had become so self-contained a monument that it could no longer serve as a material instrument. It could not tolerate any addition.

IS IT SCULPTURE?

The basic difference between architecture and sculpture emerges clearly from examples that play on the ambiguity between the two. A fountain as a useful object is a glorified waterspout, and as such its expression should be limited to the function of holding and emitting water. But when the fountain becomes a piece of sculpture, whether representational or abstract, it ceases to serve the water as a building serves its inhabitants. Instead, it uses the water for its own purpose. The water becomes a component of the fountain, an integral part of its expression. With their water turned off, the fountains of the Piazza Navona would become fragments. But the water's function varies. When a Baroque fountain is considered as a work of sculpture, the water

217

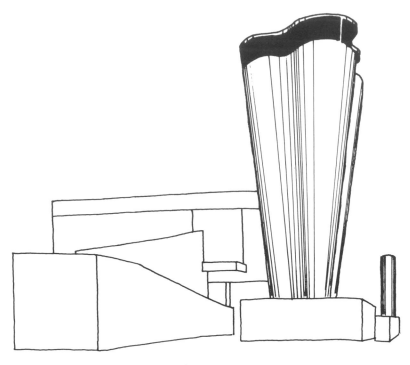

Figure 109

spewing forth from a naiad's breasts is an extension of the life-giving function of woman, expressed in the figure. Viewed as a practical implement, the bronze woman becomes a spout, serving the water.

Wright's Kaufmann House, "Falling Water," would probably be misinterpreted if it were seen as a structure offering a berth to both human inhabitants and water. The water is not served by the building, but is engaged by the house as a component that extends the centrifugal dynamics of its concrete slabs into the actual motion of the water. Thus, Falling Water is liquid architecture, not a combination of human habitation and springhouse.

Conversely, the exhaust tower on the roof of Le Corbusier's *Unité d'habitation* in Marseille can be seen as a fine piece of sculpture, dominating a configuration of other sculptural objects, cubes, steps, a cylinder (Fig. 109). At the same time, this sculptural form does not go beyond its function of channeling the flow of depleted air. The tower's entire shape can be said to be derived from, and devoted to, that function. But notice how the form of the object changes, depending on whether it is seen as a piece of sculpture or a

218

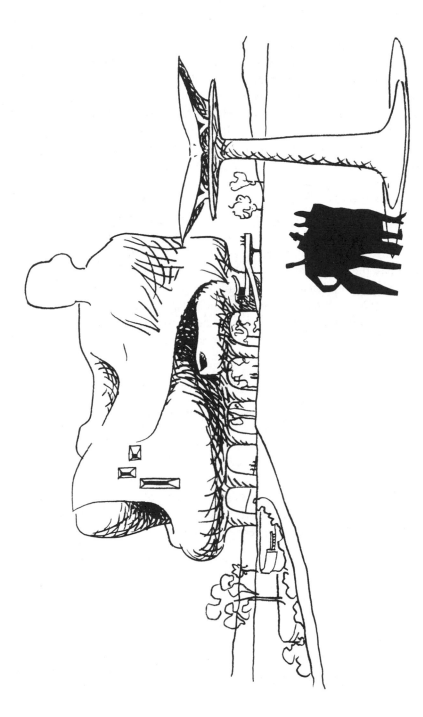

Figure 110. Drawing by Robert Sowers.

chimney. As sculpture it is complete in itself, held together by the cover on top and the opening, which serve as a kind of cornice. There is a center of gravity somewhere halfway up the tower. As a chimney, the form becomes hollow. Now the crescendo of its outline continues beyond the rim into the sky as an ever-widening discharge of air, from which the concrete spout derives its perceptual meaning. A drawing by Robert Sowers (Fig. 110) humorously illustrates what happens when sculpture is thought of as a building and when architecture pretends to be sculpture.

Buildings as utilitarian objects serve their inhabitants. But the converse can also be true: crowds of people sometimes enrich and complete the architectural structure, as the water serves the fountain, by conforming to it and thus becoming a part of it. The crowds that fill squares or flow in orderly procession toward or away from the entrance of a public building, look like a subordinate but indispensable part of the architecture. This reversal of emphasis comes about because a building is so much larger than the people it serves and therefore makes such a conspicuous, attention-riveting statement. Goethe was impressed by the dominating power of architecture when he watched the Italian populace fill the Verona amphitheater for an opera (cf. p. 269).

DYNAMIC PROPORTIONS

Dynamic expression is not the exclusive property of form in the fine and applied arts, such as architecture. It is the primary quality of any perception. This makes it all the more surprising that it has attracted so little explicit attention. Since the pioneering work of Lipps, psychologists and philosophers have ignored the subject. It goes without saying, however, that critics and art historians have constantly described particular manifestations of the phenomenon. I select a passage from James Ackerman's description of the vestibule of Michelangelo's Laurentian Library:

Continuity in the design of the wall heightens the shocking effect of the stairway, which pours out into the vestibule as an alien intruder . . . There is, after all, a dramatic if not a formal harmony between the stairway and the walls, because both conspire by their aggressiveness against the observer's ease; the wall planes, emerging forward from the columns, seem to exert inward pressure on the confined space in response to the outward pressure of the stairs.

So directly appropriate are these references to flow, intrusion, pressure, and expansion that we hardly consider them metaphorical. They are simply

Figure 111

apt descriptions of percepts, even though the objects they apply to are made of inert stone.

The examples given throughout this book illustrate various principles of architectural dynamics. This lightens the burden of the present chapter. I can confine myself here to mentioning a few additional aspects.

Perhaps the most important of these aspects concerns size relations between visual shapes. Proportions, which artists and architects judge so sensitively, would not provide us with any standard if they were only measurable quantities and not carriers of forces. Why, for example, is the golden section so widely considered, for certain purposes, the optimal ratio between two lengths (Fig. 111)? We describe it as the best balance between compactness and elongation of a rectangle, but why should this particular ratio be better than any other? Obviously because a ratio approaching the centric symmetry of a square does not bestow ascendancy on any one direction and therefore looks like a static mass; whereas too great a difference in the two dimensions undermines the equilibrium: the longer dimension is deprived of the counterweight provided by the shorter. A ratio approaching the golden section lets the shape stay in place while giving it a lively inherent tension. The very words we use to describe the determining factors indicate we are dealing with a dynamic relation. Equilibrium is the counterbalancing of forces; it has no application to mere quantity.

The same consideration applies to perceptual weight. Around 1850, the American sculptor Horatio Greenough launched a spirited protest against an early design for the Washington Monument by Robert Mills, in which a tall obelisk rose from a low circular building whose exterior presented a Doric colonnade (Fig. 112):

The prominent peculiarity of the design before us is the intermarriage of an Egyptian monument—whether astronomical, as I believe, or phallic, as contended by a Boston critic, matters not very much—with a Greek structure, or one of Greek elements. I do

221

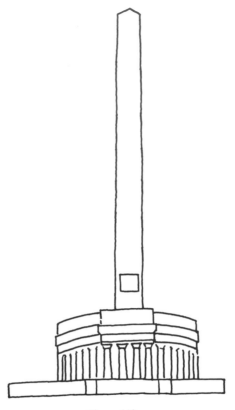

Figure 112

not think it is in the power of art to effect such an amalgamation without corrupting and destroying the special beauties and characters of the two elements. The one, simple even to monotony, may be defined a gigantic expression of unity; the other, a combination of organized parts assembled for a common object. The very perfection of their forms as exponents of so distinct characters makes them protest against juxtaposition.

Greenough objected not only to the mixture of styles but to the discrepancy between "the complex, subdivided, comparatively light Greek structure" and the heavy Egyptian mass of stone above it. He rightly rejected the argument that the slender columns were to veil a massive foundation and that therefore the combination of the two architectural elements offered no risk. "The pillars hide the strength of the structure, hence their impertinence as an architectural feature. It is incumbent upon edifices, first, to be strong; secondly *to look strong*." The physical statics of a building and an observer's

a   b

Figure 113

knowledge of it have next to no influence on the visual dynamics created by the relations between perceptual weights.

I remember walking into the cathedral of Sens, built at the transition from Romanesque to Gothic, and being struck by the discrepancy between the heavy columns of the nave and the slender ribs springing from them toward the vaults (Fig. 113a). Again, in purely quantitative terms there is nothing

223

wrong with a thin colonnette standing on a heavy support. What hurts is the inappropriate relation between perceptual cause and perceptual effect. We know from the explorations of the psychologist Albert Michotte that causality is a phenomenon directly inherent in the relations between shapes. He showed that when a geometrical shape, for example, a black square moving across a screen, hits another shape, which thereupon starts moving, the viewers experience a perceptual force that leaps from the primary agent across to the secondary object and thereby animates it. Our architectural examples indicate that a similar causal relationship gives life to juxtaposed immobile shapes. In the Sens example, the supporting columns, because of their visual heaviness, serve as the base of a dynamics that moves one-sidedly upward. The slender shaft springs from that base but is unable to counteract by pressing downward as a load, and the disproportion between the two produces the effect of a mountain giving birth to a mouse.

Otto von Simson, referring to this contrast, mentions that "to the master of Chartres such lack of homogeneity constituted an aesthetic flaw," which he overcame by composing his piers "of four slender colonettes that surround a powerful central core" (Fig. 113b). This invention "eliminates the contrast between the heavy monolithic shape of the column and the soaring bundle of shafts above it." A similar development occurred in our own century, when the transition from one style to another produced supports too slender to carry a heavy visual load. The early use of piloti columns, for example, in Le Corbusier's 1927 Weissenhof houses in Stuttgart, created a disproportion, not simply because viewers were unaware of the strength of reinforced concrete and therefore underestimated the physical staying power of the piloti, but because the visual weight of the fully enclosed cube of the building crushed the slender stilts (Fig. 114). When later architects, such as Mies van der Rohe, exposed the solid of the building as a steel skeleton, its visual weight was sufficiently reduced to eliminate the discrepancy between load and support.

Similarly, the effect of a cantilevered outgrowth is not so much a matter of how big a canopy or balcony the viewer thinks the building can keep aloft, but derives from the ratio between the visual weight of the building and the outward push of the horizontal protrusion.

In this connection, the peculiar expressive effect of supports deprived of their loads should be mentioned. In the ruins of classical buildings, isolated columns, without their entablature, look awkward. Their upward-directed power shoots unchecked into empty space, while their shape does not permit them to find balance within their own limits. The same is true for tall arcades

224

Figure 114

reaching all the way to the roof, with nothing to carry. Lipps defines ugliness of geometrical shapes as what results when the free effectuation (*Sichauswirken*) of a mechanical activity is impeded or fails to carry out the role accruing to it from its appearance.

THE OPENNESS OF BUILDINGS

Another factor that becomes truly architectural only when it is considered dynamically is the openness and closedness of buildings. In purely quantitative terms one can calculate how much of an outside wall is open, how much closed. Apart from the technical utility of such data for, say, purposes of insulation or lighting, statistics on the ratio between closedness and openness could also serve as an indicator of style. In order to describe the resulting expression, however, one would have to begin by remembering that the closedness of a wall or mass obstructs our progress through space. Openness makes the surroundings accessible to inhabitants of a building and exposes them to intrusion from the outside. In early societies, amulets were often hung at entrances or in windows to protect a house in the same way they protect a person. "Because all openings in, and boundaries of, whatever has been imbued with sacrality—whether they are openings of the human body or transition boundaries of man-created spaces—are considered vital and vulnerable, they are also the foci for protective patterns" (Prussin and Travis, writing on the environmental arts of West Africa). As a separation of outside

225

from inside, the wall creates an abrupt juxtaposition of the two worlds. I have spoken of the fundamental change of perceptual character a wall undergoes when it switches from belonging to the outside to belonging to the inside. Our imagination must make an effort to realize that the west wall of a church interior is its façade seen from behind. Openings mediate between the worlds separated by architectural barriers.

As one approaches a human settlement, openness is increasingly beset with obstacles. Buildings become more frequent, and often they also become larger. Open space loses its ubiquity, becoming mere corridors between blocks of masonry. The openness and closedness of any particular building is experienced as part of this great environmental interplay between access and obstacle. A compact building devoid of openings will look much more forbidding when it stands amidst contrastingly open space than when it borders on a narrow street. Conversely, the outgoing openness of a Wright house would be conspicuously inappropriate if there were heavy stone walls next to it.

The perceptual character of openings is strongly influenced by a difference between two types of buildings, to which I referred earlier. A building is thought of either as a closed container, into which holes are punched as needed, or it is a set of units—boxes, boards, and posts—added to one another until the space is sufficiently closed. Every architectural design dwells somewhere between these two extremes. Accordingly, there is a perceptual ambiguity about wall openings. In the traditional masonry wall a window or door interrupting the solid surface displays a positive shape of its own. Surrounded by large wall space which serves as "ground," the opening stands out as "figure," even though physically it is a hole. This prominence is underscored when the window or door is given an architectural frame of its own by means of jambs, lateral columns or pilasters, cornices, pediments, etc. In such a building both the volume of the whole and its openings have positive roles. There is a rivalry between them, which must be carefully balanced, lest the heavy cube of the solid smother the openings or, inversely, the expansive openings destroy the unity of the whole.

The French architect Boullée, who enjoyed uninterrupted walls, was jealous of what openings threaten to do to the outer shell of buildings. A building for a large number of people is necessarily a beehive, he said, and he complained about the spindliness (*maigreur*) of what remained between the many windows. The building looked like a lantern. This is the view of an architect who designs containers.

226

In a typical Frank Lloyd Wright house, by contrast, we see an airy arrangement of horizontal slabs and uprights with plenty of space left open between them. It is essentially negative space, as neutral and nondescript as the surrounding outside. In fact, the building's openings are continuations of that outer space, reaching into the building, below the overhanging roofs and terraces and between the uprights.

The windows and doors of a Renaissance palazzo, like the building itself, look out into space. They have been compared to eyes. The openings of a Wright building, on the other hand, are not in opposition to the surrounding space but extensions of it. As Wright said, "There is no longer any sense in speaking of doors and windows." His openings are like those in a textile weave: they are what is left between the shapes.

This negative role, however, is counterbalanced by the positive quality awarded to channels of access. Just as we observed earlier that streets are perceived as positive ducts of action, so the entrances and other functional spaces in the Wright house are filled with in-and-out motion. In this case, the rivalry between closed and open spaces is of quite a different nature than the one Boullée envisaged for his containers. The material slabs and cubes must be kept from reducing the open spaces to mere interstices, unable to assert their positive function visually. A door must be permitted to look like a door, that is, to be a positively defined opening. A window must look like a window. Therefore, if man's right to walk in and out and to look in and out is to be confirmed by visual form, it continues to make sense, after all, to speak of doors and windows. On the other hand, the open spaces must be kept from reducing the material slabs and cubes to mere scaffolding, thereby depriving the building of its virtue as shelter.

When open and closed spaces are given equal shares, the effect is of a screen which is dynamically neutral and simply provides the surface of the building with some transparency. In modern architecture, such screens may stand in front of the actual wall as a protection against too much openness. More often the walls themselves appear as semi-transparent screens, in which open and closed spaces alternate rhythmically. The curtain walls of the International style offer this quality of a permeable weave, as do the surfaces of Gothic buildings, for example, the lacework of the Venetian palazzi on the Grand Canal.

The effect of such screens depends on the ability of their open and closed spaces to act together as a partition, which is a flat plane or more nearly a surface layer of some depth. This effect is obtained in accord with a basic

227

Figure 115

perceptual principle, namely that a line or plane need not be spelled out entirely, but will complete itself in the observer's mind if its structure is sufficiently represented. The image of a square can be produced by four dots establishing the corners, and similarly on an architectural scale a city square can be adequately staked out by four corner buildings. Thus, although more than half of an architectural screen's surface may consist of openings, it will be perceived nevertheless as a coherent wall.

Similarly, two rows of columns separating the nave of a Romanesque church from the aisles create transparent but firmly present partitions. Or take the case of a crenelation. It delimits the top of a wall at two levels: more strongly at the bottom level (Fig. 115*b*) but quite visibly also at level *a*. At both levels the horizontals are spelled out only intermittently, but the eye is forced to complete the edges by the power of the implicit pattern.

A crenelation tops the solid wall with a border of transparency or medium density. More closely related to the screens of the modern architect is, for example, the portico surrounding the ground floor of the temple in the background of Raphael's painting *Marriage of the Virgin* (Fig. 116). The cylindrical core of the building is so solidly established that the portico is little more than a fence. On the other hand, one might find that the iron lace balconies of nineteenth-century buildings in New Orleans establish the building's outer shell, behind which the open spaces of the balconies line the walls with a kind of transparent bark. The buttresses surrounding Gothic churches form a meandering contour, which can be described as a crenelation in the horizontal. Here the two surface levels can be of about equal strength, and the open spaces they enclose represent a row of air shafts alternating with the solid buttresses.

The variety of solutions available to the architect who wishes to puncture the boundary of the solid block can only be hinted at here with a few random examples. The façade of Palladio's Palazzo Chiericati in Vicenza is established by a tenuous screen of widely spaced columns (Fig. 117). Since the colonnades are not substantial enough to create a sufficient frontal screen, the interspaces of the central part, at the level of the *piano nobile*, are filled in with a wall and windows, solid enough to let the frontal plane serve as the façade.

228

Figure 116

A complex modern example is offered by the library designed by William L. Pereira Associates for the University of California, San Diego (Fig. 118). The building is based on the shape of a spheroid, whose boundary is outlined, however, only by the corners of the cubicles the actual structure consists of. The border zone between the spheroid, which is created by the integrative power of perception, and the zigzag shapes actually built results in a layer of medium density, half-filled, half-open. This zone intervenes between the solid body of the building and the empty airspace surrounding it. The effect is strongly enhanced by the transparency of the glass walls. Conforming to the elliptical shape of the vertical section, the floors, which are cantilevered from the central core of the building, reach increasingly outward up to the third level, and then contract toward the roof. Just as in the horizontal contours, the vertical boundary is indicated in the profile by a zigzag of triangular shapes. In addition, however, the oblique contours are fully spelled out by the sixteen

229

Figure 117 Palazzo Chiericati Vicenza *Photo* Alinari

Figure 118. Library of the University of California, San Diego. *Photo*, Robert Glasheen.

powerful slope-beam columns, which support the protruding floors at an angle of 45°. Not being slanted walls but colonnades, these rows of bents present still another transparent screen effect.

The point I am trying to make here is that buildings are rarely separated from the surrounding space by a complete boundary. The mere puncturing of the walls by windows and doors tempers the solidity of the enclosure, and this leads to the various ways of sheathing the building with a layer of transparency or medium density, created by the alternation of solids and openings. The most irregular way of filling this outer layer is offered by Baroque buildings, which, in this respect, resemble sculptural reliefs. Sculptural reliefs are generally enclosed between a back plane formed by the ground between the figures and a frontal plane created by the outermost protrusions. In the space between these boundaries, the figures are deployed in all their various shapes. Rather similarly, in Baroque façades the multitude of columns, pilasters, cornices, and wall planes generally fits in with a unify-

231

ing order by confining all the sculptural turmoil to the area between two sufficiently defined planes. It is as though a plate of glass placed against the relief would touch the outer edge of the major convexities.

Openness, looseness, transparency, are well known as characteristic features of much modern architecture. The basic dichotomy between empty space and impermeable architectural solids is softened. No rigid boundary separates the two. In extreme cases the building is reduced to a skeleton, which traces the outlines of a delicate pattern against the sky—a mere apparition. The Crystal Palace and the Eiffel Tower are the obvious early examples. For our particular purpose it is of interest that in such structures surfaces are defined not by their opaque solidity, but by systems of lines—stanchions, mullions, trusses, cables—which act as visual vectors and indicate the directions of forces. Surfaces and volumes are presented as dematerialized dynamic systems. The parallel hatchings of the steel skeletons that spell out the transparent volumes of glass buildings or connect the catenary arches of suspension bridges with their base can be compared with the strings and wires with which sculptors like Gabo, Pevsner, or Henry Moore have created harplike surfaces. It may seem paradoxical that the technology of forged steel and the influence of engineering on architectural style should have led to products of such diaphanous delicacy, enlightening to the eyes but almost elusive to the touch. But we remember that in modern physics, the reduction of matter to systems of forces entails a similar sort of disembodiment.

Let me mention finally that openness explicitly overcomes the dichotomy between outside and inside—and not just in the sense that it permits us to look into interior spaces from without and to look out from within. More radically, the opening of boundaries reveals the architectural volume as three-dimensional by leading the eyes, and indeed the viewer himself, into the interior space. To be sure, a building presents itself as three-dimensional even when it displays only its outer cubic shape, or when a composite of cubes emphasizes that along with height and width, depth is one of its spatial properties. But this demonstration remains confined to the outer skin of the building, a flat surface however much it bends and folds in all directions. The true consummation of volume, namely, its continuation beyond the skin into the interior, is withheld from the viewer outside. He has to accept it on faith unless architectural features meet the boundary perpendicularly and pierce it.

I have spoken of the immaterial flatness of doors and windows, which

232

figure as mere thin lines on the architect's plan, even though they fulfill the powerful function of connecting outside and inside. A bridge or corridor remedies this immaterial flatness by presenting penetration as an explicit visual dimension. The function of leading in and out is given a material channel. The same spatial function is fulfilled by brise-soleil shutters and similar transversal slabs, which lend depth to window openings and guide the eye from the outside through the wall to the interior. And it is worth re-membering that Le Corbusier gave a dynamic impetus to the deep window channels of the chapel at Ronchamp by splaying their openings from a constricted outside to a broad inside.

Here again a comparison with modern sculpture imposes itself. Henry Moore, Jacques Lipchitz, and others have pierced the sculptural block with holes in order to transcend the two-dimensionality of an unbroken outer surface. These holes add depth to the dimensions of the external shape. The architect Portoghesi has observed that certain ruins, for example, those of Roman amphitheaters, reveal their sections to the viewer and thereby explain essentials of their internal structure, such as the relations between the open funnel of the terraced seats in the Colosseum and the ambulatories hidden underneath (Fig. 119). Sections also clarify the spatial relations between the outer façade of the ampitheater's huge cylinder and the radial aspects of its interior form—not merely for our intellectual edification but also as an expressive counterpoint between antagonistically oriented features of a truly three-dimensional structure. Portoghesi speaks of the "cognitive fascination derived from the transparency of the structures, which display themselves to our eyes in the fullness of their architectural potential."

EXPANSION FROM A BASE

Dynamically, a building is not simply a solid object sitting on its plot of land. It actively displaces space. This displacement remains a permanent feature of the building's appearance. It is a dynamic phenomenon that shows up to different degrees, as we shall see, depending on the building's shape. Even an elementary cube, when perceived dynamically, expands from an interior center in the directions that offer freedom.

Any such expansion requires a base of operation, from which the outgoing forces issue. Perceptual forces cannot emerge from nowhere. The most common base of architecture is of course the level of the terrain on which the building stands. We observed earlier that buildings rise from the ground as

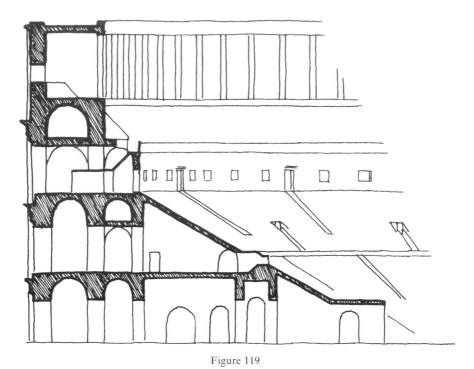

Figure 119

though they sprouted like trees. But this biological analogy had distinct limitations. First of all, the boundlessness of the ground level prevents us from perceiving the earth as a three-dimensional mass. The ground appears as a flat, two-dimensional plane. It is a base, but has no visible bulk and therefore is not a suitable generator of perceptual forces. Even a tree is not really seen as sprouting from the ground, but from its own roots if knowledge of their existence enters into the image of the tree. Then the ground is seen as concealing and containing the roots, but contributing little or nothing to the perceptual base of growth.

This is even truer for buildings. In point of physical fact, a building may be immersed in soil "up to its waist," as Victor Hugo says of medieval churches, palaces, and bastilles. "The substructure of a building was another building to which one descended, instead of climbing, and which arranged its subterreanean floor levels under the pile of the external floors of the edifice, as forests and mountains reverse themselves in the reflecting water of a lake

234

beneath the forests and mountains along the shore." But whereas reflections in water are visible, a building is commonly designed as starting from the ground and standing on it. The reader will recall our discussion in connection with the Baptistery in Pisa (p. 41).

This means that a building must provide in its own bulk the base from which the perceptual forces issue, as well as those forces themselves. It must be archer and arrows at the same time, and these functions are not segregated in the form of the building. Most parts of most buildings embody both dynamic functions. The simple shape of a pyramid is a heavy, compact mass resting on the ground, but at the same time it is the wedge-shaped manifestation of an upward force. Both dynamic themes are jointly present everywhere within the pyramid, and the same ratio between base and vector seems to be maintained throughout.

We know that all dynamics reads both ways. The rising of the pyramid is counteracted by a downward pressure, which, starting at the top as a mere point, grows into an ever-larger base as it proceeds toward the ground. This downward movement, however, is clearly secondary because whenever a visual pattern is anchored in a solid base, the direction toward the free end dominates. Two-way dynamics is more clearly active in the horizontal layers of the pyramid, as it contracts while rising from the ground or, conversely, expands from the top down. Contraction and expansion in the horizontal dimension have no relation to the pyramid's base and therefore can alternate in perception.

The complementary relation between rising and descent, contraction and expansion, constitutes the internal dynamics of the pyramid. More broadly, this internal behavior is embedded in the relation between the building and its surroundings. The pyramid displaces the air as it pushes upward. At the same time, the surrounding space can be seen as compressing the building, for example, by progressively reducing its bulk until, at its greatest height, the pyramid comes to a mere point and vanishes entirely. The building's immobile shape is perceived dynamically as resulting from the equilibrium between the expansive forces generated from within and the compressive forces converging from without.

The pyramid performs as a compact, uninterrupted whole. The shape of most buildings, however, is subdivided, and their different parts fulfill different dynamic functions. A step pyramid falls in between. It may not be

235

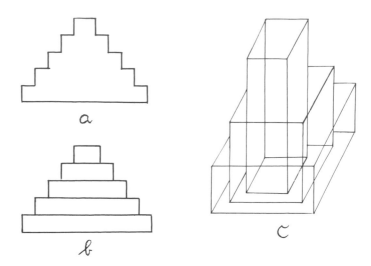

Figure 120

strong enough to bring about a real subdivision. Its steps may be seen as the ribbed surface of an otherwise compact polyhedron (Fig. 120a). But the steps can also transform the solid into a pile of slices (b). In that case, the task of contracting or expanding is seen as distributed among the members of a group of participants, which act concertedly but at different levels of efficiency. The bottom slice, having the largest bulk, protrudes farthest into the surrounding space. With increasing height, the expansive power of the layers diminishes.

It is also possible, although this version receives less support from the shape actually seen, to perceive the step pyramid as a set of cubic shapes, reaching to different heights and nesting within one another (Fig. 120c). In that case, the team performs a crescendo of upward pushes: the broader a member's base, the more sluggish its power to rise; the slimmer the base, the more energetic its upward push. The ratio between bulk and force varies from unit to unit.

A similar effect of steplike form can be found in the roof edges of Frank Lloyd Wright. Compared with a compact triangular shape, such gradients of slabs display, first of all, more subtlety: the total push is composed of several finer ones and is broken down into a number of phases, each displaying a particular degree of the effort. Although such a subdivision splinters the compact push, it also makes the gradient more explicit and more visible,

236

Figure 121. Paolo Portoghesi. Chiesa della Sacra Famiglia. Salerno.

especially when seen not in profile, but from below or in front (Fig. 121). Portoghesi, who has used such steplike gradients in many of his own works, describes them as echo effects, and mentions as examples, in addition to Wright, the cupolas of the Pantheon and of Borromini's St. Ivo at the Sapienza in Rome, as well as Michelangelo's studies for the steps of the Laurentian library.

When all the components of such a concerted effort perform the same

237

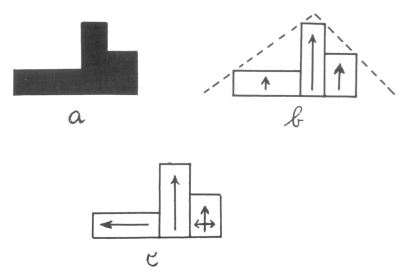

Figure 122

function with the same strength, the result is not an echo but a chorus of voices in unison, confirming one another without losing their separate existence. Any row of columns presents such parallelism. One function of a row of columns is to spell out the dynamic character of walls, which are devoid of expression when their surface is empty and therefore unstructured. A row of columns defines a surface as a pattern of vertically oriented forces. Crenelations contribute a similar effect, though of course much more weakly.

A further step leads us to the inexhaustible wealth of dynamic relationships obtainable by varying the horizontal and vertical dimensions of rectangular or cubic elements. Reduced to two-dimensional flatness, Fig. 122a can be subdivided into three components. When we take our cue from the tall upright in the center, we slice the structure vertically and perceive a trio of vectors, parallel in direction but differing in strength (Fig. 122b). The two lower ones flank the tower, but not symmetrically. The tower is not in the center, and the wings are not equal. This produces a dynamic lean toward the right, a tilted triangle formed by a short, steep ascent from the right and a longer, gentler slope from the left. Here again the variety of the effect is enhanced by the different ratios between bulk and force in the individual units. The one on the left, read vertically, is heavily expansive, but sluggish in its effort. The tower is slim and energetic. The third unit, on the right, mediates between the two.

238

The most intricate application of such rows of vertical units is found, of course, in skylines. The accidental juxtaposition of the buildings makes us look at them one by one, while at the same time they are grouped in a more or less irrational profile. Lacking a consistent order, such a chorus of vertical thrusts is often perceivable only as visual noise, that is, as a largely unstructured sensory stimulus, which can be invigorating or disturbing, depending on who is looking.

As the example of the skyline illustrates, a sequence of elements in space may be read in different directions. One can read it from left to right, or vice versa; one can try to select one element as the center and move from it in both directions or approach it from both sides. The eyes can also jump irregularly back and forth, discovering ever-new relations. Although each of these approaches provides a different experience, none rules out the others. As a spatial pattern, a skyline exists in the simultaneity of its parts. The path of sequential exploration is introduced by the roving glance of the observer.

In a more orderly pattern some such sequences are imposed by the structure while others are not. In looking at a row of organ pipes grouped symmetrically around the tallest, the eyes of the observer, which must scan in order to see at all, may start from the peak and descend to the left or to the right; or contrarily they may climb toward the peak. When the eyes take off from some other place in the pattern, the exploration is experienced as more subjective, accidental, and transitory because it is not in accord with the structure—stimulating though the adventure may be for the explorer.

A set of organ pipes, with all its elements pointing in the same direction and arranged in a single plane, does not match the dimensional variety found in architectural shapes. We turn once more to Figure 122a and note that the low, flat unit at the left lends itself only reluctantly to being viewed as rising upward like the other two. Its main axis forms itself more readily along the horizontal dimension because that is the longest. This alters the dynamics of the whole pattern (Fig. 122c). We now see the left unit and the central tower as placed at right angles to each other. They thereby describe the two principal dimensions of space, while the unit to the right now mediates not only between their heights but also between their directions.

CEFALÙ IN THREE DIMENSIONS

Detailed descriptions of complex visual shapes inevitably make tedious reading. I shall therefore limit myself to a single example, for the purpose of indicating the wealth of dynamic relations displayed by a truly three-

Figure 123. Cathedral of Cefalù. *Photo. Alinari.*

dimensional work of architecture. What do we see when we approach the magnificent Romanesque cathedral of Cefalù near Palermo in Sicily (Fig. 123)?

The theme of vertical rising is entrusted to the two towers. They fulfill this task more compellingly than the building as a whole could, because they are relatively slim in relation to the height they attain. A slight crescendo builds in the upward movement of their main mass as the single window gives way to double ones. Looking upward along the vertical axis of the towers, one is stopped rather brusquely by the rim. One may overshoot it because it comes without warning, and in comparison with the vigor of the upward sweep it is weak. The rim serves as a ritardando; it provides a first contraction of the tower's bulk, before the pointed tops apply an ultimate squeeze, which sends the upward movement forth into the sky.

In comparison with the lateral pointers, the central mass, nearly square-shaped, looks heavy and inert. It thereby provides the building with a solid core and keeps it anchored to the ground. A cornice emphasizes the division of this central mass into two layers, each of them wider than it is high. They act as horizontal counters to the vertical towers. The solidity of this central core is modified, however, by the setback from the porch to the upper levels—an echo of the contraction acted out at the top of the towers. This setback is an acknowledgment of the vertical ascent. It makes the eyes step upward. Similarly, the rows of arches create a vertical gradient of diminishing sizes: from the three tall openings of the porch one rises to the overlapping arches at the second level and finally to the even smaller arcade at the top. This upper arcade does not provide much of a closure: the central structure, in spite of its function as a counterweight, is not held down by any roof or lid, and therefore floats, with a vertical aspiration of its own, on the slender columns of the porch.

Earlier, when I compared the architectural dimensions of elevation and plan, I suggested that the vertical supplies the visual image of a building as a monument, whereas the horizontal plane interprets the physical interaction between man and building. Horizontally, as we approach the cathedral of Cefalù, we are first met by the towers, which precede the central part of the building on the plan, just as they dominate it in the vertical. The towers are sternly closed and exhibit a self-contained independence in the compact centric symmetry of their squarish section. Their shape takes no cognizance of the visitor's approach, and they offer neither doors nor windows at the ground level. The visitor is given his welcome at the recessed center—a

241

setback that was even more abrupt before the porch was added in the late fifteenth century as a mediator between the two frontal levels. The porch offers a hospitable openness as well as a prelude to the interior of the church. It supplements the compact solidity of the towers with the announcement that the building is a container, with its principal function fulfilled inside.

THE DYNAMICS OF ARCHES

One more look at Cefalù will make us aware of differences in the three arches of the porch, the central one being semicircular, the lateral ones, pointed. Their metric dimensions are similar, since they are of equal height although the lateral ones are somewhat narrower; but the difference in their dynamics is fundamental. The semicircular curvature above the springing of the central arch spreads its vectors equally in all directions, showing preference for none. It acts like rose windows or wheels, which ignore the vertical-horizontal framework and, all but untouched by the pull of gravity, are suspended somewhere in a wall. Rose windows often act as a center around which architectural masses group themselves in an arrangement that to some extent ignores the difference between up and down. The semicircular arch is combined with the supporting columns and thereby becomes a participant in the vertical dynamics. However, as the observer's eyes, guided by the columns, rise upward, they find that the movement concludes by spreading in all directions. Unlike the pointed arches, the central one echoes the function of the building's central body, which, as we observed, counteracts the upward drift as an anchoring weight.

The slight pointing of the lateral arches suffices to continue the direction initiated by the supporting columns. I enjoyed reading in the *Encyclopedia Britannica* that the Hindus objected to the pointed arch as a structural feature because they say it *"never sleeps,* meaning that it is always exerting a thrust which tends to its destruction." This is why pointed arches do not stack well. They poke into the base of whatever is above them and interfere with the solidity of the wall.

To return to circular arches: their expression depends on how much of the circle is used. The half-circle offers enough of the structure to create the radial spreading of which I spoke (Fig. 124a). At the same time, however, it meets its supports at the point where it approaches the vertical direction asymptotically. Without a break, it slips from circularity into straightness and creates a structural ambiguity at the springing. When capitals are used at the junction they help mark the structural switch. They also remedy the awkward

242

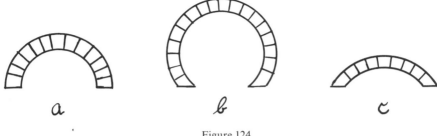

Figure 124

problem that arises when cylindrical columns are combined with arches. It has often been remarked that arches call for piers as their natural supports. As Konrad Fiedler aptly put it, piers are basically nothing but the pieces of the wall remaining when the arches are "cut out." Columns destroy the communion between supports and wall.

As soon as the circular curve of the arch passes the halfway mark, that is, as soon as its center is placed above the springing, the circle's tendency toward closure exerts its power, which creates the characteristic tension of the Moorish horseshoe arch (Fig. 124b). It threatens to snap closed, breaking its connection with the vertical supports. It also tests the very verticality of the columns or piers by trying to bend them inward.

When the segment of a circular arch covers less than 180°, it increasingly loses circularity and approaches straight lines (Fig. 124c). Note here that a curve which is a part of a circle geometrically is not necessarily perceived as such. In a segmental arch the curved top, framed by vertical supports, tends to lose the constancy of its curvature and to look instead as though it had its maximum bend at the center and straightened toward the sides. This means that the circular curve relinquishes its own centric symmetry and conforms instead to the vertical symmetry axis of the structure it is part of. Its central voussoir is redefined as a peak, and the whole curve adapts itself to this reading.

In consequence, a segmental arch hints at pointedness, although weakly. As a pointed shape it looks blunted and soft; but viewed by itself, it preserves its geometric hardness as part of a circle. There is something ambiguous and evasive about such a shape. It rises, but without conviction, and it attempts pointedness without breaking its circularity.

The circle is the most unified, the least breakable of all geometrical shapes. It is vulnerable only to the tangent, which can make it slide into straightness, but it is not easily combined with other curves or with circular lines of a

243

Figure 125

different radius. Lipps has pointed out that regularity does not suffice to create a beautiful curve. He objects to a suggestion by an unnamed "modern aesthetician" that a waveform composed of semicircles is beautiful (Fig. 125). Lipps maintains that such a combination is ugly. It pretends to offer a unitary flow but instead combines its parts, each of which has a regular shape, by an abrupt reversal of direction. A semicircle has so much of the circular structure that it is all but impossible to combine with another curve and produce a unitary form. Actually, of course, Figure 125 is not a regular curve at all, but a patchwork of regular ones. A curve obeying the same formula throughout, e.g., a sine curve, expresses its mathematical unity in the kind of visual flow that Lipps rightly insists on.

Although the pointed arch derives historically from the semicircular arch, it should also be related to the simpler triangular opening that is used traditionally to relieve the pressure on the lintel of a door. The prototype of the triangular solution is, of course, the Lion Gate at Mycenae (Fig. 126). In comparison, the pointed arch, which consists of two circular segments, makes the opening convex and thereby strengthens its "figure" character (Fig. 127a). The combination of curvature and straightness also enriches the shape; and when the centers of the two segments lie at the level of the springing, the segments continue smoothly in the perpendicular supports, whereas a triangular pediment produces breaks.

As in a segmental arch, the circular halves of a pointed arch lose some of their identity by being subjected to a vertical structure. The two sides of a pointed arch are perceived as parts of circles only if one artificially isolates them from their context. In context, they appear as gradual deviations from the vertical. In this respect, they resemble the triangular pediment; but the dynamics of the pointed arch is more forceful because the deviation of its

244

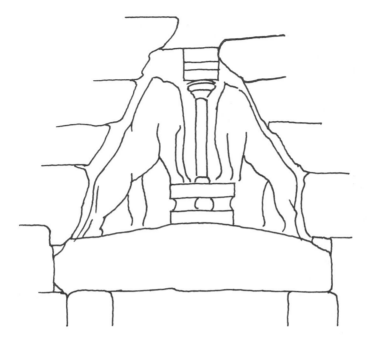

Figure 126

curved sides begins slowly and grows at an increasing rate toward the peak. This crescendo is more dynamic than the steady inclination of a triangle's straight sides.

In a drop arch, the centers of the two segments lie relatively close together at the level of the springing (Fig. 127b). Their combination, therefore, resembles a semicircle, especially when the point at which they would meet is hidden by a lantern. I have pointed elsewhere to the particular quality of the resulting effect in the profile of the cupola of St. Peter's (Fig. 128). The circular hardness of the segments combines with the slight rise at the top to convey the expression of a solid mass whose rigidity is subtly tempered by a dynamic vector at the center.

Most arches are adapted to a building's vertical dimension by being combined with supporting columns or pilasters. The visual importance of this practice becomes evident if one considers, in comparison, parabolic or catenary arches, which combine upward motion and roundness in a unitary curve. The absence of straightness leads to an effect that shows up most radically in circular windows. They appear as holes in the wall or as appli-

245

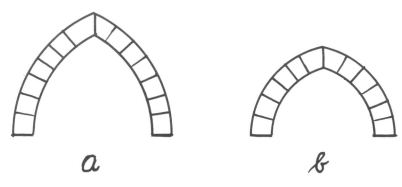

Figure 127

qués on it, but they do not partake in the structure of the wall itself in the same sense that rectangular windows can, as parts of a checkerboard pattern of open and closed spaces. Similarly, a parabolic or catenary arch appears as an aperture in the wall, not as a part of it. There can be no objection to this relationship, just as there can be none to the effect of circular windows, but its perceptual nature needs to be acknowledged. Pointed and semicircular arches are grounded in the vertical-horizontal framework of a building by

Figure 128

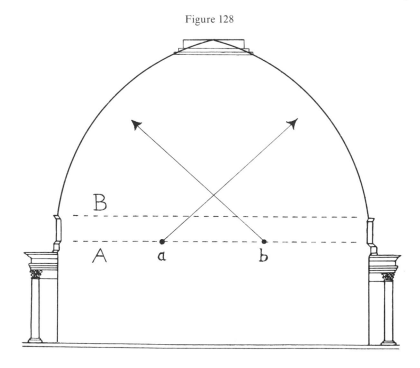

246

Figure 129

virtue of their perpendicular stilts, but they emerge from that commitment in their curved tops, which are free from a direct bond with the wall.

Notice in this connection the dynamic effect obtained by the combination of triangular gables and semicircular arches in the pediments of doors and windows. Is there a characteristic stylistic difference between the triangles cupped by semicircles, as we see them in Renaissance buildings such as the courtyard of the Palazzo Farnese or on the façade of Giulio Romano's house in Mantua, and the reverse form used, for example, by Michelangelo at the Porta Pia (Fig. 129)? When the semicircle envelops the gable, it shields the surrounding wall against the piercing vector of the triangular wedge and thereby weakens the dynamics of the thrust. When triangle and arch are switched, the curved arch below or within the gable looks like an initial phase of the thrust that becomes explicit in the triangle. The dynamics is not subdued but enhanced. Michelangelo attains a related effect by alternating curved and triangular pediments on the windows of the vestibule in the Laurentian library.

VIII. EXPRESSION AND FUNCTION

T HROUGHOUT this book, my principal concern has been to show that visual expression is an indispensable and indeed inescapable attribute of all architectural shapes. From this point of view there is no difference of principle between the expression of unadorned straightness in a concrete column and that of the stucco fantasies of a Baroque interior. Each satisfies a sensory need in accordance with the architect's and the client's philosophy of life. The difference is purely stylistic.

ORNAMENT AND BEYOND

A distinction between structural necessity and ornament is made necessary, however, by two other approaches to the nature of architecture. The more primitive approach defines the function of buildings simply as the physical requirements of shelter. From that point of view there seems to be a reasonably clear-cut difference between what is needed to erect a stable enclosure and what is added to these essentials. However, a psychologist may be permitted to point out that the difference between physical and mental needs is less self-evident than it might appear. All physical requirements of man express themselves as mental needs. The very desire to survive, to quench thirst and hunger, is a mental demand developed in the course of evolution to insure the survival of the species. A creature not possessed of these yearnings would peacefully die from lack of food within hours. Thus the needs served by the architect are exclusively mental. The occupants of a building would be hard put to make a reasonable distinction between protection from the rain, enough light to read the newspaper, enough verticals and horizontals to satisfy the sense of balance, and walls and floors covered with the colors and shapes necessary to convey, through the eyes, the gaiety of a full life.

Actually the traditional criterion for functionality refers not to the satisfaction of the client's "physical" needs, but more simply to the elements needed to create and uphold the building's physical structure. This is quite evident in the fundamental statement on the subject, Vitruvius's chapter on the ornaments of the orders. Vitruvius distinguishes the contribution of the carpenter from that of the artist: as a carpenter, the builder sets up the columns, pilasters, beams, and walls; as an artist, he cuts off projecting ends and creates an even surface, carves the vertical grooves for the triglyphs and paints them blue, etc. He endeavors to provide "beauty more than usual" and to avoid "an ugly look."

A very similar distinction is reached by a second approach, intent on defining what one might call the Platonic *eidos* of the building, that is, the bare essentials of its being. For this purpose Marc-Antoine Laugier, in his essay on architecture, resorted to the notion of the primitive hut—not to derive standards from the historical origin of architecture, but to establish a principle permitting him to distinguish essentials from non-essentials. The elements of the primitive hut designate columns, entablature, and pediment as the essential components of any building. "From now on," writes Laugier, "it will be easy to distinguish between those parts that are essential to an architectural composition and those introduced by necessity and added to by caprice." Since Laugier excludes the needs of the inhabitants, as distinished from those of the structure, his criteria for what is essential are rigorous indeed. Even the walls are counted among the *licenses*. They are not needed to hold up the roof as long as there are four corner posts.

The severity of the standards advocated by Laugier at least in theory can be understood only as a reaction to a tendency among architects toward excessive "ornamentation." In our own century a similar reaction suggested the stripping of architectural form to the bare geometry of its bones. We realize now that such abstinence is not the necessary corrective of the abuse but simply a stylistic alternative.

A better perspective on the problem can be obtained by consulting Ananda K. Coomaraswamy's observations on the meaning of ornament. Coomaraswamy recalls that in the world's great cultures "ornament" or "decoration" did not stand for gratuitous prettification but, on the contrary, referred to necessary attributes of an object or person. This is evident even in the original meaning of these terms and their equivalents in other languages. Ornament refers originally to necessary equipment, such as the ornaments of a ship or an altar, or in rhetoric to what is needed for effective communication by speech. Decoration comes from decorum and indicates what is needed for a thing or person to perform its function properly. Even in our own time, says Coomaraswamy, "if, for example, the judge is only a judge in act when wearing his robes, if the mayor is empowered by his chain, and the king by his crown, if the pope is only infallible and verily pontiff when he speaks *ex cathedra*, 'from the throne,' none of these things are mere ornaments." He also notes that what we call charming is originally something that exerts a charm, namely a magic power, and that "cosmetic" derives from *cosmos* and therefore designates what is needed for proper order.

The original meanings of these terms, by now as sadly cheapened as the functions to which they refer, preserve an attitude to which our crude distinction between what is needed to perform physical functions and what gratuitously pleases the senses is entirely alien. The pair of eyes painted on the prow of a boat in ancient Greece or in New Guinea is as essential to a safe journey as the proper shape and wood for the boat "itself." Similarly a building relies on the entirety of its shapes to serve the human mind. Viewed in this way, the ribs indicating the structure of a vault in a Gothic church or in a sports arena by Nervi are as indispensable as the vault itself, and the foliage of the Corinthian capital is as necessary as the column.

Only when this principle is recognized may one look for criteria by which to distinguish the "ornaments" that enhance the visual efficiency of a building from others that interfere with it. Only then, looking for example at Santa Maria della Salute in Venice, might one ask whether the large volutes surmounted by statues, the so-called *orecchioni* on the terrace around the cupola, support or disrupt the relation between the cupola and the church's octagonal base (Fig. 130).

Under the title *Integral Ornament at Last!* in a few important pages Frank Lloyd Wright defined integral ornament as "the developed sense of the building as a whole, or the manifest abstract pattern of structure itself. Interpreted. Integral ornament is simply structure-pattern made visibly articulate and seen in the building as it is seen articulate in the structure of the trees or a lily of the fields." And he aptly referred to Beethoven's Fifth Symphony, developed from a four-tone theme, the implication being that nobody in his right mind would describe, and perhaps dismiss, all the music beyond those four tones as ornaments of dubious validity.

There exist, in fact, ornaments in music, but significantly they do not serve to distinguish between the essentials of a composition and gratuitous additions, but instead derive from a division of labor between composer and

Figure 130. Santa Maria della Salute. Venice. *Photo*, Gerald Carr.

performer that is alien to modern concert practice. Starting in the days of the Gregorian chant, when singers "indulged in extemporaneous ornamentation of the traditional melodies" (Apel), and culminating a thousand years later in the virtuoso performances of singers and instrumentalists, this practice assigned the composer the task of providing the basic structure of the piece, whose execution in fully developed form was the performer's responsibility (cf. Fig. 68). Architectural parallels can be found when building does not proceed autocratically from a fully developed blueprint but takes off from a

251

generic plan of overall shape and function and leaves the execution to the imagination and practical skill of what we would call the contractor and his masons. In neither case does "ornament" refer to something that could be done without.

Musically, the distinction between the composer's task and that of the performer clarified the structural skeleton of a composition. Willi Apel reports that when composers began to write out in explicit detail just what they wanted the audience to hear, the innovation was decried as

detrimental to the visual clarity of the melodic line. J.S. Bach, for instance, was severely criticized by at least one contemporary musician on the ground that "he writes down in actual notes the ornaments and embellishments that performers are accustomed to supply instinctively, a habit which not only sacrifices the harmonic beauty of his music but also makes the melody totally indistinct."

The difficulty indicated by this criticism is familiar to architects as well. Any architect unwilling to limit his statement to a few elementary shapes faces the problem of ensuring that his design's underlying formal theme emerges and visibly determines all elaboration. Implicit here is the basic principle of order that governs all perceptual form. Successful patterns are organized in such a way that all details are understood as elaborations—*diminution* was the term used by the medieval musicians—of superordinate forms, and that these, in turn, similarly conform to their superiors. This leads to a hierarchic structure, which permits the viewer or listener to grasp a complex whole as the gradual unfolding and enrichment of a theme, the bearer of the design's basic meaning. In the interplay between that fundamentally simple assertion and the rich consequences resulting from its realization lies the substance of an architectural statement.

Note here that the particular quality of a particular work resides neither in its basic theme, which it may share with other works, nor in the surface texture of its style, but, as the musicologist Heinrich Schenker has taught us, in the "middleground" of the design, which tells what the artist has accomplished by applying a style to a theme.

EXPRESSION FROM DYNAMICS

Of the two key concepts, function and expression, the former is most familiar to architects, although there is no agreement on its meaning. The latter, expression, although equally fundamental, is all but absent from most systematic discussions of architecture and appears only in the narrow sense of traditional symbolism. Given this state of affairs, it is not surprising that the relationship between the two concepts is far from clear. When an architect decides that "function" should be limited to what satisfies bodily needs, he is narrowing the meaning of the term to accord with his own attitude or style. In practice it is fairly obvious what he means when he says that all he wants his building to do is to protect its inhabitants against rain and snow, heat and cold, burglars and snoopers. As I observed earlier, however, such a limitation attempts to slice a fragment from the indivisible totality of human needs. Let me assert once more that the needs of the body become needs only by being felt by the mind as discomfort, and that there is no sensible way to distinguish between the protection of the body from heat and the mind's preference for curtained windows, or between the material safety of one's belongings and the feeling of being securely encased. Different means may be called upon to meet these different demands: insulating materials to obtain the desired room temperature, appropriate colors and spatial dimensions to make the room *feel* warm. Any separation of these needs from one another, however, is arbitrary, and is not admissible when the design's rationale is the well-being of the client. Function must refer to the totality of the needs the building is to meet.

Expression, on the other hand, relies on what I have described as the dynamics of visual form. Dynamics is a property supplied by the mind spontaneously and universally to any form that is perceivable, i.e., organized in such a way that its structure can be grasped by the perceiving nervous system.

Dynamics has generic qualities, such as straightness or flexibility, expansion or contraction, openness or closedness. These dynamic qualities are perceived not only as particular visual characteristics of a particular object, but as properties of a very general nature. They are experienced as ways of being and behaving, to which we may find analogies, for example, in our own mind. The human mind also can be straightforward or flexible, expansive or retiring, etc. Perceptual dynamics serves as the carrier of expression in the broader sense of exemplifying and illustrating ways of being and behaving, found in nature and in man-made things, in physical and mental processes.

To distinguish this view of expression from those of other theorists, let me assert that the objects and events we perceive are not simply endowed by us subjectively with human qualities, as the theory of "empathy" has it. Rather, the dynamic qualities come along with the percepts of objects and events, and characterize them as possessing in themselves some particular way of being or behaving. When a building is nearly devoid of windows and other open-

253

ings, it conveys the particular quality of closedness—a quality we may also know, for example, as a tightness of mind. (In fact, I shall have occasion to mention at the end that the kind of expressive behavior we find embodied in architecture enables us to reason concretely about such nonsensory properties as human strivings, relations, or attitudes.)

The capacity to perceive the expressive qualities of things inheres spontaneously in the human mind. It is found most purely in children, at early stages of civilization, and in persons of highly developed intuitive sensitivity, such as artists. It is hampered by a civilization that favors practical utility in a purely physical sense and hesitates to acknowledge the existence of phenomena that cannot be measured or counted.

Even in our civilization, however, full perception is by no means beyond retrieval in the average person. It is favored by folkways that promote the "poetic sense" of human experience. When the public imagination is acquainted with the thought that "a mighty fortress is our God," buildings are more readily seen as carrying metaphoric meaning. But it must be admitted that in present-day public education, the cultivation of sensitivity to perceptual expression is grievously neglected.

FUNCTION CANNOT MAKE FORM

If expression is a quality inherent in the perceptual appearance of objects and events, how is it related to what architects call function? Clearly, expression is not identical with a building's physical properties: a building may be soundly built yet look flimsy and precarious. Nor is expression identical with what the viewer, rightly or wrongly, believes the physical structure of a building to be. And yet there is some connection. We say, for example, that the amphitheater in Epidaurus reveals by its shape its suitability for assembling large groups of people to receive a common message. At the same time, the building presents a symbolic image of concentration, of democratic unity, unanimity, and equality.

But how does the symbolism get into the building? In the nineteenth century, for example, the art theorist Konrad Fiedler spoke eloquently about the process of spiritual assimilation, by which all traces of the building materials' characteristics and all contingencies of structural technique are expunged from the viewer's mind. What remains is the pure form of the building, the vehicle for its spirit. This sounds right, but how are we to understand the transformation of the sight of a material object, an arrange-

254

ment of cement, stone, or wood, into something immaterial, as the spirit evidently is? And what are we to understand by pure form?

When architects discuss form, they are generally content to describe it as physical shape. The have not worried explicitly about the psychological problem of how shape can transmit spiritual meaning, except by pointing, for example, to harmonious proportions as conveyors of beauty. They have also acknowledged that certain shapes are conventionally associated with certain meanings—for example, when Vitruvius observes that the Doric order fits the "virile strength" of a Minerva, Mars, or Hercules. It is true that in such examples there reverberates the intuitive realization of a visible affinity between the look of things and their character; but essentially architectural thinkers have been occupied by the question of how form, whatever its meaning, relates to function.

William James, in his *Principles of Psychology*, mentions "the celebrated French formula of 'La fonction fait l'organe,' " and architects are well known to have applied this biological principle to their own trade. But it has become evident by now that neither in biology nor in the applied arts can form ever be fully determined by function. The reason is, as the designer David Pye has explained with great clarity, that function consists in abstract principles, not in shapes. For example, the function to be fulfilled by a wedge can be described verbally. The principle designates a range of shapes as suiting the purpose, but it declares no preference for any particular embodiment.

In most cases this range of shapes, serving a particular function, is defined not only intellectually, but also perceptually. Perception, too, is not primarily concerned with particular shapes but with kinds of shapes. What we see, first of all, when we look at an object is what kind of thing it is. This follows simply from the biological purpose of perception, which is essentially that of learning about kinds of things. Even in dealing with unique individuals, man and animal are mainly concerned with the question: What kind of person, what kind of thing or event is this? Thus when one surveys the wedges presented by Pye in an illustration, one not only understands by intellectual abstraction but perceives directly what they all have in common as members of a class—with the important proviso, however, that some of the shapes display the character of a wedge more clearly than do others.

Pye realizes, of course, that the more specific the functional requirements of the object are, and the stronger the constraints imposed on it, the narrower the range of choices available to the designer. Thus an engine offers less

255

freedom than a flower vase, and a jet airplane less than a paper kite. Pier Luigi Nervi has pointed out that, for example, buildings exceeding 300 feet either in height or in span "have static and construction requirements which become ever more determining with the progressive increase in these dimensions." If technological progress is irreversible, asserts Nervi, the style determined by it "can never again change." However, even Nervi believes that despite technical constraints, "there always remains a margin of freedom sufficient to show the personality of the creator of the work and, if he be an artist, to allow that his creation, even in its strict technical obedience, become a real and true work of art."

The "margin of freedom" left open by the constraints of physical function is what concerns us here. How is the architect to use this margin? A desire to display the creator's own personality must certainly not be the prime mover—we are all too well acquainted with the distressing results of such motivation. Then is the freedom to be used to make the building "a real and true work of art"? But what is such a work of art like? The typical answer, in our own tradition even to the present day, has been that form should provide formal beauty. And if we press further and ask what is meant by beauty, we find, for example, Leone Battista Alberti defining beauty as "a harmony of all the parts, in whatsoever subject it appears, fitted together with such proportion and connection that nothing could be added, diminished, or altered, but for the worse."

This harmony of proportion, *concinnitas universarum partium*, is considered even today the designer's one and only "aesthetic" obligation, and it is thought of as quite separate from, indeed unrelated to, the requirements of practical function. In our own time, beauty of form is sometimes reduced to meaning nothing more than attractive workmanship. Pye, for example, after enumerating the practical requirements of use, ease, and economy, adds "the requirements of appearance," by which he means the "useless," although not worthless, qualities of surface finish, smoothness, flatness, fairness of curves, neat fitting, etc.

Such accounts of the matter are sadly incomplete. The demand for harmony and good proportion does not tell us what kinds of form are to be harmonized and proportioned; nor does insistence on neat workmanship. Physical function does not sufficiently determine form and no such determination explains why a visible kinship should result between function and expression. The meaning of beauty, as I hope to indicate, emerges only if we understand beauty as a way of perfecting expression.

256

WHAT VESSELS EXPRESS

Buildings, says Etienne-Louis Boullée at the begining of his essay on architecture, should in some way be poems: "The images they offer our senses should arouse sentiments analogous to the use to which those buildings are dedicated." The emphasis must be on the word *analogous*. But how are we to understand the kind of analogy in question, and how is it to be brought about? Let me use for a somewhat systematic demonstration a functional object that is simpler and therefore more easily described than most buildings, namely ceramic vases.

Figure 131 gives the outlines of a few types of ancient Greek vessels. They were made to hold wine, water, or oil, and sometimes to display flowers. For argument's sake, I shall assume that they all perform their physical function adequately, and that the great variety of shapes, of which I give but a small sample, cannot be explained simply by the different uses to which the vases

Figure 131

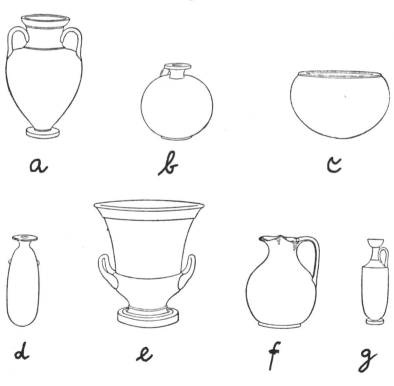

are put. They all serve the three basic functions of receiving, containing, and dispensing, and they all have handles.

The common way of dealing with the shape of such objects "aesthetically" has little reference to either their function or their expression. By investigating the shapes "in themselves"—their proportions, curvatures, etc.—one may arrive at certain formal criteria, which accord with our intuitive sense of pleasantly proportioned and shaped objects. Two observations are in order with regard to this procedure.

First, the discovery of geometric regularity in an object does not *explain* the positive qualities experienced in the concomitant perceptual relations. The obvious musical examples are the simple spatial ratios discovered by the Pythagoreans for the tones of the musical scale, when produced on a string. Neither the relations between linear distances on a string nor the similar ratios found later among the wavelengths of sound vibrations explain why those intervals display a simple harmony when they are heard. The correspondences strongly suggest a causal relation between structural properties of the physiological stimulus and those of the percepts, but further theorizing is required to explain the nature of the relation.

Similarly, the geometrical formulae of the Fibonacci series or the golden section neither prove that the corresponding spatial ratios, picked perhaps from Le Corbusier's Modulor series, are agreeable to the human eye, nor explain why this should be so. A good deal of fancy biological and psychological speculation would be required to make the causal link between stimulus and percept plausible.

More important for our purpose is a second observation. There is no point in evaluating the harmony of pleasant relations between forms "in themselves" when these forms are meant to embody a functional theme, such as that of receiving, containing, and dispensing. The particular dynamics of each shape and each relation between shapes is influenced by that function. Perceptual appearance varies accordingly. The neck of an amphora may look elegantly slender when it is seen as the channel through which wine is poured (Fig. 131a); but the same relative size may look humorously stocky when it is seen as belonging to a human neck. This is not simply because humans generally have a slenderer neck. Different standards of relative size apply to the function of being the stem of a head than to the function of being a duct leading to an opening.

The mathematician George Birkhoff, testing his "aesthetic measure" on Greek and Chinese vases, stipulates a range of measurements that vases must not transcend if they are to avoid instability and injury and are to be handled easily. Within these limitations he treats the dimensions of a vase as geometric entities in their own right, as though they could equally well belong to some other object or to none at all. He seems never to consider that when, for example, two parts of a vase are of the same size, it makes all the difference for their dynamic relations whether they are the neck and the foot or whether they embody some other functions.

When Le Corbusier, playing a venerable game, discovers that two pairs of the principal diagonals on the façade of Michelangelo's Palazzo Senatorio in Rome meet at right angles, he has not unlocked the secret of the beautiful composition (Fig. 132). That simple relation between the rectangles of the façade works well only because the building as a whole has just the right dimensions for its place and function on the Capitoline square. The same relation would look squeezed or bloated if the shape of the building were not appropriate to its function or if the size of the two projecting bays were not in keeping with their role in the total structure. The underlying geometric regularities may contribute to the pleasant effect, but they would not look right if the shapes to which they apply did not serve the building's purpose.

What, however, is that purpose? Surely not just the requirements of practical utility. Let us return to the Greek vases. If we observe that their contours embody the functions of receiving, containing, and dispensing, what do we

Figure 132

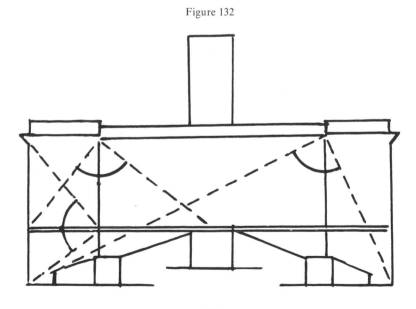

259

mean by embodiment? Not merely that the vessel's shape is physically suited to meeting these requirements—a necessary, but not a sufficient, condition. Rather we mean to point out, for example, that roundness as a visual dynamic quality expresses containing. The convexity of the boundary gathers the contents of the vessel around the center. This function is most fully expressed in the spherical aryballos, an oil bottle intended to contain a good deal and to dispense little at any one time (Fig. 131b). Here the dynamics of concentric containing is so dominant that the small neck looks almost like an unwonted interruption.

In the other examples of Figure 131 the theme of concentricity is combined with the themes of receiving and dispensing. These are expressed visually by the dynamics along a vertical axis. In the lebes, a bowl, this upward direction is indicated only by the slicing off of the container's top (c). As a subtlety of this particular shape, the curvature starts at the bottom with a rather large radius; but toward the top, as though suddenly aware of the approaching challenge to its closure, it intensifies its curvature to the extent of almost reaching closure before the opening can interfere.

The alabastron, a perfume bottle, modifies containing with dispensing all the way through its elongated shape (d). In the calyx-crater, used for the mixing of wine, the contour wholly subordinates the large upper part of the container to the function of receiving and pouring by employing a crescendo toward the opening as the principal theme and replacing convexity with concavity (e). Here, the action interrupted by the rim is not closing but further expanding.

Note that what we are discussing in these descriptions are purely visual characteristics of the functions as visual themes. The physical aspects of receiving, containing, and dispensing are only items of practical information, which contribute "subject matter" to the visual dynamics of the image.

Perhaps the particular nature of my approach will be clarified by a reference to the so-called conservation experiments, devised by Jean Piaget. In these experiments, a child is presented with two identical beakers, each filled with the same amount of liquid. The contents of one of them is poured into a third beaker, which is taller and thinner (Fig. 133). A young child will assert that the taller beaker contains more water even though he has watched the pouring. A somewhat older child will realize that the quantity has remained the same. Psychologists tend to assume that the younger child is simply wrong, that the correct judgment of equality and inequality concerns only physical quantity. Thus they fail to acknowledge that the perceptual in-

Figure 133

equality of the same amounts in the two differently shaped containers is a legitimate phenomenon in itself. The naive observer declares that there is more liquid in the taller container, not simply because appearance deceives him—which may indeed be the case—but because the perceptual experience is the primary reality and therefore quite naturally the first thing to talk about. He will be backed by any visual artist, for whom perceptual facts preserve their primacy; and the older child, no longer "deceived by appearance," may be well on his way to acquiring practical efficiency at the price of crippling his senses. The primary perceptual evidence is what we must consider in the present discussion.

I spoke of the three main functions represented visually through the shapes of the vases. Let me add here that the types of vases differ in their way of representing these functions. Most of them offer a clear visual distinction between the belly, as the representative of containing, and the neck, which stands for receiving and pouring. This distinction can be made by a gentle and gradual turn of the curve from convexity to concavity, as in the oinochoë, a wine jug (f). Or it can be expressed by a sudden edge, interrupting the body of the container, swinging inward to form the neck and then, with the same suddenness, outward again for the spout. These pointed turns give the lekythos, a slender ointment jug, its look of nervous intelligence (g). However, a vessel may also lack such differentiation of function. It may look like a primitive creature which has not yet attained that more elaborate level

261

of organization. Or it may display the sophisticated elegance of a solution that has passed beyond the simple-minded formula of a separate shape for each particular function and has succeeded in combining several functions in a common complex design.

To combine different functions in a common design, however, is a special art. It requires that these various functions be kept visually present, in spite of their fusion. When Frank Lloyd Wright, in his Guggenheim Museum, combined the horizontality of floor spaces with the gradual transition from one floor to the next, the resulting spiral kept both functions in sight and demonstrated their union in a strikingly intelligent solution. This is quite different from the sort of reckless primitivism that forces a variety of functions into an arbitrarily simplified shape. There may be some justification for Vincent Scully's remark that Eero Saarinen's auditorium for the Massachusetts Institute of Technology forces "all functions, appropriately or not, into a single geometric shape." Whatever the architect's solution, we have reasons to scrutinize it with interested participation, because the problem of how to unite different activities in a common enterprise is a constant concern of all of ours.

SPONTANEOUS SYMBOLISM: MIES AND NERVI

One cannot describe the dynamic qualities of shape without at the same time invoking their spontaneous symbolism. Functions such as receiving, containing, and dispensing are by no means limited to vases, or to physical activities more generally, but are immediately relatable also to fundamental aspects of human social behavior, to qualities like generosity and exploitation, acquisitiveness, stinginess, husbandry, etc. It is my contention that these symbolic overtones accompany perception not only in rare moments of aesthetic contemplation but whenever we look at an object and handle it with some involvement of our natural sensitivity. For the most part, these are open symbols, as I have called them earlier, in that they do not signify specific applications but refer to the broad range of possible examples for which the generic perceptual properties stand.

At the same time, these open symbols differ from some conventional symbols by their compelling necessity. As Lipps pointed out, there is nothing esoteric, nothing arbitrary, about them. "Especially the formal symbolism of particular shapes becomes a very simple matter, so simple that in the end it looks like a mere tautology. In fact, what could be more redundant than the observation that something upright rights itself, that a bent shape bends, or

262

that a widening shape expands?" It is necessary, however, continues Lipps, to acknowledge these qualities with the greatest seriousness and to be aware of what they imply and what necessarily follows from them.

Another characteristic of the spontaneous symbolism of perceptual form needs to be pointed out here. Verbal language accustoms us to thinking of the properties of objects as adjectives, that is, as things attached to things. However, as soon as we consider these properties dynamically, we find that they belong to activities rather than things, and are therefore adverbial rather than adjectival. When we call the shape of a teapot graceful we mean, more accurately, that the teapot pours gracefully. Or we may observe that it contains pompously, or that, in the act of receiving, it surrenders unreservedly. This is why I suggested earlier that perceptual expression conveys ways of being and behaving.

The relatively simple examples of ceramic vessels have served to illustrate the relation between form and function. Form, it turns out, is not simply the physical facilitation of function. Rather, it *translates* an object's functions into the language of perceptual expression. The visible capacity to contain and to pour in a certain characteristic way is not simply what we observe when we become aware of what takes place physically. It is a visual *analogy* —Boullée's term—to the object's practical functions.

Let us examine now an example closer to architecture, namely a piece of furniture. When one looks at Mies van der Rohe's famous Barcelona chair of 1929, one notices first of all the absence of vertical and horizontal components (Fig. 134). The pattern shuns the easy stability of upright legs and the reliable horizontality of the conventional seat. Especially when compared with the uncompromising framework of a Mies building, this piece of furniture, by tilt and curve, introduces the presence of man as an element of life. In keeping with a particularly modern behavior, this chair does not require the user to adapt his body to the rigidity of the basic framework but adapts itself to his comfort. The right-angular straightness of back and seat is tempered by the tilt, a partial concession to the pull of gravity, and this tilt makes the back of the chair serve as a support rather than as a brace enforcing straightness. Throughout the chair's design, strict adherence to principles of order is combined with flexible yielding. The two longer steel bars fuse the verticality of a supporting back with the horizontality of a floor base, and the resulting curve expresses the yielding to the weight of the user's body.

The same curve, however, displays enough firmness to sustain the weight safely. Visually, assurance of unflagging support is given by the curve's being

263

Figure 134. Barcelona chair. Knoll International, New York.

part of a circle. Circles are the hardest, most inflexible curves. More generally, the design attains visual stability by conforming to simple geometrical relations. Mies seems to have inscribed the profile of his chair in a square (Fig. 135). The upper right corner of the square serves as the center for the circular curve of the principal steel bar, which thereby acts as a curved diagonal. At its middle the circular curve is touched by the seat cushion; and the crossing of the two bars divides the square at the ratio of 2:3.

All this geometry comes as a surprise after one has been intuitively caught up by the superb blend of leisurely grace and reliable sturdiness in the chair's appearance. The complexity of the dynamic theme is embodied also in the geometry of the shallow S-curve in the lower steel bar which comes close enough to a straight line to endorse the austere simplicity of the design but plays around that straightness like an arabesque, a descendant of Hogarth's serpentine "line of beauty." The S-curve once again combines the dimensions of verticality and horizontality, the upward rising of the support and the horizontal base; it sustains and also yields to the weight carried by the seat.

There is finally the contrast between the substantial volume of the pliable pillows and the immaterial abstractness of the hard metal curves, a meeting

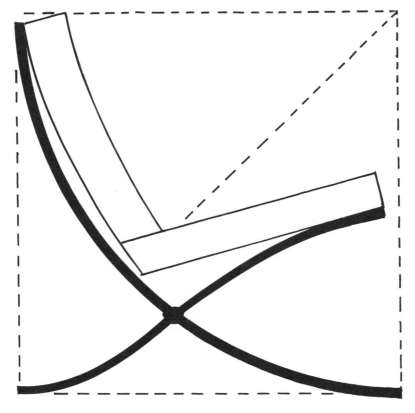

Figure 135

between weighty substance and disembodied energy, which keeps the user safely suspended above the ground by means of intangible forces—symbolic allusions to our bold modern ways of dispensing with load-bearing walls and keeping airplanes aloft.

Perhaps these examples have begun to show concretely what takes place when good design makes an object appear as pure form—the spiritualization of which Konrad Fiedler spoke so mysteriously, yet persuasively. The compelling dynamics of the Mies chair dematerializes the physical object by transforming it into the carrier of a constellation of forces. The validity of the constellation goes far beyond the expression of the particular chair. It symbolizes a way of life, the cultural circumstances under which the object was conceived.

A somewhat comparable theme, simple enough to yield to verbal analysis

265

Figure 136. P. L. Nervi. Municipal Stadium. Florence.

and sophisticated enough to epitomize architectural expression, is the section through Pier Luigi Nervi's grandstand of the Municipal Stadium designed for the city of Florence in 1928 (Fig. 136). The section is directly accessible in the photograph because the building was under construction when it was taken. But the visual pattern it reveals serves as an inherent skeleton even in the completed building. In Nervi's design, the visual stability of the vertical-horizontal framework is explicitly stated. Even the relation between the roof and the vertical supports of the back is close to a right angle—close enough to make the slight curvature of the rooftop surface appear as a deviation from the horizontal. This reference to the flat horizontal increases the expressive strength of the rise.

Within the basically rectangular framework the inclined plane of the seats acts as a sturdy diagonal. The openness of the box toward the front answers the need of the spectators to have their view unimpeded by columns. But this openness would leave the roof looking precariously unsupported were it not for the cantilevered beams, which transform the roof into a gracefully bent wedge. The weight of this wedge is centered in the well-supported back of the building, and the wedge diminishes in bulk as it swings toward the opening. Like the steel bars of the Mies chair, the profile of Nervi's roof translates the combined theme of rising and supporting into visible dynamics by an elastic combination of curvature and straightness.

Through the freedom of its outreach, this graceful shape demonstrates modern man's power to emancipate himself effortlessly from the pull of gravity, while at the same time obeying the laws of terrestrial existence. The simple validity of this solution is highly original, yet free from arbitrary individuality. The shape and arrangement of the building's components faithfully adhere to the requirements of physical statics; but they also translate the play of forces into a visual pattern that interprets the dynamic theme to the eyes of the viewer. And the spontaneous symbolism conveyed by this pattern carries an expressive message about the condition of twentieth-century man. This is a way of saying that the design of the grandstand in Florence fulfills the task of architecture. It does so with such purity of form and intelligent simplicity of invention that I would not hesitate to count Nervi's works among the very few that will survive untouched by cultural change.

The example of this simple, two-dimensionally interpreted theme may stand here for the infinite ways in which the role of a building is conceived through the ages. Simple or complex, reposing or rising, open or closed, austere or playful, compact or sprawling, each building meets essentially similar tasks by displaying the variety of attitudes man brings to the challenges of his existence.

BUILDINGS MOLD BEHAVIOR

One cannot do full justice to the visual expression of architectural objects by treating them as detached sights, as though they existed merely to be looked at. Such objects not only reflect the attitudes of the people by and for whom they were made, they also actively shape human behavior. Some years ago, the Vietnam peace talks in Paris were delayed by a problem of *ébénisterie diplomatique*, as the French called it, a problem of diplomatic cabinetmaking. The representatives of the United States and North Vietnam haggled over the shape of the table at which the negotiators would sit. Should it be angular or round, shaped like a diamond, a doughnut, or a double crescent? The discussion aroused much hilarity, but it was ridiculous only in length of time. It was a substantial matter because it involved visual acknowledgment of who was dealing with whom. The United States, in the interest of the Saigon government, refused to accept the Vietcong as a contending party. According to the *New York Times*, it therefore proposed a bilateral grouping, with the Americans and South Vietnamese seated opposite the representatives of North Vietnam and the Vietcong. Hanoi insisted on a four-sided arrangement; it was willing to accept a round table, which would seat the parties in four groups, but this was agreeable to the Americans only if a line were painted across the table. Hanoi refused to accept the dividing line, which would have transformed the centric symmetry of the table into a bilateral one.

The physical layout of a situation has been considered important through the ages for all ceremonial occasions. It not only influences the behavior of the participants, it also defines their social status. The questions of how many parties there are, how they are grouped, the distance between them, who is at the head and who below, are symbolized by spatial relations involving shape, distance, height, etc. The acceptance of the spatial arrangement is primary evidence for the acceptance of the corresponding social pattern. This has always been true, and architecture has played a prominent part in providing an appropriate setting.

Whether a person is confined to a narrow path or given wide latitude determines the role assigned to him and his way of playing it. It will be remembered that Mussolini received his callers in a large hall in the Palazzo

Venezia. The visitor had to cross the entire empty space, unaided by any guiding support and scrutinized by the dictator, who sat ensconced behind his monumental desk at the other end of the room. Or again, the entrance door to a traditional Japanese tea ceremony house is kept very low, so that each participant has to humble himself before gaining admittance.

When people face one another around a table they testify to their convivial status, that is, to their "living together" for the occasion. The audience in the usual theater or lecture hall professes a mere parallelism of purpose and target, which is quite different from doing things *with* other people. When Goethe reported on his Italian journey, he remarked on the arena of Verona that "an amphitheater is truly suited to impressing the people with themselves and letting them serve as a spectacle for one another." The architect

had provided by his art a crater, as simple as possible, so that the people themselves might serve as its ornament. When they saw themselves gathered in this fashion, they had to marvel, for they had been accustomed elsewhere to seeing one another running back and forth in a disorderly and undisciplined confusion. But in the theater, the wobbling, roaming animal of the many heads and the many senses sees itself unified in a noble body, shaped into unison, fused in one mass and stabilized as one form, and animated by one spirit. The simplicity of the oval is felt by every eye in the pleasantest manner, and every single head serves as a measure for the immensity of the whole. Seeing the building empty, one has no standard by which to tell whether it is large or small.

Here again one thinks of Wright's Guggenheim Museum, in which man is distanced from man by the central court. He sees his fellow visitors as a detached picture of people looking at pictures and presenting him with part of the same crowd with which he himself is mingling. At the same time, by its spiral shape, the building programs the visitor's action as a linear path through a one-dimensional environment, which is particularly appropriate when the exhibition itself calls for a one-dimensional sequence, for example, when the work of an artist or period is shown in chronological order.

But the channeling of traffic is only the most tangible aspect of the building's impact on its users. Buildings have a large share in determining to what extent every one of us is an individual or a member of a group, and to what extent we act out of freely made decisions or in obedience to spatial boundaries. All these conditions amount to configurations of forces. Only because the building itself is experienced as a configuration of forces, namely, as a particular pattern of constraints, dimensions of freedom, attractions and repulsions, can the architectural setting serve as a part of the dynamic whole that constitutes our lives.

HOW IDEAS GAIN SHAPE

Let me return once more to the structural theme or skeleton of every piece of design. I have described it as the carrier of the building's principal meaning, which the viewer must grasp if he is to understand the design as a whole. We need to add here that this basic theme is also the germ of the idea that guides the architect in developing his design. This does not necessarily mean that in the actual chronological course of events every architect starts with this relatively simple core concept and proceeds gradually to more and more detail. In actual practice, the first spark of an invention may come from the specific image of a particular aspect, from which one may work one's way back to the central theme. More often than not, the creative process moves fairly erratically back and forth between conceptions of the whole and of the parts. Only when one surveys the process in its entirety does one become aware of the logical order that leads from the basic theme to its final embodiment. It is like watching a young child's manner of running back and forth and yielding to peripheral distractions while making for a goal: looked at as a whole, these disorderly spurts are integrated into a sequence of goal-directed behavior.

The germinal theme is crucial to all human inventions. Whether it be a work of art, a piece of machinery, a scientific theory, or a business organization, they all sprout from a central idea and grow around it. In the case of architecture, however, the central theme also serves as the bridge between the program for a building and its design. The relation between these two fundamental components has been something of a puzzle in architectural theory. It is also a source of friction between the client, who speaks the language of his needs, and the architect, who thinks in terms of visual shapes and physical materials. How the needs of the one can be translated into the resources of the other is not obvious. For example, the program for a library may speak of the number of books and readers to be accommodated, the variety of materials to be provided, the services to be offered, the requirements for access, ready connection, and separation, and perhaps also the state of mind the building should evoke and the idea it should stand for within the community.

None of these functions is directly visual, and not all of them can be, or need be, met by the architecture. A building cannot teach French or manufacture high-quality typewriters. It can serve the user's purposes only to the extent that they can be translated into architectural means, the most important of which are spatial sizes, shapes, and relations. But how is the translation into spatial properties to be accomplished? The problem encountered here in theory and in practice may be illustrated by a definition given in the mid-1960s by Tomás Maldonado, then director of the *Hochschule für Gestaltung* in Ulm. He defined industrial design as "an activity whose ultimate aim is to determine the formal properties of the objects produced by industry. By 'formal properties' is not meant the external features, but rather those structural and functional relations which convert an object into a coherent unity from the point of view of both the producer and the user"; and he went on to state that "the merely external features are often only the result of the intention to make an object superficially more attractive, or to dissimulate its constitutional deficiencies, and thus they represent an accidental reality, neither born nor developed together with the object." The question arises: If design is not to consist of tangible, visual shapes—a rather remarkable stipulation on the part of the man heading an institution that, as the successor of the Bauhaus, was dedicated to *gestaltung*—in what medium are those "structural and functional relations" to be conceived?

And here it is essential to realize that, quite apart from architectural design, the "program" of a building is itself bound to assume the form of a visual pattern if it is to make the raw data of entities and quantities apply to any form of organization. This is evident if one thinks of a flow chart, any tree of a business organization or administrative hierarchy, or the analysis of any process, be it the organic functions of the human body or the logical development of an argument. They all need to be laid out spatially, and more often than not the spatial image is given actual visual shape on paper in a chart or diagram.

It is at that stage of the thought process that programming can make contact with the search for the basic theme of a building's design. If, for example, the function to be performed requires that a number of branch activities all have equal access to a central control office, the mind automatically conceives of a circular arrangement around a center. From there, the translation into the plan for a building becomes feasible, even though the building is not a figment of disembodied spatial relations but a material object, dependent on the laws of nature and the physical and psychological properties of materials and human inhabitants. Now project and design speak the same language of visual thinking.

It is quite true that at early stages of a conception the thought model does not commonly assume the definitive shapes of the final object. Just as the relational pattern of Figure 83 is only a configuration of dynamic forces,

271

which could be depicted on paper as an arrangement of squares or triangles rather than of disks, so the structural theme of a building often takes the form of a system of arrows, of volumes defined by directions, overall proportions, and purely topological relations. This, however, does not prevent the skeleton from being visual. In fact, vision is the only medium in which the mind can apprehend it. And once a particular building is the final target, there is no stopping at a particular stage of the designing, no point at which the "structural" turns into the "visual," no point at which essence gives way to "external" shape. The conception is visual throughout, and it remains an organization of dynamic forces all the way to the final shape, which alone admits the project to physical reality and presence. References to bad design, which may indeed aim for superficial attraction or the dissimulation of deficiencies, are beside the point when the nature of architecture is under discussion.

ALL THOUGHTS TAKE TO BUILDING

When the human mind organizes a body of thought, it does so almost inevitably in terms of spatial imagery. This will have become evident from what I said about programs for buildings, and I can think of no more appropriate point with which to complete the argument of this book. The design of a building is the spatial organization of thoughts about its functions. Conversely, any organization of thoughts assumes the form of an architectural structure. Thus Kant, toward the end of his *Critique of Pure Reason* writes a chapter on what he calls the architectonics of pure reason. By architectonics he means "the art of systems." Although Kant speaks of pure thoughts, the architect will persuade himself that what is here under discussion is his business. Kant's principal paragraph deserves to be given completely:

Under the rule of reason, our cognitions must not be rhapsodic but must form a system, which alone enables them to support and promote reason's principal purposes. By a system I mean the unification of the manifold cognitions under one idea. This idea is the rational concept of the form of a whole, to the extent to which it determines *a priori* the range of the manifold and the position of the parts in relation to one another. This is to say that the rational scientific concept contains the purpose and the form of the whole, which is congruent to it. Owing to the unity of the purpose, to which all the parts refer and in view of which they also relate among themselves, any one part can be missing as long as all the others are known; and no accidental addition can be made, nor can any dimension of the completed totality be undefined, that is, not determined *a priori* by definite boundaries. It follows that the whole is articulated and not aggregated; it can grow, but only through internal action, not

272

externally, just as the body of an animal does not grow by adding limbs but rather strengthens each of them and makes it better suited to its purpose without any change of proportion.

All good thinking, then, can be said to aspire toward the condition of architecture. Thus André Maurois praises Marcel Proust's main work by saying that it has the simplicity and the majesty of a cathedral, and he quotes from a letter Proust wrote Jean de Gaigneron in 1919:

I had meant to give each part of my book such titles as *porch, stained-glass windows of the apse*, etc., in anticipation of the stupid criticism that books whose sole merit, as I shall show you, consists in the solidity of their slightest parts, are lacking in structure. However, I gave up these architectural titles right away because I found them too pretentious.

To demonstrate what is meant by the architectural organization of thought, I cite one of the very few drawings Sigmund Freud made as a means of illustrating his concepts, which throughout his work are highly visual and spatial (Fig. 137). In what he calls "a modest drawing," Freud undertakes to describe the complex interrelation between two sets of fundamental psychoanalytic concepts, namely unconscious, preconscious, and conscious, and

Figure 137

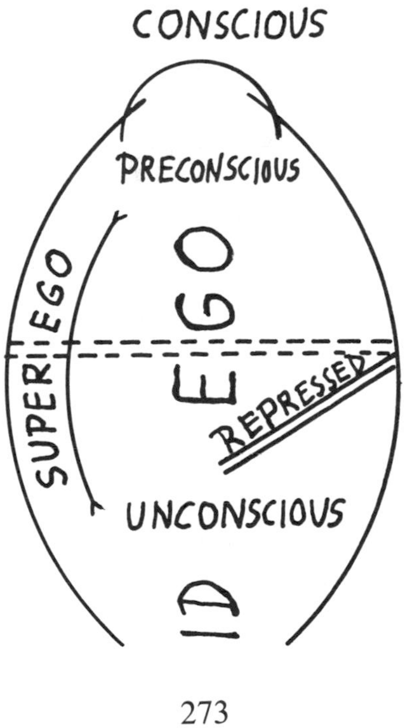

273

id, ego, and superego. The principal dimension to be represented is that of the distance from the station point of consciousness, i.e., the dimension of depth. Hence an elevation is more appropriate than a horizontal plan. The representation is not quite true-to-scale: Freud observes that the realm of the unconscious ought to be much larger. This flaw, however, is of minor importance, because the drawing is topological rather than metric. The size ratios are mere approximations, and the circular shapes serve simply to convey the notion of containing, just as the dotted straight line merely indicates the distinction between the unconscious and the preconscious. Freud emphasizes that no precise boundaries are intended: "We cannot do justice to the particular nature of the psyche by linear contours, such as the ones used in my drawing or found in primitive paintings. The diffuse color fields of the modern painters would do better."

The drawing inevitably commits itself to particular shapes, but it illustrates a level of reasoning concerned with general spatial relations, such as contiguity, sequence, connection, separation, overlap. Even so, the conception is entirely visual, and if it were to be executed as a building, the working-out of the actual shapes and dimensions could continue from here without a break.

Two observations are pertinent. First, although Freud's drawing consists inevitably of shapes, it is actually the translation of a system of forces into a perceptually tangible medium. Forces are visible only through their embodiment, just as a wind needs clouds or water or trees to show up. Freud's drawing depicts the upsurge of buried energy from the depth of the id toward the liberating realm of consciousness. It shows the horizontal barrier that blocks this upward motion. It also shows the opening provided by the superego, which acts as a bridge. Underlying the construct of shapes, just as in architecture, is a configuration of forces.

Second, the visual model is not simply a pedagogical device, not simply an analogy, a directly perceivable metaphor used to facilitate understanding of the complex dynamics of interacting forces. The drawing indicates the medium in which Freud himself thought because no other medium is available for studying the configuration of psychic forces. The drawing is metaphorical in the sense that no such architecture exists in the human brain, but it is also factual in the sense that it directly illustrates the relations between the forces Freud was concerned with.

Since all human thoughts must be worked out in the medium of perceptual space, architecture, wittingly or not, presents embodiments of thought when it invents and builds shapes.

NOTES

CHAPTER I

P. 9. Plato's *Timaeus*, 50/51. From *The Dialogues of Plato*, transl. B. Jewett (New York, 1892).

P. 18. For visual attraction and repulsion, see Arnheim (4) ch. I. (Numbers in parenthesis refer to the Bibliography.)

P. 19. The social aspects of proxemics are described by Hall (48) and (49), ch. 10.

P. 24. Zucker (126), pp. 7 and 16.

P. 26. Robert Musil (80), ch. 87, p. 630.

P. 28. Portoghesi (94), pp. 80, 82.

CHAPTER II

P. 34. Lodovico Dolce on clock towers (32), p. 119.

P. 34. On the relation between visual and kinesthetic orientation, see Witkin (122).

P. 35. Norberg-Schulz on verticality (83), p. 21; on rooted huts (84) p. 110.

P. 35. Wright on the horizontal plane (125), pp. 67, 17.

P. 36. Bachelard (19), p. 34.

P. 37. Fig. 17 is traced from a 1929 still life by Morandi. Private collection.

P. 41. The baptistery in Pisa, designed by Dioti Salvi, was built between 1153 and 1278. According to Fletcher (37), its arcade is "surmounted by Gothic additions of the 14th century, which disguise the original design" (pp. 319–20). Donato Bramante's Tempietto (1502–10) stands in the cloister of San Pietro in Montorio, Rome.

P. 45. The quotation on Laugier in Herrmann (53), p. 30.

P. 45. Portoghesi on directions in walls (94), p. 125.

P. 46. On visual weight in relation to location, see Arnheim (4), ch. 1.

P. 47. Northwick Park State Hospital after Banham (20), p. 11.

P. 51. On the entasis of columns see Vitruvius, *The Ten Books on Architecture*, ch. 4. Vitruvius also notes that the level of the stylobate must be increased along the middle, otherwise "it will look to the eye as though it were hollowed a little."

P. 52. Neutra (82), p. 48.

P. 52. On Nervi's Unesco building, Persitz (89).

P. 55. Le Corbusier's Carpenter Center for the Visual Arts at Harvard University was completed in 1964.

P. 57. On the spatial conception of early sculpture, see Arnheim (4), pp. 215ff.

P. 59. Robert Wiene's *The Cabinet of Dr. Caligari* is a German film of 1919.

P. 61. Scheerbart (103), p. 53.

P. 64. Golding (46), pp. 84, 103, 213.

CHAPTER III

P. 67. For an introduction to Wertheimer's discussion of gestalt psychology, Wertheimer (120), and Asch (17).

P. 68. Perception of figure and ground, Koffka (61), ch. 5, and Arnheim (4), ch. 5; also Kennedy (60), ch. 6.

P. 69. Figure and ground in Escher's prints, Teuber (114).

P. 70. Fig. 37 is freely adapted from the outlines of a relief by Jean Arp.

P. 71. On Archytas, Jammer (59), p. 8.

P. 71. Lipps on the countertendency (67), p. 50.

P. 72. Exhibition of David Carr's stalactites at the Bertha Schaefer Gallery, New York, 1969.

P. 72. Aristotle defining space, *Categories*, ch. 6.

P. 73. Contour rivalry, Arnheim (4), p. 223.

P. 76. Detached houses, Kruse (62), p. 54.

P. 76. Nature of the street, Norberg-Schulz (83), p. 83.

P. 78. Function of streets, Berndt, et al. (21), p. 17.

P. 79. Portoghesi (94), p. 34.

P. 79. Heidegger (50), p. 152.

P. 81. Fig. 43 is reproduced from Schaefer-Simmern (102), p. 42.

P. 84. On Mondrian, Sweeney (113), p. 25.

P. 84. Object lines, Arnheim (4), p. 219.

P. 85. Quattro Fontane, Zucker (126), p. 158.

P. 86. Lipps on expansion (67), p. 54.

P. 91. Centralized churches, Wittkower (123), p. 29; for early Christian examples, see Guyer (47).

P. 91. Symposium on Inside and Outside: (57).

P. 92. W. Zucker (57), p. 158.

P. 92. Adolf Portmann: *Entlässt die Natur den Menschen?* Part I. Munich: 1970.

P. 94. Bachelard (19), p. 210.

P. 94. Tao Tê Ching, Waley (117), ch. 11.

P. 95. Brinckmann (26), p. 11.

P. 95. Hagia Sophia: Watterson (57) and MacDonald (71), plate 56.

P. 97. Animal architecture, von Frisch (43), p. 197.

P. 97. Rasmussen (98), p. 50.

P. 99. Wright on folded planes (125), p. 19.

P. 100. Quotation from Musil (80), ch. 21. Translation mine.

P. 102. St. Sernin, Focillon (38), p. 20.

P. 104. Portoghesi's theater in Cagliari (94), p. 160.

P. 104. Early Christian tombs, Guyer (47), p. 30.

P. 107. Ronchamp, Bolle-Reddat (23).

P. 108. Venturi (116), p. 88.

CHAPTER IV

P. 111. Frankl (39), pp. 144, 151.

P. 112. Norberg-Schulz (84), p. 93.

P. 112. Perspective projection, Arnheim (4), pp. 287ff.

P. 114. Rasmussen (98), p. 39.

P. 117. Dome of Florence, Lynch (70), p. 102.

P. 118. Piaget (91), ch. 8.

P. 118. Clock towers, Proust (95), pp. 214ff.

P. 119. Butor (27), "Les 'moments' de Marcel Proust."

P. 121. Geminiani, *Sonata in E-minor for oboe and basso continuo.*

P. 124. Lévi-Strauss (65), p. 35.

P. 124. Experiments on mental images, Shepard and Metzler (109).

P. 124. Stevens on allometry (111), the effect of scale, pp. 16–33; see also Thompson (115), ch. 2, "On Magnitude."

P. 133. Additive seeing, Schubert (104), ch. 3.

P. 133. Le Corbusier's modulor (64), and Arnheim (14).

CHAPTER V

P. 145. Mobile homes, Scully (106), p. 61.

P. 146. Alberti (2), VII, p. 17.

P. 147. Freud on the prosthetic god (41), sect. III.

P. 149. Frankl on circulation paths (39), p. 15.

P. 152. Design of steps, Fitch et al. (36).

P. 152. Goethe, *Baukunst* (fragment).

P. 153. Child's floorplan, Church (29), p. 9.

P. 154. Lym (69).

P. 156. Pevsner on Bruchsal (90), p. 284; on Sant' Andrea, p. 196.

P. 159. Motion perspective, Gibson (44).

P. 159. Nerval's poem, Pichois (93), p. 11. I am indebted for this reference to Prof. Marcel Muller, University of Michigan.

P. 159. Vézelay, Venturi (116), p. 54.

CHAPTER VI

P. 162. Order and disorder in landscaping, Arnheim (12).

P. 164. Order in closed systems, Arnheim, *Entropy and Art*, Berkeley and Los Angeles: 1971.

P. 166. Hôtel de Matignon, Pevsner (90), p. 334, Venturi (116), p. 88.

P. 170. Anonymous architecture, Rudofsky (101), Portoghesi (94), p. 134.

P. 173. Certosa in Pavia, Fletcher (37), p. 684.

P. 177. Memorial Church, Berlin, architects Egon Eiermann and R. Wiest, 1959–63.

P. 179. Wieskirche, Venturi (116), p. 69.

P. 180. Nuclear square, Zucker (126), p. 14.

P. 183. Porta Pia, Rasmussen (98), p. 58. Burckhardt quoted after Schwager (105); translation mine.

P. 191. Inflected shapes, Venturi (116), p. 91.

P. 192. Children's drawings, Arnheim (4), Figs. 132, 133.

P. 197. Branchings in plants, Weiss (118), p. 806.

P. 203. Life space, Lewin (66).

CHAPTER VII

P. 207. Symbols and signs, Arnheim (5), ch. 8.

P. 207. Gothic symbolism, Pevsner (90), p. 116; Simson (110), p. 134.

P. 207. Lorenzer (21), p. 89.

P. 208. Law court, Boullée (24), p. 113.

P. 209. Jean Giono (45), p. 27.

P. 210. Indian Sikhara, Frey (42), p. 72.

P. 211. Presbyterian church, Stamford, and TWA Terminal (79).

P. 211. Lipps on empathy (67), ch. 1.

P. 211. Wölfflin (124), p. 15.

P. 212. Visual expression, Arnheim (4), chs. 9, 10, and (11).

P. 213. Moholy-Nagy (77), p. 208.

P. 214. Plato's five solids, *Timaeus* 55, 56.

P. 215. Wallace Stevens, *The Collected Poems* (New York, 1974), p. 76.

P. 215. Self-image and likeness, Arnheim (10), p. 325.

P. 217. Malraux (74), p. 56.

P. 220. Laurentian Library, Ackerman (1), pp. 117, 120.

P. 221. Greenough, *Form and Function* (Berkeley and Los Angeles, 1947), pp. 23–24.

P. 224. Simson on Chartres (110), p. 206.

P. 225. Prussin and Travis (96).

P. 226. Boullée (24), pp. 30, 117.

P. 227. Wright on doors and windows (125), p. 81.

P. 233. Transparency, Portoghesi (94), p. 102.

P. 234. Victor Hugo (55), vol. II, p. 90.

P. 242. Hindus on arches, Encycl. Brit., 11th ed., 1910–11, p. 343.

P. 243. Fiedler (35), p. 472.

P. 245. Cupola of St. Peter's, Arnheim (4), Fig. 278, after Wölfflin.

CHAPTER VIII

P. 249. Vitruvius, *The Ten Books on Architecture*, book IV, ch. 2.

P. 249. Laugier, Herrmann (53), p. 46.

P. 249. Coomaraswamy on ornament (30), pp. 85–99.

P. 250. Wright (125), pp. 63ff.

P. 250. Ornamentation in music, Apel (3), p. 629.

P. 252. Schenker system, Apel (3), p. 754.

P. 253. Psychology of expression, Arnheim (4), chs. 9, 10, and (11).

P. 255. Doric order, Vitruvius, book II, ch. 2.

P. 255. William James (58), vol 1, p. 109.

P. 256. Nervi (81), pp. 184, 187.

P. 256. Alberti on beauty (2), book VI, ch. 2.

P. 257. Buildings as poems, Boullée (24), p. 47.

P. 257. Athenian vases, Richter and Milne (99).

P. 258. Le Corbusier (64), p. 26.

P. 260. Conservation of liquid, Piaget and Infelder (92).

P. 262. Scully (106), p. 36.

P. 264. Line of beauty, Hogarth (54), ch. 9.

P. 268. Peace talks table, *New York Times*, Jan. 16, 1969.

P. 269. Goethe, *Italienische Reise*, Sept. 16, 1786.

P. 271. Maldonado (73), p. 133.

P. 273. Maurois (75), p. 175.

P. 273. Freud (40), XXXI, p. 110.

BIBLIOGRAPHY

1. Ackerman, James S. The architecture of Michelangelo. Baltimore, 1971.
2. Alberti, Leone Battista. Ten books on architecture. New York, 1966.
3. Apel, Willi. Harvard dictionary of music. Cambridge, Mass., 1944.
4. Arnheim, Rudolf. Art and visual perception: the new version. Berkeley and Los Angeles, 1974.
5. _____. Visual thinking. Berkeley and Los Angeles, 1969.
6. _____. The genesis of a painting: Picasso's *Guernica*. Berkeley and Los Angeles, 1973.
7. _____. Lemonade and the perceiving mind. *In* Moorhouse (78), pp. ix-xii.
8. _____. Inverted perspective in art: Display and expression. Leonardo, Spring 1972, vol. 5, pp. 125-35.
9. _____. From function to expression. *In* Arnheim (10), pp. 192-212.
10. _____. Toward a psychology of art. Berkeley and Los Angeles, 1966.
11. _____. The gestalt theory of expression. *In* Arnheim (10), pp. 51-73.
12. _____. Order and complexity in landscape design. *In* Arnheim (10), pp. 123-35.
13. _____. The robin and the saint. *In* Arnheim (10), pp. 320-34.
14. _____. A review of proportion. *In* Arnheim (10), pp. 102-19.
15. _____. The dynamics of shape. Design Quart. #64. Minneapolis, 1964.
16. _____. and Eduard Sekler. Review of Schubert (104). Journal Soc. of Arch. Hist., March 1969, vol. 28, pp. 77-79.
17. Asch, Solomon E. Max Wertheimer's contribution to modern psychology. Social Research, March 1946, vol. 13, pp. 81-102.
18. _____. The metaphor: a psychological inquiry. *In* Henle (52), pp. 324-34.
19. Bachelard, Gaston. La poétique de l'espace. Paris, 1964. (Engl.: The poetics of space. New York, 1964.)
20. Banham, Reyner. A clip-on architecture. Design Quart. #63, 1965.
21. Berndt. Heide, Alfred Lorenzer, and Klaus Horn. Architektur als Ideologie. Frankfurt, 1968.
22. Birkhoff, George D. Aesthetic measure. Cambridge, Mass., 1933.
23. Bolle-Reddat, Abbé René. Our Lady of the Height, Ronchamp. Munich, 1965.
24. Boullée, Etienne-Louis. Architecture. Essai sur l'art. Paris, 1968.

25. Bower, T. G. R. The visual world of infants. Scient. Amer., Dec. 1966, vol. 215, pp. 80–92.
26. Brinckmann, Albert Erich. Plastik und Raum als Grundformen künstlerischer Gestaltung. Munich, 1922.
27. Butor, Michel. Répertoire, vol. I. Paris, 1960.
28. Chase, William G., ed. Visual information processing. New York, 1973.
29. Church, Joseph. Language and the discovery of reality. New York, 1961.
30. Coomaraswamy, Ananda K. Figures of speech or figures of thought? London, 1946.
31. Cooper, Lynn A. and Roger N. Shepard. Chronometric studies of the rotation of mental images. *In* Chase (28), pp. 75–176.
32. Dolce, Lodovico. Dialogo dei colori. Lanciano, 1913.
33. Edwards, Arthur Trystan. Architectural style. London, 1926.
34. Ellis, Willis D. A source book of gestalt psychology. New York, 1939.
35. Fiedler, Konrad. Bemerkungen über Wesen und Geschichte der Baukunst. *In* Schriften über Kunst, vol. 2, Munich, 1914.
36. Fitch, James M., John Templer, and Paul Corcoran. The dimensions of stairs. Scient. Amer., Oct. 1974, vol. 231, pp. 82–90.
37. Fletcher, Banister. A history of architecture on the comparative method. New York, 1961.
38. Focillon, Henri. The life of forms in art. New York, 1948.
39. Frankl, Paul. Die Entwicklungsphasen der neueren Baukunst. Leipzig, 1914. (Engl.: Principles of architectural history. Cambridge, Mass., 1968.)
40. Freud, Sigmund. Neue Folge der Vorlesungen zur Einführung in die Psychoanalyse. Vienna, 1933. (Engl.: New introductory lectures on psychoanalysis. New York, 1965).
41. _____. Das Unbehagen in der Kultur. Vienna, 1930. (Engl.: Civilization and its discontents. New York, 1958.)
42. Frey, Dagobert. Grundlegung zu einer vergleichenden Kunstwissenschaft. Darmstadt, 1970.
43. Frisch, Karl von. Animal architecture. New York, 1974.
44. Gibson, James J. Motion picture testing and research. Report #7. U.S. Army Air Forces Aviation Psych. Program. Washington, D.C., 1947.
45. Giono, Jean. Que ma joie demeure. Paris, 1949.
46. Golding, William. The spire. New York, 1964.
47. Guyer, Samuel. Grundlagen mittelalterlicher abendländischer Baukunst. Einsiedeln, 1950.
48. Hall, Edward T. The hidden dimension. Garden City, N.Y., 1969.
49. _____. The silent language. New York, 1959.
50. Heidegger, Martin. Bauen Wohnen Denken. *In* Vorträge und Aufsätze. Pfullingen, 1954.
51. Helmholtz, Hermann von. Popular scientific lectures. New York, 1962.
52. Henle, Mary, ed. Documents of gestalt psychology. Berkeley and Los Angeles, 1961.

53. Herrmann, Wolfgang. Laugier and eighteenth century French theory. London, 1962.
54. Hogarth, William. The analysis of beauty. Oxford, 1955.
55. Hugo, Victor. Notre-Dame de Paris, Paris, 1949. (Engl.: Notre Dame de Paris, New York, 1953.)
56. Huxtable, Ada Louise. Pier Luigi Nervi. New York, 1960.
57. Inside and outside in architecture: a symposium. Journal Aesth. Art Crit., Fall 1966, vol. 25, pp. 3–15.
58. James, William. The principles of psychology. New York, 1890.
59. Jammer, Max. Concepts of space. Cambridge, Mass., 1954.
60. Kennedy, John M. A psychology of picture perception. San Francisco, 1974.
61. Koffka, Kurt. Principles of gestalt psychology. New York, 1935.
62. Kruse, Lenelis. Räumliche Umwelt. Berlin, 1974.
63. Lashley, K. S. and J. T. Russell. The mechanism of vision: a preliminary test of innate organization. Journal of Genet. Psych. 1934, vol. 48, pp. 136–44.
64. Le Corbusier. The modulor. Cambridge, Mass., 1954.
65. Lévi-Strauss, Claude. La pensée sauvage. Paris, 1962. (Engl.: The savage mind. Chicago, 1966.)
66. Lewin, Kurt. Principles of topological psychology. New York, 1936.
67. Lipps, Theodor. Raumaesthetik und geometrisch-optische Täuschungen. Schriften d. Gesellschaft f. psychologische Forschung, II. 1897.
68. Loos, Adolf. Gesammelte Schriften. Munich, 1961.
69. Lym, Glenn. Images of home at Peabody Terrace. Unpubl. dissertation, Dept. of Psychology and Social Relations, Harvard University, 1975.
70. Lynch, Kevin. The image of the city. Cambridge, Mass., 1960.
71. MacDonald, William. Early Christian and Byzantine architecture. New York, 1962.
72. Maertens, H. Der optische Massstab oder Die Theorie und Praxis des ästhetischen Sehens in den bildenden Künsten. Berlin, 1884.
73. Maldonado, Tomás. Design education. In Gyorgy Kepes, ed., Education of vision. New York, 1965.
74. Malraux, André. Antimémoires. Paris, 1967. (Engl.: Anti-memoirs. New York, 1970.)
75. Maurois, André. A la recherche de Marcel Proust. Paris, 1949. (Engl.: Proust: portrait of a genius. New York, 1950.)
76. Michotte, Albert. La perception de la causalité. Louvain, 1946.
77. Moholy-Nagy, L. Von Material zu Architektur. Munich, 1929.
78. Moorhouse, Charles E., ed. Visual education. Carlton, Victoria, 1974.
79. Museum of Modern Art. Four new buildings: architecture and imagery (MOMA Bulletin, 1959, vol. 26, #2).
80. Musil, Robert. Der Mann ohne Eigenschaften. Vienna, 1931. (Engl.: The man without qualities. New York, 1953–65.)
81. Nervi, Pier Luigi. Aesthetics and technology in building. Cambridge, Mass., 1965.

82. Neutra, Richard. Survival through design. New York, 1954.
83. Norberg-Schultz, Christian. Existence, space, and architecture. New York, 1971.
84. ———. Intentions in architecture. Cambridge, Mass., 1965.
85. Ost, Hans. Studien zu Pietro da Cortonas Umbau von S. Maria della Pace. Römisches Jahrbuch für Kunstgeschichte, 1971, vol. 13, pp. 231-85.
86. Paivio, Allan. Images, propositions, and knowledge. Research Bulletin #309, University of Western Ontario, October 1974.
87. Panofsky, Erwin. "Idea": ein Beitrag zur Begriffsgeschichte der älteren Kunsttheorie. Berlin, 1960. (Engl.: Idea: a concept in art theory. Columbia, S. C., 1968.)
88. Parr, A. E. Problems of reason, feeling and habitat. Arch. Assoc. Quart., July 1969, vol. 1, #3, pp. 5-10.
89. Persitz, Alexandre, with Danielle Valeix. Le siège de l'Unesco à Paris. L'Architecture d'aujourd'hui, Jan. 1959, #81.
90. Pevsner, Nikolaus. An outline of European architecture. Harmondsworth, Eng., 1943.
91. Piaget, Jean. La représentation de l'espace chez l'enfant. Paris, 1948. (Engl.: The child's conception of space. New York, 1967.)
92. ———. and Bärbel Inhelder. Le développement des quantités physiques chez l'enfant. Neuchâtel, 1962.
93. Pichois, Claude. Vitesse et vision du monde. Neuchâtel, 1973.
94. Portoghesi, Paolo. Le inibizioni dell'architettura moderna. Rome, 1974.
95. Proust, Marcel. Du côté de chez Swann. Paris, 1954. (Engl.: Swann's way. New York, 1928.)
96. Prussin, Labelle and Karen Travis. Environmental arts of West Africa. Research News, University of Michigan, May 1975, vol. 25, #11.
97. Pye, David. The nature of design. London, 1964.
98. Rasmussen, Steen Eiler. Experiencing architecture. Cambridge, Mass., 1959.
99. Richter, Gisela M.A. and Marjorie J. Milne. Shapes and names of Athenian vases. New York, 1935.
100. G. Rietveld Architect. Catalogue by the Stedelijk Museum, Amsterdam, and the Arts Council of Great Britain, 1972.
101. Rudofsky, Bernard. Architecture without architects. Garden City, N.Y., 1964.
102. Schaefer-Simmern, Henry. The unfolding of artistic activity. Berkeley and Los Angeles, 1948.
103. Scheerbart, Paul. Glasarchitektur. Berlin, 1914. (Engl.: Glass architecture. New York, 1972.)
104. Schubert, Otto. Optik in Architektur und Städtebau. Berlin, 1965.
105. Schwager, Klaus. Die Porta Pia in Rom. Münchner Jahrbuch der bildenden Kunst 1973, vol. 24, pp. 33-96.
106. Scully, Vincent. Modern architecture. Rev. ed. New York, 1974.
107. Sedlmayr, Hans. Zum Wesen des Architektonischen. *In* Sedlmayr. Epochen und Werke, vol. 2, Vienna, 1960.
108. Sekler, Eduard F., ed. Le Corbusier's Visual Arts Center for Harvard University: a history and evaluation of its design. Cambridge, Mass., (in press).

109. Shepard, Roger N. and J. Metzler. Mental rotation of three-dimensional objects. Science 1971, vol. 171, pp. 701–3.

110. Simson, Otto von. The Gothic cathedral. New York, 1962.

111. Stevens, Peter S. Patterns in nature. Boston, 1974.

112. Straus, Erwin W. The upright posture. Psychiatric Quart. 1952, vol. 26, pp. 529–61.

113. Sweeney, James Johnson. Mondrian, the Dutch and De Stijl. Art News, Summer 1951, pp. 24–62.

114. Teuber, Marianne L. Sources of ambiguity in the prints of Maurits C. Escher. Scient. Amer., July 1974, vol. 231, pp. 90–104.

115. Thompson, D'Arcy. On growth and form. Cambridge, Eng. 1969.

116. Venturi, Robert. Complexity and contradiction in architecture. New York, 1966.

117. Waley, Arthur. The way and its power. New York, 1958.

118. Weiss, Paul A. One plus one does not equal two. *In* G. C. Quarton, ed., The neurosciences. New York, 1967.

119. Werner, Heinz. Comparative psychology of mental development. New York, 1948.

120. Wertheimer, Max. Gestalt theory. Social Research, Feb. 1944, vol. 11, pp. 78–99.

121. ——. Untersuchungen zur Lehre von der Gestalt. II. Psychologische Forschung 1933, vol. 4, pp. 301–50. (Engl. *in* Ellis [34], pp. 71–88.)

122. Witkin, H.A., et al. Psychological differentiation. New York, 1962.

123. Wittkower, Rudolf. Architectural principles in the age of humanism. New York, 1962.

124. Wölfflin, Heinrich. Prolegomena zu einer Psychologie der Architektur. *In* Kleine Schriften. Basel, 1946, pp. 13–47.

125. Wright, Frank Lloyd. The natural house. New York, 1954.

126. Zucker, Paul. Town and square. New York, 1959.

ACKNOWLEDGMENTS

The author is indebted to:

George Allen and Unwin Ltd., London, and Barnes & Noble, New York, for a quotation from Arthur Waley, *The Way and Its Power.*

the University of California, San Diego, for a photograph of its library (Fig. 118).

the Regents of the University of California for a quotation from Horatio Greenough, *Form and Function.*

Miss Prunella Clough and Mr. Patrick Carr for a photograph of David Carr's sculpture (Fig. 38).

Knoll International, New York, for permission to reproduce Mies van der Rohe's Barcelona chair (Fig. 134).

Prof. William L. MacDonald for the photograph of a plaster cast model of the Hagia Sophia (Fig. 52).

Dott. Pier Luigi Nervi and the Harvard University Press for a photograph of Nervi's grandstand for the Municipal Stadium in Florence (Fig. 136).

Prof. Paolo Portoghesi for photographs from his book, *Le inibizioni dell'architettura moderna* (Fig. 14, 57, 121).

Random House, Inc. Alfred A. Knopf, Inc. for permission to reprint "Anecdote of the Jar" from Wallace Stevens's *Collected Poems.*

Prof. Henry Schaefer-Simmern for a photograph from his *The Unfolding of Artistic Activity* (Fig. 43).

Prof. Eduard F. Sekler for photographs and ground plan of the Carpenter Center for the Visual Arts, Harvard University (Fig. 13, 69).

Mr. Robert Sowers for his drawing (Fig. 110).

Dr. H. van den Doel, Ilpendam, for permission to use a photograph of his home (Fig. 101).

INDEX

285

286

287

Weiss, Paul, 197
Weissenhof, Stuttgart, 224
Wertheimer, Max, 67, 114
Whitney Museum, 138
Wieskirche, 179
Wittkower, Rudolf, 91
Wölfflin, Heinrich, 211

Wright, Frank Lloyd, 35, 38, 43, 44, 68, 99, 145,
    149, 193, 214, 218, 227, 236, 250, 262, 269

York University, Toronto, 34

Zucker, Paul, 24, 25, 85, 180
Zucker, Wolfgang, 92